The Life and Death of Stalin

Books by Louis Fischer

THE LIFE OF MAHATMA GANDHI

THE GOD THAT FAILED *(Co-author)*

THIRTEEN WHO FLED *(Editor)*

GANDHI AND STALIN

THE GREAT CHALLENGE

EMPIRE

A WEEK WITH GANDHI

DAWN OF VICTORY

MEN AND POLITICS *(An Autobiography)*

STALIN AND HITLER

THE WAR IN SPAIN

SOVIET JOURNEY

MACHINES AND MEN IN RUSSIA

WHY RECOGNIZE RUSSIA?

THE SOVIETS IN WORLD AFFAIRS *(Two Vols.)*

OIL IMPERIALISM

The Life and Death of STALIN

by LOUIS FISCHER

HARPER & BROTHERS, PUBLISHERS
New York

THE LIFE AND DEATH OF STALIN

Printed in the United States of America

FIRST EDITION

F-B

Library of Congress catalog card number 52-5433

TO GLORIA AND VICTOR

Contents

Illustrations

These illustrations will be found in a group following page 114

THANKS TO

AVRAM YARMOLINSKY and his associates in the Slavonic division of the New York Public Library for devotedly assisting in my research work,

HANNAH D. RABINOWITZ who typed the manuscript,

GEORGE FISCHER, my son, who listed the bibliography,

SIMON MICHAEL BESSIE, CASS CANFIELD, HARRY SIGMOND, and others who helped me with their frank criticism of the manuscript.

LOUIS FISCHER

The Life and Death of Stalin

CHAPTER I

From Mountain Hovel to Moscow Kremlin

Amid the Caucasus Mountains, where Europe ends and Asia begins, stands Gori, a rock-strewn town with a population of five thousand. There, on December 21, 1879, a son was born to Catherine and Vissarion Djugashvili, and they called him Joseph. He later assumed the name of Stalin, "Man of Steel."

Joseph's father was a shoemaker who earned little and drank much and receives only passing mention in the official Soviet biographies of Stalin. It is reported, however, that he gave Joseph many "frightful and undeserved beatings."

But Catherine was a loving mother and affectionately called Joseph "Soso." Her parents were village serfs who married her off young. When Joseph was born she was twenty and had already had three children who died in infancy. Joseph was raised as an only child.

The family home was a cheap, rented stone house consisting of one room with a stone floor and an alcove kitchen. Vissarion had his cubicle where he repaired shoes. Sometimes he worked in a shoe factory in Tiflis, the capital of Georgia, fifty miles from Gori. Catherine took in laundry and mended clothes for the neighbors. At the age of seven Joseph fell ill with smallpox and his mother nursed him at home. The disease permanently branded Joseph's face with circular pockmarks.

Henri Barbusse, the French Communist author whose official biography of Stalin, published in 1935, had Stalin's approval, writes that "as a child" Joseph "was small and slim, with a bold, almost brazen expression" and "slightly Asiatic eyes." He seemed to tease, or defy, the bigger boys who frequently bullied him. Either in a youthful fight, or in an accident, his left arm was badly hurt. The wound festered and blood poisoning developed. He almost died. "I don't know what saved me," Stalin said later. "It was either my healthy constitution or the salve of the village medicine woman. But I got well." This is Stalin's own story about his rigid elbow and short left arm as told to his sister-in-law Anna who recorded it in her memoirs published in Moscow in 1946. But Leon Trotsky, writing in 1940, says he often saw Stalin wearing a warm glove on his left hand at Politbureau meetings and that "rheumatism was the generally accepted reason." Other authors assert the arm was short from birth. All authorities agree, however, that the second and third toes of Stalin's left foot were grown together from birth. Since the poor shoemaker's child usually went barefoot, the boys often noticed it and made fun of him. He had reason to be resentful.

Stalin spent his boyhood in a little world where nature was rugged and beautiful and man was rugged and poor. Georgia, the province of his birth, had retained many characteristics of the feudal Middle Ages. The men of the Khevsur tribe wore coats of mail and regarded themselves as descendants of the Crusaders. The cities abounded in impoverished nobility and the villages in princes who owned nothing more than a house on stilts, two goats, and a cow. Bandits filled the wild countryside. The blood feud was an honored tradition; the family of a murdered person pursued the suspected culprit unto death. Forgiveness was regarded as unworthy of this hard-living, meat-eating, wine-drinking, gay, and otherwise hospitable mountain folk.

Georgia, once an independent country, has been invaded by Alexander of Macedon, Pompey, Genghis Khan, Tamerlane, and others. Like the Caucasus Isthmus of which it forms a part, it is a crossroads of history and therefore an ethnic and linguistic Tower of Babel. Dozens of nationalities inhabit the Caucasus, and while they all have distinguishing tongues and traits, their blood cannot have remained pure throughout the churning centuries. The rights which serfdom gave to landlords over their desirable young women slaves reduced racial purity still further.

The population of Stalin's home town was mixed. Many of the

more prosperous citizens were Armenian and Tartar merchants. Some scholars suggest that Stalin's mother was not a Georgian but an Ossetian from a region farther north in the Caucasus. Though Stalin considers himself a Georgian, and is always considered a Georgian, he is less genial, less handsome and lackadaisical, less flamboyant and demonstrative, and more ambitious than most Georgian men. An admixture of non-Georgian blood may explain the difference.

"My parents were uneducated people," Stalin said later in life. The father planned to apprentice Joseph to a cobbler, but he died when the boy was eleven, and even before that Catherine's will was stronger. She hated the trade of her husband and of her husband's father; it proverbially led to poverty and drunkenness. She wanted her son to be educated. A devout Christian, she dreamed of making Soso a priest. A student for the priesthood could get free schooling. The church offered the prospect of a good livelihood and good social status.

When Joseph reached the age of nine Catherine accordingly enrolled him in the little local religious preparatory school. The first volume of Stalin's collected works, published in Moscow in 1946, states that this school was a four-year institution which Stalin entered in September, 1888, and finished in June, 1894. It thus took him six years to pass the four grades. He may have been a bad student or he may have been ill. Upon his graduation, his mother sent him to the Greek Orthodox Theological Seminary in Tiflis.

Within a year, he joined the underground revolutionary movement. Joseph the divinity student thereupon abandoned God and Jesus for Marx and Lenin. His bible was Karl Marx's *Capital.* Yet he remained at the seminary for five years. He lived in two worlds. In the formative, impressionable period of his life between the ages of fifteen and twenty, Stalin led a double life, one open and untrue, the other furtive and absorbing. He learned to dissimulate. The seen was unreal, the real was unseen.

The theological seminary was a seedbed of rebellion; it would have required courage for Stalin to remain outside the revolutionary movement. In 1883, a Georgian student named Sylvester Djibladze rose from his seat, walked up to the Russian director who had spoken slightingly of the Georgian language, and smacked his face. The student received a three-year prison sentence, and the school was temporarily closed. Three years later another Russian principal was stabbed to death by a nineteen-year-old Georgian student. The police reported that most of the Georgian students and teachers sympathized with the assassin. Many of them were expelled.

The Georgians, who number between two and three million, are a proud people and have always resented Russian domination. Patriotism made them revolutionists. But Stalin was moved by personal motives. When Emil Ludwig, the German author, asked Stalin, in an interview on December 13, 1931, what made him a rebel, he replied, "Out of protest against the humiliating regime and Jesuitical methods which existed at the seminary."

"For instance," Stalin explained, "there was spying in the dormitories: At 9:00 A.M. the bell rings for tea; we go to the dining room, and when we return to our rooms we see that in the short time our closet drawers have been searched and ransacked. . . ."

In his first year at the seminary, now the Palace Hotel, Stalin's conduct was exemplary, and his report card shows that he received the highest mark for it. Later, according to the school's archives, "the Student Djugashvili is disrespectful and rude in his relations with persons of the administration." Once, one of his teachers, a monk, locked the young Stalin in a solitary-confinement cell for five hours for a breach of discipline.

Having joined the rebels, Stalin attended secret revolutionary meetings and read illegal anti-Czarist literature when he should have been studying scriptures. His new allegiance whetted his appetite for knowledge unobtainable in class. An entry in the seminary's discipline book notes that young Joseph was found on the chapel stairs reading *The Literary Evolution of Nations* by Letourneau, and adds, "This is the thirteenth time this student has been discovered reading books borrowed from the Cheap Library."

Ultimately the religious authorities tired of Stalin's transgressions, and he was expelled on May 29, 1899. Greek Orthodoxy lost a priest; orthodox communism found its high priest.

The expulsion shattered his mother's dreams. Thirty-one years later, when Stalin, dictator of Russia, had established her in a room in the former palace of the Czar's Viceroy in Tiflis, she told reporters, "Soso was always a good boy. . . . He was not expelled. I brought him home on account of his health. When he entered the seminary he was fifteen and as strong as a lad could be. But overwork up to the age of nineteen pulled him down, and the doctors told me he might develop tuberculosis. So I took him away from school. He did not want to leave. But I took him away. He was my only son. . . ."

This pathetic statement has all the ingredients of self-administered balm for a broken heart. Catherine Djugashvili scarcely had the money to consult "doctors"; the willful Joseph would hardly have obeyed her and gone home to Gori. The fact is he stayed in Tiflis.

According to another version he was expelled because of poor marks and inattention to studies. The *Album of Bolshevik Party Leaders*, published in Moscow in 1927, gives "untrustworthiness," in the quotes presumably of the seminary, as the reason. The explanation now authorized by Stalin himself is: punishment for "making Marxist propaganda."

No longer a candidate for the priesthood, Joseph Vissarionovitch Djugashvili found a job as a minor clerk in the Tiflis Observatory. It did not even pay for his food; students at the seminary often made collections to buy his meals. "He lived," a contemporary writes, "in a small, squalid, poorly furnished room on Mikhailovskaya Street," and dressed in a plain black Russian blouse with red necktie and a peaked Russian cap. In winter he wore an old brown cape. He paid no attention to his dress, his blouse was always "dirty" and his shoes "unpolished." This was the "Bohemian," antibourgeois appearance frequently affected by the revolutionists of the day.

Stalin's talent was for organization. He was a man of action. He felt a special attraction for secrecy and subversion. Many of the anti-Czarist revolutionists adhered at the time to the Social Democratic party. Early in the twentieth century the party began to divide into a large, mild, populist faction—the Mensheviks—and a smaller, more extremist, conspiratorial faction—the Bolsheviks. When this division hardened into a definite split, Stalin joined the Bolsheviks. The Bolshevik party stressed strict discipline, clandestine work, and violent action. That is where Stalin belonged. Lenin wanted the party to become "a stable organization of leaders . . . consisting chiefly of people professionally engaged in revolutionary activity . . . and trained in the art of combating the political police." This attracted Stalin more than a party based on popular appeal, oratory, and public meetings.

Stalin, a minor neophyte, thus became a devout disciple of Lenin, who, thirty-three years old in 1903—only nine years Stalin's senior—had already gained recognition as the master mind of the Bolshevik movement of all Russia.

Stalin launched strikes and taught discontented workingmen the tactics of revolt. When the Bolsheviks lacked funds he helped to stage bank robberies. These were highly melodramatic affairs with gun duels, prancing steeds, decoys, and hairbreadth escapes. Stalin never actually took part in them. His department was behind-the-scene management.

In 1905, at the age of twenty-six, Stalin made one of his few early speeches. A popular upheaval had shaken Russia after her defeats in the Russo-Japanese War. The revolutionists were sanguine of success. "What do we need to really triumph?" Stalin asked in his now well-known question-and-answer rhythm. "For this we need three things: first, arms; second, arms; third, again and again arms." He called the Bolshevik party a "fortress"; politics was a military operation.

"The aim of every struggle is victory," Stalin wrote in 1904. This seems a simple thought, yet it made Stalin what he is. His wish to win overwhelms others and it so overwhelms him that he lets no scruples bar the way to success. Stalin rose to supremacy by the use of force, but also by the force of his bulldozer personality. He is full of spurting animal vigor. "The philosophy of *Weltschmerz* is not our philosophy," Stalin wrote Demyan Byedni, the Soviet poet, in a letter dated July 15, 1924, and first published in 1947. *Weltschmerz* is agonized concern for suffering humanity. "Our philosophy,"

Stalin continued, "was rather precisely described by the American Whitman." There follows Stalin's Russian text from Walt Whitman: "We are alive. Our red blood boils with the fire of unexpended strength."

This is a better key to Stalin than Marxism. He is the product less of ideology than of temperament. He is a primitive who despises weaklings. Reminiscing once about his Siberian exile, he said, "Have you ever seen fishermen before a storm on a big river like the Yenisei? I have seen it many times. There is one kind of fisherman who, facing the approaching storm, mobilizes all his strength, inspires his people, and courageously speeds his boat to meet the storm. 'Hold fast, boys,' he shouts, 'grip the wheel tightly, cut the waves, we will win out.' But there is another sort of fisherman who, fearing the storm, becomes discouraged, whines, and demoralizes his own ranks. 'What a pity,' he cries, 'there's a storm coming up, lie down, boys, in the bottom of the boat, close your eyes, maybe somehow we will be carried to the shore.' "

Stalin knew Maxim Gorki's poem, "The Stormy Petrel," written in 1901; he liked its stirring call to battle:

> Look, the storm, the storm is coming.
> Proudly soars the Stormy Petrel,
> Over raging sea, 'mid lightning
> Shrieks the prophecy of triumph:
> Hail the mighty coming tempest.

Stalin loves talking about war with military officers. When a foreign statesman mentioned the Pope, Stalin said derisively, "How many divisions has he got?" He respects guns, not spirit. The presence of fighting men inspires him to emotional heights. He visited the Soviet cruiser *Red Ukraine* lying in the naval basin of Sebastopol, on July 25, 1929, and watched an amateur performance by the crew. Then, in typical style, he wrote in the visitor's book: "Was on the cruiser *Red Ukraine*. Present at the amateur evening performance. General impression: excellent people, brave, cultured comrades, ready for anything in the interest of the common cause. Pleasant to have to do with such comrades. Pleasant to fight the enemy in the rank of such fighters. With such comrades it is possible to conquer the whole world of exploiters and oppressors. I wish you success, comrades of the *Red Ukraine*. J. Stalin."

Pacifists bore Stalin. In 1930, Maxim Gorki wrote him from abroad suggesting the publication of stories which would teach the Soviet people the horrors of war. ". . . we," Stalin replied in a letter first published in 1949, "are not against all wars. We are against imperialist wars because they are counterrevolutionary wars. But we are for a liberating, anti-imperialistic, revolutionary war, although, as is known, such a war is not only not free of the 'horrors of bloodshed' but is full of them to overflowing."

In August, 1945, General Eisenhower stood on the Lenin Mausoleum with Stalin watching a mass display of physical-culture exercises. "This develops the war spirit," Stalin said to the General. "Your country ought to do more of this."

Struggle fascinates Stalin. Competition sharpens his wits. The Bolshevik party, born to fight, bound to be persecuted by the Czar's government, was Stalin's natural home. He rose in its ranks quickly. The police was on his trail. In 1902, on a visit to St. Petersburg, he rented a furnished room. In the early hours of the morning, there was a loud knock on his door. "Why don't you let me sleep?" he groaned, half-awake. The reply was Russia's traditional night call: "Open up, it's the police." This was one of many arrests.

Six times Stalin was banished to Siberia between 1902 and 1913. Five times he stayed a short while and then escaped to his secret haunts and work. He was too brimful with energy to remain confined. (The Siberian cold, Henri Barbusse writes, cured Stalin of tuberculosis.)

By 1905, Stalin's drive as an organizer had earned him his spurs in the Bolshevik party many of whose top leaders were in Siberian prisons or foreign exile; he became a medium-sized fish in a small pond. In December of that year he was delegated to the annual party congress in Finland. He also attended the 1906 party convention in Stockholm, and the 1907 annual meeting in London. These, and a visit to Cracow in 1912 and Vienna in 1913, were Stalin's only trips abroad until 1943 when he met President Roosevelt and Prime Minister Churchill at Teheran. Each stay was as brief as he could make it. He felt less at home in the intellectual circles of Europe than among the tough workers and rough mountaineers of the Caucasus. He knew no foreign language. In a Baku jail, once, he studied German and Esperanto but mastered neither. Even his Russian was spoken with a thick Georgian accent. He had little acquaintance with world literature or world history. The West did not attract him. He wanted to get back to work.

During this period, as he himself admits, Stalin was a "practitioner," a political organizer. Ambition or envy had stimulated his desire to be a writer, but what writing he did in the local party press was dull, superficial, and un-Communistic. He advocated, for instance, the division of large feudal estates into small, private-capitalistic peasant holdings; in common with the moderate Mensheviks, he believed that since Russia had few industries the working class would not soon win a popular majority. Therefore a socialist revolution had to be ruled out. His highest hope was the overthrow of the monarchy.

This made him a poor Bolshevik but a bad enough criminal in the eyes of the Czarist police which seized Stalin again in 1913 and transported him beyond the Arctic Circle where the chances of flight were few. There, in the silent, inhuman white expanses of the frozen North, the future ruler learned of the outbreak of the First World War. He remained a prisoner throughout 1914, 1915, and 1916. He spent the summers fishing and hunting and laying up stores for the long polar winter. Once he sent a letter to his future father-in-law, who revealed the fact in the Moscow *Pravda* of December 22, 1939, asking for money to buy food supplies. His winters were devoted to reading, trapping and sleeping. He wrote no books or tracts as Lenin, Trotsky, and other revolutionary leaders did in Siberian confinement. Stalin's sister-in-law, Anna Alliluyev, records that he liked to walk several miles for the prisoners' mail because fetching the mail excused one from housework. (Political prisoners sometimes lived in groups which enjoyed comparative freedom.) She says he himself recounted later how he would lie in bed mornings and feign sleep so that others would do the chores on the day when he was orderly.

Though a prisoner and disloyal, Stalin was called up by the army in 1916 but rejected as physically inadequate.

The World War so weakened the rotten, unintelligent, unpopular Czarist regime that the parties of the moderate center led by Prince Lvov, Paul Miliukov, Irakli Tseretelli, and Alexander Kerensky easily forced Nicholas II to abdicate in March, 1917. This was the signal for the antimonarchists, including the Bolsheviks, in Siberian and foreign exile to return to Petrograd. Stalin was one of the first. He became co-editor, with Leo Kamenev, of the *Pravda*, the daily newspaper of the Bolshevik party.

Under Stalin-Kamenev supervision, *Pravda* pursued a middle-of-the-road, cautious policy until Lenin, accompanied by Zinoviev, Radek, and other top Bolsheviks, arrived in the famous "sealed train" from Switzerland, in April, 1917. Lenin stepped out of the Finland Station in Petrograd, climbed on an armored car and, surprising friendly listeners, attacked the new democratic government for keeping Russia in the war and failing to introduce radical reforms. Later, in party councils, he excoriated Stalin and Kamenev for their sympathetic attitude to Prince Lvov and Kerensky. Lenin insisted on the organization of local and regional soviets which would rule in defiance of and in competition with the federal government. He envisaged the establishment of a Bolshevik regime.

Lenin was a tiny, bald man with a giant personality. He had faith in victory and tremendous drive. He knew what he wanted. He knew how to use his opponents' weakness and the Russian people's impatient yearning for peace, land, and adequate food. He had a plan of attack. He painted a simple, clear, appealing goal: power. He skillfully gathered his limited forces for a quick, sharp blow. Few followers could resist his certitude, clarity, and intensity.

The Bolsheviks overthrew the Kerensky regime on November 7, 1917, with comparatively little bloodshed. During the preparations for this revolt, Stalin, as he subsequently admitted in a pamphlet, hesitated conservatively and advised against the plunge. Under Lenin's pressure, however, he reversed himself, and thereafter, until Lenin died, gave every appearance of supporting the leader.

The Bolshevik revolt is vividly described in John Reed's *Ten*

Days That Shook the World. Lenin read it twice and wrote an introduction recommending it. The book does not mention Stalin. Stalin's part in the Bolshevik uprising was important, but not nearly as important as Trotsky's. Lenin directed. Trotsky, his chief assistant, strode the stage and stirred the multitudes with fiery, purposeful oratory. Stalin worked in the rear.

Within a few months of its birth, the Soviet regime was attacked by domestic reactionaries and foreign powers. Leon Trotsky became Commissar of War and organizer of the Red Army. Joseph Stalin was one of his political commissars. Rivalry flared between them immediately.

The Trotsky-Stalin joust of giants, one of the greatest feuds of all time, played a major role in Soviet history and in world history. Through the polemical smoke screen of the 1920's and 1930's it seemed that the two men and their followers clashed on such issues as village collectives, kulaks, world revolution, China, and industrialization. But long before these problems had arisen or been thought of, Stalin's competitiveness and jealousy brought him into conflict with the temperamental Trotsky.

Stalin "always repelled me," Trotsky wrote in his autobiography, published after he had left the Soviet Union. Trotsky held Stalin in contempt for his vulgarity, lack of culture, and narrow outlook. Stalin disliked Trotsky and called him "an actor." He envied Trotsky. Once the supreme Politbureau voted to grant Trotsky the Order of the Red Banner for defending Petrograd during the civil war. Trotsky describes what followed. Leo Kamenev, assistant Prime Minister under Lenin, proposed that the same decoration be conferred on Stalin.

"What for?" Michael Kalinin, subsequently President of the Soviet Union, exclaimed.

"Don't you understand," Nikolai Bukharin explained. "Lenin thought this up. Stalin cannot live if he hasn't got what the other fellow has. He cannot forgive it." This applied especially when the other fellow was Trotsky.

The haughty Trotsky and the envious Stalin were bound to come to blows.

"I insist categorically on the removal of Stalin," Trotsky wired Lenin from the fighting front on October 8, 1918. Stalin was at Tsaritsyn (now Stalingrad) acting as political supervisor of Voroshilov. Trotsky charged that Stalin and Voroshilov were refusing to obey orders from headquarters.

Lenin transferred Stalin to the Ukrainian front. Stalin took Voroshilov with him. Again Stalin and Trotsky collided. "The Tsaritsyn methods," Trotsky telegraphed Lenin on January 10, 1919, "which led to the complete disintegration of the Tsaritsyn army cannot be permitted in the Ukraine." Lenin advised Trotsky to reach a compromise with Stalin. It could not be done. In June, 1919, Stalin asked the Central Committee of the Bolshevik party to dismiss Trotsky from the command of the Red Army. Trotsky offered to resign. The Central Committee gave him a vote of confidence.

Trotsky underestimated Stalin and regarded him as a "provincial." But the provincial, with a sharp eye to the future, took the job of General Secretary of the Communist party. It was a minor job, usually held by lesser men. Lenin dominated the party, and the secretary was a subordinate. But Stalin understood that in a highly centralized state controlled by the party the General Secretary would be a key man after Lenin's death. Meanwhile the position enabled Stalin to work assiduously and in the dark gathering a band of henchmen who would be loyal to him because he appointed them and could dismiss them. On the other hand, Trotsky, always a prima donna, held his head so high in the clouds that he never stood on the solid ground of party organization. He was a Gibraltar without a hinterland, a lone lion, a battleship sailing political seas without an escort and therefore vulnerable to subsurface attack. Meanwhile Stalin was laying plans and mines.

Lenin knew the deep antagonism between Stalin and Trotsky. He had witnessed many manifestations of it. In 1919, for instance, Trotsky complained to Lenin that Stalin had been drinking wine from the well-stocked cellars of the Czar in the Kremlin.

Lenin summoned Stalin. Trotsky argued the matter with Stalin in Lenin's presence. "If the rumor reaches the front that there is drinking in the Kremlin," he said, "it will make a bad impression." The sale of alcohol was illegal at that time in Russia.

"How can we Caucasians get along without wine?" Stalin protested.

"You see," Lenin interjected laughingly, "the Georgians cannot do without wine." Lenin did not intend to discipline Stalin.

That ended the discussion. "I capitulated without a struggle," Trotsky wrote in a *Life* article in 1939.

But what would happen without a Lenin to break the tension with a smile and joke? Lenin sensed the coming strife between the two colossi. In December, 1922, when he had recuperated from his first stroke, he wrote his last testament and addressed it to the party congress. "Comrade Stalin," Lenin warned, "having become General Secretary of the Party, has concentrated tremendous power in his hands, and I am not sure he always knows how to use that power with sufficient caution."

Lenin, trusting no outsiders, gave the testament to his wife for safekeeping. But the matter did not let him rest; he feared that the Stalin-Trotsky antagonism would split the party. So a few days later he asked for the document and appended a decisive postscript. "Stalin," he declared, "is too rude. . . . I therefore propose to the comrades to find a way of removing Stalin from that position [of General Secretary] and appointing another who in all respects differs from Stalin only in superiority—namely, more patient, more loyal, more polite, and more attentive to comrades, less capricious."

For Bolsheviks, the party was everything. A small shock troop usually operating against popular resistance, it had to be harmonious. A sly, unfriendly, bad-mannered, intriguing General Secretary might disrupt the organization. Yet the testament's appendix shows that Lenin knew it would be difficult to dislodge Stalin. It proved impossible. He held too many of the hidden strings of power.

To become Soviet dictator, Stalin had to surmount the tremendous handicap of Lenin's last injunction against him. He had to crush the towering Trotsky. He had to remold Russia. He did all of these. That is the measure of his genius.

The battle for the succession to Lenin commenced while he

was still alive. Stalin combined with the shrewd, demagogic Gregory Zinoviev and the hard-working, intelligent Leo Kamenev to oust Trotsky, then ailing with a mysterious infection which kept his temperature high. Lenin died on January 21, 1924. The triumvirate intensified its work.

Trotsky was on his way for a cure in the Caucasus when he received the news of Lenin's death. He immediately wired the Kremlin asking when the funeral would take place and saying he wanted to return. In reply he received a telegram signed "Stalin" stating, "The funeral takes place on Saturday. You will not be able to return in time. The Politbureau thinks that because of the state of your health you must proceed to Sukhum." The funeral actually took place on Sunday, January 27. Trotsky could have been there. He has stated that Stalin kept him away deliberately. Stalin wanted to weaken the association in people's minds between Lenin and Trotsky. But why did Trotsky allow Stalin's deception to succeed? Why did he even ask when the burial would occur? On hearing of Lenin's death he should have flown to Moscow. Trotsky's illness perhaps weakened his will. His lack of resolution, in any case, contrasts revealingly with Stalin's determination not to have him at the politically important funeral.

Trotsky nevertheless retained much of his popularity. The Red Army's party organization had adopted a resolution in January, 1924, backing Trotsky, its chief. The university students were overwhelmingly for him. The central departments of the Soviet government were honeycombed with Trotskyist oppositionists. Large groups of workingmen expressed sympathy for his program of democracy within the party.

The Stalin-Zinoviev-Kamenev trio met this challenge in their own way. In the absence of Trotsky, they gave him a first assistant, Michael Frunze, who had fiercely attacked him in the press. General Muralov, commander of the Moscow garrison, a partisan of Trotsky, was transferred to a remote provincial post. Army Commander-in-Chief Serge S. Kamenev, an intimate co-worker of Trotsky, suffered a demotion. Petrovsky, a staunch friend, was dismissed from the war office. Other leading Trotskyists were ordered to distant posts:

Ossinsky to Stockholm as Soviet commercial representative, Preobrazhensky to the London Anglo-Soviet negotiations, Sapronov to Vladivostok, and Antonov-Avseyenko to China.

Thus relieved of large embarrassments, the triumvirate proceeded to crush the Trotskyist rank and file. Stalin's position in the party facilitated this task. Wherever possible, he replaced loyal Bolsheviks with loyal Stalinists as the secretaries of party units. The party membership was diluted by the rapid, wholesale enrollment of unassimilated new members who, out of inexperience or fear, would obey orders.

Having prepared the ground, the triumvirate called a national congress of the party for May, 1924. So skillfully had Stalin, Kamenev, and Zinoviev operated in the four months since Lenin's death that not a single delegate voted for Trotsky. The era of machine-made unanimity had dawned.

After listening to the reading of Lenin's last testament, the congress voted unanimously against publishing it. It has never been published in Russia. But it was smuggled out of the country.

By virtue of his position as the party's General Secretary, Stalin was now the strongest leg of the ruling triangle.

Stalin's four simple rules of success were already discernible: any method is justified if it helps achieve the desired end; men must be discarded when no longer useful; alliances are made to be broken; ideas have no existence unless chained to the chariot of power.

Stalin's rise from mountain hovel to Moscow Kremlin was a triumph of organization harnessed to will power. It attests to the primacy of will power in leadership. His will enabled Stalin to conquer Himalayan obstacles.

CHAPTER II

The Trotsky-Stalin Feud

Trotsky was defeated 748 to 0 at the May, 1924, party Congress. But he remained a popular giant. Boris Souvarine, of the French Communist party, told the delegates that "to the world proletariat Trotsky's name is synonymous with the revolution." He might have added: and to the Russian people as well.

The older generation remembered Trotsky as the young man who appeared suddenly, like a bright star, during the 1905 anti-monarchist revolution. The younger generation fought victoriously under Trotsky in the 1918-1920 civil war. His personality, if theatrical, had strong public appeal. His presence excited. His speeches excited. His writings stirred the heart and brain. The country coupled Trotsky with Lenin as the two men who made the 1917 revolution. At that time the people did not know Stalin. Stalin's name was unknown to the masses even in 1924.

Stalin therefore continued to dig the ground from under Trotsky's political feet. Trotsky moved away; he did not fight back. He was biding his time. Lenin, in his last testament, had called Trotsky "the ablest man" in the party but noted, too, his "excessive self-confidence." Trotsky rested on his laurels and sickbed.

Presently, feeling weaker, Trotsky launched a flank attack on Zinoviev and Kamenev; he published a two-volume book entitled *1917*. It appeared at the end of 1924 and raised a dust storm which did not subside for years. In its introduction, Trotsky attacked Zinoviev and Kamenev for their resistance to the Bolshevik uprising of November, 1917. Rather than participate in it they had resigned from the Bolshevik Central Committee. Lenin fell upon them like a tiger. He denounced them as "deserters and strike-breakers." Trotsky now recalled those facts.

Trotsky's book made him vulnerable. Theretofore the ruling

Stalin-Kamenev-Zinoviev trio had criticized him for trying to convert the party to "Trotskyism." But their definitions of this sin were vague. Now he had given his enemies a new weapon; he was splitting the party by maligning its leaders. Bolsheviks worship unity.

Responding to pulls from Stalin's headquarters, thousands of like-worded resolutions poured into his office from local and regional party groups, and from foreign Communist parties, condemning Trotsky's "aggression" against the party.

Encouraged, the triumvirate dismissed Trotsky as Commissar of War and appointed Michael Frunze in his stead. But they did not yet dare to remove Trotsky from the supreme Politbureau of the Bolshevik party. The colossus had to be crushed piecemeal. Stalin was not deluded by the success of his manipulations; he is always sober. He still feared Trotsky.

"Why has the party become a lifeless mechanism?" Trotsky asked Bukharin, a pro-Stalin member of the Politbureau. "We are afraid of you," Bukharin replied. "That is why there is no democracy in the party." The party, however, was not yet a completely compliant instrument, and Stalin accordingly hesitated to engage in mortal combat with Lenin's closest aide.

In the spring of 1925, Trotsky, unemployed and partially recovered from his illness, knocked at the Kremlin gate for a job. He got three: chairman of the Chief Concessions Committee, chairman of the Electro-Technical Authority, and chairman of the Industrial Commission for Scientific Research. For a person of Trotsky's past, prestige, and ability, these were minor tasks. They required meticulous attention to a million minutiae. Stalin wished to burden Trotsky with a mountain of detail. If Trotsky mishandled one detail it could be magnified into a mountain under which to bury him.

Trotsky had no choice. He refused to share responsibility for Stalin's policies, yet politically it was unwise and temperamentally it was impossible for him to be inactive. He consequently welcomed the opportunity to concentrate on technical assignments until the next wave of revolutionary fervor made a call on his special talents.

The revolution was in a trough of despair. The initial period of zeal, which ended with the defeat of the foreign and domestic enemy, had been succeeded by fatigue and Lenin's proclamation of the New Economic Policy (NEP) in March, 1921. This was an avowed retreat. The country was economically exhausted. To promote its restoration, outside capitalists were offered industrial concessions, and city capitalists or Nepmen and the one hundred and twenty-five million capitalistically minded peasants were granted new free-enterprise freedoms to produce and trade. "Is this why we fought?" many Communists asked mournfully. Some committed suicide; they felt that the revolution was dead.

Demoralization was rife in government and party and people. Trotsky published fiery articles against it. He stressed the need of personal ethics in a crisis. He advocated novel social forms. He hoped to "disencumber the family of kitchen and laundry" by "the communalization of the family household." His purpose was to "cleanse the relationship between husband and wife of all that is external, foreign, forced, accidental. Each would cease to spoil the life of the other." Trotsky also waged war on corrupt living among officials and the growing inequality in wealth. He campaigned against swearing. "One would have to consult philologists, linguists, and folklore experts," he wrote, "to ascertain whether any other people has such unrestrained, filthy, disgusting oaths as we have. As far as I know, there is no other." Stalin habitually indulges in these famous many-ply "mother oaths"; Trotsky puritanically avoided them.

While Trotsky occupied himself with these broad problems, Stalin was oiling the party machine. Trotsky wrote a notable book on literature. Stalin fastened his hold on the party propaganda press. Trotsky was waiting for a resurgence of revolutionary *élan*. He looked hopefully for signs of social upheaval in Germany, England, China. He urged the Chinese Communists to form regional soviets which would ultimately supplant Chiang Kai-shek's conservative government. Stalin supported Chiang Kai-shek.

Trotsky was a generalissimo of smashing political offensives. Stalin was a major conducting tedious trench warfare in muddy dugouts. Soviet Russia lay in a trench struggling for economic revival. There would be no offensive for years. The times were suited to Stalin. The pedestrian plodder had an advantage over the dashing horseman in brilliant armor.

Trotsky was an uneasy amalgam of ethics and power, morality and terror, literature and revolution; a split personality. Stalin is solid flint. He does not live on the plane of ideas and doubts.

At the end of 1925, a startling development occurred. Zinoviev and Kamenev abandoned Stalin and joined Trotsky. They said Stalin would wreck the revolution. Trotsky boasted that his ideas had converted them. But he himself had once remarked sarcastically that they "lacked that little detail called character." They turned their coats easily. Intimate acquaintance with the method of their fellow triumvir, Stalin, had very likely led them to suspect he was plotting to get rid of them. They accordingly rushed into an alliance with Trotsky whom they had previously attacked and persecuted. He, who had previously attacked them, was not above grasping their proffered aid. Nadiezhda Krupskaya, Lenin's widow, also joined Trotsky. Many were seeing what Lenin had foreseen: the perils of Stalin's leadership.

Stalin was too insecure to stand alone. He now formed a tight block with Prime Minister Alexei Rykov, Michael Tomsky, the head of the Soviet trade unions, and Nikolai Bukharin, editor of the Moscow *Pravda*, a peppery philosopher much beloved by the Communist youth.

The reigning Politbureau of seven was thus divided between the "Left": Trotsky, Zinoviev, and Kamenev, and the "Right": Rykov, Tomsky, Bukharin. Stalin stood at the center, on the fulcrum of the political seesaw, enjoying maximum maneuverability and accepting minimum commitments. This was an opportunist's dream. Stalin craves the freedom to zigzag.

He needed it to cope with the peasant problem. The peasants were the Kremlin's headache. Addressing them in 1925, Bukharin said, "Enrich yourself." The slogan frightened many Communists. The enrichment of one hundred and twenty-five million little capitalists might destroy the Soviet government. A peasant earning money wants to buy factory goods. But Russia's industries were just beginning to recover from the civil war, and their few products were expensive yet shoddy. The peasants demanded cheap, imported commodities. Imports, however, would strangle the struggling industries and thus ominously give capitalist farming greater weight in the national economy than socialist industry.

Stalin's power was in danger. If he sided with the "Right," the peasantry would prosper and the country would be happier, but the party might feel that Stalin was restoring capitalism. The resulting indignation among Bolsheviks could sweep him from office. If, on the other hand, he sided with the "Left" the peasantry might revolt.

Stalin sided with both "Right" and "Left."

To please Rykov, Tomsky, and Bukharin, his "Rightist" partners, Stalin curtailed government subsidies to industry and implemented their "enrich yourself" policy. Indeed, wealthier farmers, or kulaks who were naturally anti-Communist, received the legal right to enlarge their holdings by renting the land of less successful peasants.

To steal the thunder of the "Left," Stalin promoted several spectacular development projects like the huge Dnieprostroi hydroelectric station and began to decapitate the kulaks; the moment a peasant grew so rich as to arouse the hatred and envy of his neighbors he was taxed out of existence, or dispossessed outright, or arrested. The same measures were applied to the private capitalist merchants and industrialists. This killed the geese which were laying the country's golden eggs. The peasants produced less and hoarded their produce. In 1928, all Soviet cities were short of bread. Long queues besieged the government's urban employment agencies.

The country had made considerable progress. There had been three good harvests since 1922. But pressing problems still plagued the nation. Trotsky stressed the difficulties. Stalin emphasized the material improvement and booked it to his credit. A considerable segment of the Communist party, however, felt that the progress was due to the NEP compromises with capitalism. On this issue Stalin faced a decisive battle in the arena of party politics.

Slowly, silently, Stalin cleansed the party, the central source of political authority; whoever was critical or independent had no place in his system. Frantically, secretly, the Trotskyists mobilized their strength. Foreign correspondents in Moscow found anti-Stalin literature in their mailboxes. Opposition gatherings took place underground, in factory cellars, in a wood near Moscow, in workingmen's apartments. Trotsky sometimes addressed four such meetings a day. The great orator who had thrilled whole divisions at the front before sending them into battle and stirred multitudes in assembly halls now appeared in a crowded living room where the baby's crib and the table and chairs had been piled on the bed to make place for fewer than a hundred listeners. Sometimes, however, the Trotskyists dared to convene large open meetings attended by thousands.

This could not continue long. Bolshevism, and Stalin, are intolerant of organized opposition. Yet it was not Stalin who made the first impatient move. Trotsky did.

November 7, 1927, was the tenth anniversary of the Bolshevik revolution. Soviet Russia celebrated the event with bigger-than-ever festivities.

On the eve of the celebration, oppositionists circulated rumors that during the customary army review on the Red Square, while Stalin watched from the Lenin Mausoleum, a courageous officer or soldier would shout, "Down With Stalin." The massed battalions would join the demonstration, and then the military would surround Lenin's tomb and arrest and depose Stalin. Nothing happened.

After the military parade had ended, a gigantic procession of workingmen, government officials, and youth passed before Stalin. The Trotskyists expected these civilians too to demonstrate against Stalin. On the march through the Red Square, a group of Chinese Communist students of the Moscow Sun Yat-sen University lifted the long, sinuous papier-mâché dragon off their heads, threw Trotskyist proclamations into the air, and shouted, "Death to Stalin." GPU men quickly arrested them. Nobody else demonstrated.

Near the Red Square, at the corner of Vozdvizhinka and Mokhovaya streets, is a government building with a second-story grillwork balcony. Many of the civilian marchers passed this spot on their way into and out of the square. At about 2 P.M., Trotsky appeared on the balcony with several associates. A picture of Trotsky was hung from the grillwork and he commenced to harangue the citizens who immediately congregated below. But a young man climbed up to the balcony from the pavement and pulled down the picture. In a few minutes Trotsky was silenced by boos. This was his last public appearance in Russia.

At six that afternoon, I saw Trotsky with his brother-in-law Kamenev in a large, black, angular limousine being driven by their driver along Tverskaya Avenue toward Kamenev's suburban home. They were defeated men.

Trotsky's effort was naïve. Had he imagined that the flood of his oratory would check the tide of history? Eight days later Trotsky was expelled from the Communist party. As a result he lost his political status in the country. But Stalin made no other move. The next move required careful preparation. It required a shifting of officials in the GPU. Trotsky had friends in the GPU.

One day in January, 1928, nine weeks after Trotsky's unsuccessful coup at the Red Square, two automobiles filled with armed men stopped in front of the apartment house on Granovsky Street where Trotsky lived. They were GPU agents. Four of them went upstairs. They knocked at Trotsky's door, were admitted, and asked him to follow them. "You are under arrest," they said. The man who, with Lenin, had started the revolution was being arrested by four policemen. He refused to go. They seized him and lifted him up. He fought and kicked and bit. As they carried him downstairs one of his secretaries banged at all apartment doors and yelled, "They are arresting Comrade Trotsky." They arrested him too.

The same month, Leon Trotsky was banished to Alma-Ata, a town in Soviet Turkestan. That ended his career in Russia. He was forty-eight, the same age as Stalin. For Stalin it was a beginning. The death of Lenin had stirred his unfathomable ambitions. The eclipse of Trotsky opened the door to their fulfillment.

CHAPTER III

Mummy and Deity: Lenin and Stalin

When Lenin died, his widow was in favor of cremation and simple burial. But against her opposition and that of other Bolshevik leaders, Stalin ordered the body submitted to a complicated chemical process, lasting many months, which enables it to defy decay if not shrinkage. The small shriveling corpse now lies permanently embalmed in a hermetically sealed showcase within the beautiful marble mausoleum in Moscow's Red Square where hundreds of thousands view it each year.

The mummy needed a mausoleum to house it and a deity to guard it. The mausoleum is Stalin's temple.

Lenin on display in a glass case marked the decay of his ideas. Communism, which claims to be scientific, has abandoned reason to become Russia's official religion. Lenin in visible effigy and Stalin its protector are part of the paraphernalia of the cult. It has, too, a liturgy of personal adoration of the living "Great Disciple" which is as remote from the people as the obsolete Slavonic texts of the Greek Orthodox Church.

That Church also had its miracle-making mummies, and when the Bolsheviks came they destroyed them. They wanted no rival claimants on the people's credulity. The new source of miracles is Stalin; from him all blessings flow. He is the fountainhead of goodness, the father of every achievement. To judge by official odes, he makes the sun warmer and the stars brighter and brings happiness to mankind. One song to Stalin is entitled, "Live Forever." The first verse reads:

> Stronger than steel is thy name,
> Brighter than sun is thy glory,
> Sweeter than honey is thy word,
> Live forever, beloved Leader.

A "Hymn to J. V. Stalin" proclaims:

> The world has no person
> Dearer, closer.
> With him, happiness is happier,
> And the sun brighter.

Hundreds of such songs, poems, cantatas, and hymns are widely distributed by the Soviet propaganda machine.

Stalin's picture adorns offices, schools, factories, and homes, and is carried in processions as were those of saints and Czars in the days of unenlightenment.

The preservation of Lenin's corpse was the beginning of the glorification of Stalin. The dictator could not expect to be treated as a god if he treated the master as an ordinary human being.

The god of Sovietism operates an avenging apparatus more x-ray-eyed, more ubiquitous than any ever attributed to the celestial inhabitants on Olympus. In addition, he is the infallible oracle.

Most of the prophets of Leninism have been purged. There is now a new generation that did not know Lenin. They know his face in the mausoleum, but Stalin interprets his works.

Before Lenin's death Stalin was anonymous, silent, retiring. Later, he fitted his portrait into a larger medallion of Lenin; evidence of humility, above all of identity. Still later the two portraits were printed side by side and of equal size. Now Lenin's picture, like his mummy, is smaller, whereas Stalin's grows and multiplies and fills the Soviet earth.

On one occasion, Lenin was photographed with Kamenev at his right, and Stalin at his left. This picture, with Kamenev cut off, is displayed in millions of copies throughout the Soviet Empire as proof that Stalin was Lenin's closest friend.

Hundreds of thousands of statues, busts, plaques, and statuettes of Stalin have been manufactured in Russia despite material shortages. Thousands of building-high photographs and millions of smaller photographs of the *Vozhd* or Leader, have been distributed in the Soviet Union and, now, in its foreign satellite colonies. A twenty-six-foot bronze statue of Stalin, atop a thirty-two-foot-high pedestal was unveiled in Budapest on December 16, 1951, when the official Hungarian Communist daily called Stalin "the greatest figure in Hungarian history."

Seven Soviet cities and towns have been named after Stalin: Stalingrad, Stalinabad, Stalinogorsk, Stalin, Stalino, Stalinir, Stalin-aoul. In Bulgaria, Varna has been renamed Stalin. Rumania too has a Stalin town. Thousands of counties, mountain peaks, lakes, rivers, ships, factories, farms, and schools are called "Stalin."

Stalin is showered with fawning adulation and saccharinal flattery. Except perhaps some Oriental potentate in the remote past, no human being has ever lapped up so much intellectual toadying. The July, 1945, issue of *Bolshevik*, ideological organ of the party, called him "the greatest scientist of our age." *The Cultural Front* magazine declared that "certain pronouncements of Aristotle have only been fully deciphered and expressed by Stalin." "Who best understands the Russian language?" Soviet President Kalinin asked; "Stalin," he replied. The Moscow daily *Izvestia* went to the length of announcing that "without Stalin no one can understand anything or write anything of interest." Similar effusions pour from Soviet mouths and presses in nauseating abundance.

On November 7, 1922, the fifth anniversary of the revolution, when Lenin was still alive, the Moscow *Pravda* mentioned Lenin twelve times, Trotsky four times, Stalin not once. The Moscow *Pravda* of November 7, 1937, mentioned Stalin eighty-eight times, Lenin fifty-four times, and "Stalinist" fifteen times. The *Pravda* anniversary number of November 7, 1947, reduced by paper shortages from eight to four pages, cites Stalin sixty-six times.

Stalin's birthday falls on December 21. The Moscow *Pravda* of December 18, 1929, prior to his fiftieth anniversary, published two columns of preliminary matter about the coming celebration. The next day, nine columns were devoted to it, the next, five columns. In the *Pravda* of December 21, 1929, every square inch of space except four columns of the eighth and last page was given over to Stalin's birthday. (The *Pravda* is printed in the format of large American and British dailies.)

In 1939, the preliminary matter commenced to appear on December 19, when two of *Pravda*'s six pages were consecrated to the approaching birthday. The next day, all six pages except one column on the last page were devoted to his birthday. On the birthday itself, a special twelve-page edition contained not a word on any other subject. The next day *Pravda* went back to its regular six-page issue and gave five of them to Stalin's birthday, the next day two pages, the next one and a half, the next one, the next two, the next three, the next one, the next one, and on the last day of 1939 half a page.

What is said in this endless footage of repetitious, unreadable prose matters little. What matters is that it is said at such great length. Poverty of thought is concealed by a plethora of printer's ink. In December, 1949, the *Pravda* was reduced to four pages owing to newsprint shortages. Birthday preliminaries appeared on December 8, in four columns. Every day until December 18, a quarter of the newspaper's space went to Stalin's birthday, and this was apart from the usual reports, telegrams, and greetings to Stalin which are daily features of every Soviet newspaper throughout the year. On December 19, Stalin's birthday matter took two of the four pages, December 20, three and a half, December 21, every word of twelve pages, December 22, six pages minus one column, December 23, all four pages minus two columns, December 24, three of the four pages, December 25, three out of four, December 26, two out of four, December 27, two out of four, December 28, two out of four, December 29, one and a half out of four, and December 30, slightly less than one page.

Age apparently does not mellow Stalin or reduce his appetite for praise. On the contrary, the richness of diet has destroyed his taste, and now only quantity counts.

The published official text of the main address at the Lenin memorial meeting in Moscow on January 21, 1949, shows that the speaker was interrupted five times by applauses and each time it was at the mention of Stalin's name. The end of the stenographic record reads: "Thunderous applause. All rise. Cries of 'Long Live Comrade Stalin.' 'Glory to the Great Stalin.' 'Hurrah for Stalin.'" The commemoration of Lenin's death becomes a backdrop for a Stalin ovation. The same thing now happens each year.

In 1945, a typical petition of reverence was presented to Stalin with the personal signatures of 2,547,000 residents of the White-Russian (Byelorussian) Republic. The same year a similar letter was signed by two and a half million citizens of the Kazak Republic. That Asiatic state counts six inhabitants to the square mile, and it is easy to imagine the work and travel required to collect two and a half million names. But these documents—there have been dozens—are apparently what Stalin likes.

In January, 1936, Stalin and Molotov went to see *Lady Macbeth of Mtsensk,* a musical comedy by the gifted Soviet composer Shostakovich. It had been playing to full houses for two years in most Soviet cities. All newspaper reviews had been enthusiastic. The Soviet government had subsidized performances of it abroad. But when Stalin saw it he did not like it; there was not enough melody in it for him. He enjoys folk rhythms, and this was complicated music. So Stalin called David Zaslavsky to his office and in a few days Zaslavsky had an article in the Moscow *Pravda* lambasting Shostakovich's play. Immediately *Lady Macbeth of Mtsensk* and other works of Shostakovich were banned. Critics who had lauded the musical comedy now attacked it ferociously. Stalin's poor taste forced them to act in bad taste.

An ounce of humility or a dash of humor would have prevented Stalin from acting as an authority on music. It would induce him to reduce the flow of eulogies laid at his feet morning, noon, and night. But Stalin has no sense of proportion; that is what makes him totalitarian. His vanity is unlimited. He cannot look in a mirror and laugh at himself. He wants flattery. Indeed he craves flattery not only for the present but for his past. He rewrites his own biography.

Nothing so destroys peace of mind as a gnawing desire to reopen the book of life and expunge something indelibly recorded there. Stalin knows that Lenin, the father of Bolshevism, subordinated him to Trotsky and rejected him in his testament. Therefore the Kremlin machine feverishly taps out the myth of Stalin's intimacy with Lenin and of Trotsky's "Fascist treachery." And it is never enough, for no amount of repetition will make it true.

Hundreds of "Old Bolsheviks," who knew better, signed an open letter to Stalin, published in the *Pravda* of November 7, 1947, regurgitating the official version of the Bolshevik uprising: "Thirty years ago you, together with Lenin, at the head of the Bolshevik party, led the working class of our country in the assault on capitalism." Stalin and Lenin, and nobody else, living or dead, except occasionally Molotov, are mentioned as the leaders of the 1917 revolt.

By the exaltation of Stalin and the denigration of everybody else the person became the idea. Stalin became Bolshevism: all its virtues resided in him. Bolshevism is now a state religion with a god, a church, a hell, but no believers. They mutter prayers, offer up sacrifices, and bow low to the god, for he is a jealous god and his supply of thunderbolts is inexhaustible. But there is no faith; and no balm; only fear.

Lenin prohibited adulation of himself. He was loved. Stalin must be content with genuflections.

In Lenin's time the regime was weak. Now it is strong. But Stalin has a sense of inferiority. Compulsory hero worship and pagan idolatry might increase his hold on the minds of the people and his faith in himself.

By toil and talent Stalin had, before the revolution, worked himself up into the highest councils of the Bolshevik party. But he felt out of place in that company. Lenin was the thinker, Trotsky the master of style and speech, Bukharin the fine dialectician with pervasive charm. All were men of culture, broad European experience, and skill in ideological hairsplitting. Compared to them Stalin was a backwoodsman. He sensed it. It hurt. He remained behind the scenes, planning revenge on those who were close to the master, especially on Trotsky who was closest. He would rewrite the history which credited the Lenin-Trotsky partnership with making the revolution. He would substitute himself for Trotsky and liquidate those who might testify to the contrary.

Toward the same end, Stalin expurgated Lenin's collected works, for they were Stalinistically impure. Lenin was not scrupulous, yet he had some respect for history and truth. In debate, Lenin wielded the scalpel, Stalin the ax, if necessary the GPU's revolver.

Lenin was a dictator. But he shared his power. Stalin is the hundred-percenter, the monopolist. The law of Stalinism requires the extinction of all rival centers of power within the country, and if possible outside. It also requires the extinction of thought.

Lenin admitted his mistakes in public. He had enough authority to weather mistakes. But in a speech on January 26, 1924, Stalin said Lenin was "always right." This made it possible for Stalin to claim the same perfection.

Stalin cannot err; the Communist state can do no wrong. That is the Kremlin credo. It sentences intelligence to death. The only permissible mental process in Stalin's Russia is the justification of what the government has already done.

No government can be infallible. When the world Communist movement committed itself to the Soviet government's infallibility it abdicated its intelligence.

Stalin's infallibility is designed to create trust. Many acts of the Soviet government are illogical and opaque. But if the masses believe in Stalin's wisdom they will take everything on faith.

Stalin's infallibility makes the purge a permanent feature of Soviet life. Since the dictator is infallible, the system he has created is infallible, the more so since it is based on infallible doctrine. Therefore anything that goes wrong in the Soviet Union must be due to the ill will of a subordinate who maliciously perverts the system. And that is treason. Stalinism leaves no room for human error or doctrinal fallacies. It recognizes only heresy or hostility. Hence the perpetual purge. The purge is a device to deflect blame from Stalin.

Stalin aspires to political immaculacy for himself. The official Soviet stenographic records of the famous Moscow trials of 1936, 1937, and 1938, show that there was a previous agreement between the prosecution and the defendants, a *quid pro quo*. The accused would co-operate with the state, and the state would reward the accused. In pursuance of this arrangement, the men arraigned at the trials confessed to responsibility for the deficiencies, blunders, and crimes of the Soviet government. There had been hundreds of train wrecks in Siberia. An accused official confessed that he had staged them deliberately. The peasants in collective farms had complained that they were underpaid. Former Commissar of Finance Grinka confessed that he, on instructions from Prime Minister Rykov, another defendant, purposely underpaid the peasants in order to sow discontent. In White-Russia, the number of livestock had been disastrously reduced. Defendants at one Moscow trial confessed that it was done on orders from the Polish Intelligence Service. Thirty thousand horses had died of anemia in White-Russia in 1936. "My work," accused Sharangovich testified.

Thus Stalin rejects absolute responsibility while exercising absolute control.

In 1928, it was clear that the capitalistic peasants—125,000,000 out of the entire Soviet population of 150,000,000—could, by withholding grain, starve the city and weaken Communist industry and finance. This confirmed Trotsky's prophecy. Stalin had a solution. He would lock the peasants into collective farms where they would work under government control and with government-owned machinery. It was a tremendous undertaking which shook the entire country to its roots. Stalin directed the operation personally.

Minor officials, acting on his orders, forced peasants to join the collectives. The peasants resisted. There was violence on the countryside. Many peasants preferred to slaughter their cattle rather than take them into the collectives without compensation. From 1928 to 1933, according to Soviet statistics, the number of cattle in the Soviet Union dropped from seventy million to thirty-four million, horses from thirty-six million to fifteen million, and pigs from twenty-six million to nine million. As these results of peasant protest began undermining the nation's economy, Stalin decided to call a temporary retreat. The Moscow daily *Izvestia* of March 2, 1930, accordingly published an article by Stalin entitled "Dizziness with Success." Did Stalin courageously admit his own error? No, he blamed the minor officials and provincial leaders who had speeded collectivization in obedience to his instructions. Success in establishing collectives, he wrote, had gone to their heads. They were dizzy with success, they must relax the pressure, they had overdone it. Not Stalin; "they." Stalin is always right.

President Roosevelt, Prime Minister Churchill, and Generalissimo

Stalin were in a huddle at the Yalta Conference in February, 1945. The Soviet-Nazi pact of August, 1939, was mentioned. Churchill declared that he had always condemned it. Stalin motioned to Molotov. "Come here," he said. "Explain your pact with Hitler." It was of course Stalin's pact with Hitler. But Stalin has a need to escape disapproval. The dictator's perch is the best place in which to achieve it.

Stalin is afraid to open the slightest chink in his armor; through it someone might thrust home the mortal attack. Behind Stalin's facade of imperturbable personal strength, there must lie a deep weakness, a vast vulnerability.

Yet intolerance of opposition is not merely a personal trait; it reflects the Communist mentality. Indeed, in ferocity of retort and hostility to the slightest deviation, a red thread leads from Marx to Lenin to Stalin. Though Lenin disowned him, Stalin is his true heir. Stalin altered the will and squandered the legacy, but he is a chip off the old block.

Stalin's innate distrust of people is congenial to Bolshevism. His hate of rivals fits snugly into the hate which feeds the destructiveness and dynamism of the Soviet system. "It is impossible to conquer an enemy without having learned to hate him with all one's soul," Stalin said in 1946. Hate, cruelty, secrecy, dishonesty, dissimulation, and distortions are characteristics of Stalin and features of Soviet totalitarianism. The system found its man. The man adapted the system to himself. Now the two are indistinguishable. Lenin sometimes seems far away, but the differences between him and Stalin, though vast, are quantitative, not qualitative. They are differences of degree.

Lenin, like Marx, stabbed with the political pen, Stalin chops with the executioner's ax. Lenin had the brains to convince. Stalin, after he achieved full power, killed to conquer. Lenin had analytical agility and clarity of thought. Stalin is the skilled politician. But the Bolshevik intellectuals, beginning with Lenin and Trotsky, who looked down their snobbish noses at Stalin because he was a plebeian boss type, rated him lower than he deserved. His mental equipment, though neither unusual nor impressive, is adequate for a dictator who brooks no contradiction. Stalin is a master of the sneer and the commonplace. When he has an idea he chews on it endlessly. His mind is near enough to the mass mind to enable him to read it. In debate he is arrogant, cruel, sarcastic, and always conscious of the grandstand's love of blood and vulgarity. His success with these methods increased his scorn for the defeated intellectuals who had treated him with contempt. Stalin detests finesse, complicated culture, abstract thought, sensitive art, humanism, and gentleness. What he detests he destroys.

Stalin has recreated Russia in his cultural image. He has lowered the nation to his mental level. He sets the standard for the entire country. His crude taste is law. No one must be better than the dictator. What is good enough for Stalin is good for the peasant and good enough for the professor. The iron harshness of Stalin's politics carries over into art and public manners.

Russia, mother of great writers, musicians, and scientists and of a great people, deserves somebody better than Stalin. But communism could not have had a more perfect leader. A social system finds men who fit its needs. Ancient Rome produced Caesars. Medieval Italy bred artists. India grows saints. America grows engineers. Four centuries ago Albert Einstein might have been a Michelangelo, two centuries ago a Beethoven. The talents of outstanding men flow into molds that vary with the requirements of the times. In Stalin, the Soviet system found a dictator of genius. In him it attained its highest flower.

CHAPTER IV

Revolutionary Gradualness

Stalin can deify himself and impose his infallibility because he has absolute power. He achieved this power gradually. In fact, Bolshevik totalitarianism has been a gradual growth. From its birth in November, 1917, the Soviet regime, to be sure, dealt ruthlessly with persons who fought it, but its treatment of government officials, Communists, and average citizens was much milder than it is today.

Revolution is usually associated with rapid change and democracy with gradualness. Actually, Soviet despotism matured by stages. In 1918, for instance, Lenin permitted the publication of a daily newspaper, the Moscow *Communist*, founded to change his foreign policy. Having done so, he flayed its editors fiercely until his arguments and world events persuaded them to shut down. Likewise, Lenin appointed several outspoken critics to represent Soviet Russia at the Genoa Conference in 1922. For a while, Stalin, following the same pattern, sent some of his opponents as ambassadors to foreign countries. Subsequently, when he acquired adequate power, it became more stylish to get rid of them by shooting. In August, 1923, as Stalin admitted on December 2, 1923, a wave of strikes swept through some Soviet provinces. In later years, strikes were rigorously prevented. Until the middle of the 1920's, critics of the Soviet government and many citizens who wished to emigrate were allowed to leave the country. Subsequently, the exit door was closed.

Even if Bolshevism had planned from the beginning to introduce the harsh tyranny of today it would have had to proceed step by step, for the Russian people knew freedom and would have preferred to be free. The frequency with which the contrary is asserted does not make it true.

That the absolute monarchy allowed more freedom than the Bolshevik regime is demonstrable. Lenin's mother, living in Czarist

Russia, communicated through the official post office with her son, a well-known revolutionary, in Switzerland, and openly sent money to him. Exiled Bolsheviks in various parts of Siberia assembled for party conferences. These things would have been quite impossible in Lenin's or Stalin's Russia. Most startling fact of all—Lenin, Stalin, Trotsky, and a host of other rebels were in the hands of the Czarist police and survived.

For a short, tortured period, the Czarist government sanctioned a parliament or Duma in which Bolsheviks, Mensheviks, and other avowed antimonarchists participated. The flow of books, magazines, newspapers, and persons into and out of Czarist Russia was considerable. It was appreciable in the first decade of Bolshevism. It is negligible now.

In the nineteenth century, the Russian government granted George Kennan, an American writer (granduncle of the subsequent American Ambassador to Soviet Moscow), access to the detention camps in Siberia. He fiercely denounced them in a book. Stalin's government makes no such liberal slips.

The Okhrana, the Czar's political police, committed untold crimes but was by no means a ubiquitous, omnipotent instrument like the Cheka, the GPU, the NKVD, or, the latest incarnation, the MVD. Russian literary classics, as well as the existence of opposition parties, opposition newspapers, and trade unions, testify amply to the fact that the Russian people knew restricted freedom and were less terrorized under the Czar than under Stalin or Lenin.

Moreover, Russia was a very free country between the fall of Nicholas II in March, 1917, and the rise of Lenin and Trotsky in November. Lenin himself said that in that eight-month Kerensky interregnum, which he cut short, Russia was the "freest country in the world."

Not all Soviet citizens, of course, remember conditions before the Bolshevik revolution. But most of them have studied Lenin's life and the early history of the Bolshevik party. Even assuming, however, that this academic knowledge made no impression, every Soviet adult knows, from personal observation and often at his personal cost, that his own liberties have gradually been curtailed.

There was more freedom in Russia before Lenin's death than after, and more before Trotsky's banishment than after. Every passing year of Stalinism brings more tyranny. Freedom is lost in fractions. Time has helped Stalin learn his trade.

In 1929, in Moscow, I was writing a two-volume history of Soviet foreign policy. Georgi Chicherin, the Foreign Commissar, Maxim Litvinov, and Leo Karakhan, the Assistant Foreign Commissars, Borodin, Moscow's representative in China, and many other Russian policy-makers helped me collect the data for this work, and gave me access to their own and government archives. When Litvinov had taken the story of Soviet foreign relations up to and through the important Anglo-Soviet negotiations of 1924, he said, "I have told you everything I remember. The man who really knows what happened is Rakovsky."

Christian G. Rakovsky, an early Bolshevik, and Soviet ambassador in London and Paris, had been dismissed from office and banished for his Trotskyism.

"But Rakovsky," I said to Litvinov, "is in exile."

"Go and see him," he suggested.

"How can I find him?" I asked.

"He is somewhere in Saratov," Litvinov informed me. "His daughter can give you the exact address."

Rakovsky's daughter, who lived in Moscow, gave me her parents' address and a letter and suitcase of books to deliver to them.

In those days, a foreign journalist could simply go to the railway station or a travel agency, buy a ticket, and proceed to any part of the Soviet Union, except Central Asia, always a sensitive region. I bought my ticket and sleeper accommodation, but then it occurred to me that although I had met Rakovsky a number of times he might not reveal unpublished facts to me unless he knew that Chicherin, Litvinov, and others had been doing so. I brought these doubts to Litvinov.

"But what do you expect me to do," he replied. "I cannot write a letter recommending you to a banished Trotskyist."

"Then there isn't much sense in my going," I said.

"Well, let me think about it," he promised.

Two days later a courier handed me a letter signed by Litvinov and addressed to Feodor Rothstein, Litvinov's assistant and chief of the Foreign Commissariat's press department. Litvinov asked Rothstein to assist me in the preparation of my book. Rakovsky would know that this letter was intended for him, first because it would otherwise not have come into my possession, and, second, Litvinov could have given such instructions to Rothstein orally, for their offices were next to one another and they met a dozen times a day.

On arriving at the ancient Volga city of Saratov, I went to a hotel. The guest's names were inscribed in chalk on the hall porter's blackboard. On it I read, "Christian G. Rakovsky" and, again, "Christian G. Rakovsky." He and his wife occupied two rooms in the best hotel in town.

I spent eight days, six or seven hours each day, with Rakovsky. He had with him, in a huge trunk in his room, the secret protocols of the Anglo-Russian conference which he allowed me to copy. He also carried into exile a large personal correspondence. He was doing research for a book on Saint Simon and regularly received material on the subject sent at his request by the Marx-Engels Institute in Moscow.

Rakovsky usually received me at noon. He would talk to me for about two hours while I took notes. Then he would go for lunch. Several times I accompanied him to the restaurant. As he walked through the streets men would bow and tip their hats.

I would return to Rakovsky's apartment at 6 P.M. An hour or so later, a young man would come in, nod, sit down, and listen. Moments later, another person entered. By 7:30, six or seven persons had gathered. I asked him who they were. "These are my fellow Trotskyist exiles," he explained.

Today, no exile lives in the comfort of Saratov or in the luxury of a hotel. No commissar sends a foreigner or anybody to an opponent of Stalin. No citizen has the temerity or folly to display reverence for an exile. No oppositionists congregate freely together. Rakovsky himself was soon transported to Siberia. In the March,

1938, Moscow trial he was charged with being a Japanese spy and condemned on his own, unsubstantiated confession.

In the early era of comparative mildness, Stalin also treated Trotsky gently. Trotsky was not tortured or tried. He was banished on January 16, 1928, to a pleasant house in Alma-Ata, in Turkestan. A year later, Stalin deported him to Turkey, thus surrendering control over him. Before he consented to leave, Trotsky negotiated with Stalin, through the secret police, on which of his associates would accompany him.

(Stalin continued his step-by-step persecution of Trotsky. He put pressure on the Turkish government which requested Trotsky to move. Trotsky went to France. Stalin agents made life so intolerable that Trotsky left for Norway. Still pursuing the foe—in the tradition of the Georgian blood feud—Stalin protested to Norway. The Norwegian government induced Trotsky to depart. He went to Mexico. There, in 1940, he was murdered by mysterious hands suspected of being Stalinist.)

In 1928 and 1929, Stalin, reckoning with possible indignation in the party and country, did not dare shoot Trotsky. In 1936, Zinoviev and Kamenev were executed. That is an index to the crescendo of terror during the seven intervening years. In retrospect the 1920's in Russia were an era of freedom compared with the political pogroms of the 1930's and the rigors of the '40's and '50's. Stalin advanced toward absolutism slowly.

Stalin habitually moves with magnificent caution at the beginning, probing, testing his enemy's strength, noting the intensity of resistance, seeking weak spots. In the second stage, he advances to strike a trial blow and withdraws to watch the effect. Finally, when fully certain of the outcome, he makes the kill. Stalin never gambles. He collectivized agriculture gradually and, in one phase, retreated before menacing peasant hostility. He destroyed the trade unions and the party in installments. He liquidated Trotsky in more than a dozen moves. The Baltic states were seized in three moves. First move: in September and October, 1939, under Moscow pressure and in accordance with a prior agreement between Stalin and Hitler, Latvia, Lithuania, and Estonia granted bases to Russia on the Baltic sea. The Nazis, however, suspected that Moscow had further plans in this area. On October 31, 1939, therefore, Soviet Foreign Minister Molotov declared publicly, "The chatter about the sovietization of the Baltic countries is profitable only to our enemies and all anti-Soviet provocateurs." The new Russian treaties with Latvia, Lithuania, and Estonia, he added, "firmly stipulate the inviolability of the sovereignty of the signatory nations as well as the principle of noninterference in the affairs of the other nation." Molotov thus promised that the three Baltic countries would remain independent. Second move: in the spring of 1940, while Hitler concentrated on the conquest of Norway and Denmark, Stalin sent masses of troops into the Baltic states and occupied them. Third move: on July 21, 1940, when Hitler was busy occupying France and threatening England, the Baltic countries were officially annexed by Russia and sovietized as Molotov had said they would not be.

At each of these three stages, Stalin went as far as he dared. When he thought there would be no foreign opposition he took everything he wanted. Promises and treaties were forgotten.

Stalin's installment-plan politics stems from a primitive caution which tempers his natural combativeness. But he has also thought it out and formulated it, as usual, in military terms. "When," he asked in a *Pravda* article dated April 3, 1930, "can an offensive be successful, say, in the field of military affairs? When people do not limit themselves to uninterrupted advance but try at the same time to reinforce captured positions, regroup their forces in conformity with the new situation, bring up their rear, bring forward their reserves. Why is this necessary? In order to guarantee yourself against surprises, to liquidate some openings in the front which occur in any offensive, and to prepare, in this manner, the complete liquidation of the enemy. . . . The same must be said about offensives on the class-war front."

This explains Stalin's patience. While the world waits and guesses, he may be closing a breach in the home front or stiffening a satellite. What does it matter that the entire operation seems to lack finished form? To a Spaniard, the manner of killing a bull is highly important. To Stalin form is immaterial. Results count, not appearances. He would rather bend than break. He would rather retreat than court defeat. He would rather create an impression of weakness than go beyond his strength. There is nothing Stalin would not do because it might seem incongruous or without precedent. His goal is not world applause.

Without the caution which makes him indifferent to form Stalin's will and fiery bellicosity might have got him into many difficulties. But on the brink of an impetuous act he has often stopped to calculate and saved himself.

To indicate disapproval Stalin often says, "But this is Don Quixotism." He rejects quixotic methods. Rather than tilt at windmills with a long lance he would put sand in the mechanism and, as opportunities occur, take the windmill apart piece by piece.

Stalin's guiding rule is "piecemeal."

CHAPTER V

"I Am the State"

It is unfair to Stalin to call him a modern Genghis Khan or Tamerlane or Ivan the Terrible. He outranks all the autocrats of history. The monarch who said, "I am the state," was an amateur compared to Stalin.

At the Yalta Conference in February, 1945, President Roosevelt said he could not agree to certain arrangements which the United States Senate might reject. Stalin replied that he too had to consider the views of his generals and political lieutenants. The statement, designed to put him in a stronger bargaining position with the President, gave wings to the myth that Stalin, the "moderate," faced an "extremist" opposition in the Politbureau. President Truman, in fact, once expressed this view. "Joe," he said, "is a decent fellow but he is a prisoner of the Politbureau. He makes certain agreements but he can't keep them; they won't let him." Publications have spread the same notion. But though this always makes a piquant "inside story," there is no proof, nor even circumstantial evidence, of opposition to Stalin in the Politbureau or elsewhere in the party or government.

As Stalin grows older, and with the deterioration of his heart, he takes long vacations, sometimes lasting four or more months, in his villa near Sochi on the beautiful Caucasus Black Sea Riviera. Even there, a two-day train journey from the Kremlin, his hand remains on the controls. A long-distance telephone, teletype machines, and an air-courier service keep him in close touch with all major developments, and no question is decided without him unless he grants the permission.

It is the Soviet state, as it developed after 1928, that gives Stalin power unknown in history. Until 1928, the Soviet system tolerated capitalism in the cities and villages. Today, private capitalism has been extinguished. The Kremlin exercises complete control over Soviet economy and, therefore, over all the persons who work in that economy. This makes it a modern superfeudalism, the Middle Ages with tractors and electronics. It is the feudal nature of the Soviet state which explains Stalin's unprecedented power.

Sovietism is neither communism nor socialism nor Marxism. The Soviet destruction of private capitalism conformed to the precepts of Marx. But what happened after that does not. After that, thanks to Stalin, came feudalism.

Stalin has not known a capitalistic country. Czarist Russia was never predominantly capitalistic. It was largely feudal. Georgia was especially feudal. This is what the youthful Stalin knew and hated. This he resolved to destroy.

By defeating Napoleon, the Czar kept the French revolution out of Russia and thus entrenched feudalism. Later, in 1825, some Russian noblemen, impressed with the French ideas of "Liberty, Equality, Fraternity," tried to overthrow the absolute monarchy and give Russia a constitution. They failed.

In 1862, Alexander II liberated the serfs. But the landlords remained, many peasants had no land, and Russia remained a backward country. The bulk of the peasantry depended on the landlords and paid them tribute. Nor did the growth of urban industry, often financed from abroad, destroy the feudal character of Russian society. The bourgeoisie was weak, weaker in influence than the aristocracy. The worker stood cap in hand before his employer. Less wealth meant lower status. That is typical of social relations under feudalism where, moreover, the upper classes feel no public responsibility, evade taxes, and live in blinding luxury, but "love" the serf and try to establish a father-son relation with him. Even so the Indian maharaja allows the peasant to complain or beg in person. Even so the Czar, afraid though surrounded by a glittering court of fawning feudal nobles, aspired to be "Little Father" to the suffering people who could petition him for relief. Feudalism and feudal capitalism substitute paternalistic "solicitude" for good wages.

The Provisional "Kerensky" government, which succeeded the deposed Nicholas II, inherited the crippling deficiency of Czarism:

a weak capitalist class. Had it abolished feudalism by giving land to the peasants and making them little capitalists, the new liberal regime of 1917 might have resisted communism. But freedom alone was not enough to hold the loyalty of the people. Liberty without peace, without a land reform, and without a strong police department, was an open door to Bolshevism.

Many Bolshevik leaders (not Stalin) had, during their European exile, encountered the spirit of the French revolution which dethroned feudalism. But they rejected its teachings because it enthroned the bourgeoisie. Liberty, equality, and fraternity were to them synonymous with capitalism and therefore anathema.

Theoretically, the Communist alternative to capitalism is socialism. Actually, it would have been a titanic, probably an impossible, task to erect a Socialist state in Russia. The Bolsheviks never tried. They did something else. They established a modernized feudalism.

There was a natural transition from Czarist feudalism to Soviet feudalism. That is why feudal Russia became the first Communist state. Feudalism and communism have much in common, and the more feudal a country the more communism appeals to it as an improvement. In the United States, England, and Western Germany, where feudal elements are negligible, so is communism. In Italy, where capitalism is superimposed on a feudal base, communism is strong. Other conditions too may produce a big Communist, or Fascist, movement: the despair of an impoverished middle class, or industrial stagnation or national degradation. But where feudalism is widespread and capitalism puny, as in Russia, communism always gains.

The feudal character of the Soviet system manifests itself unmistakably in village and town.

In the villages, the Soviet revolution nationalized land and gave it to the peasants for use but not as their property. That was the first Bolshevik land reform of 1917. It was a capitalist revolution. It created a mass of small private capitalists. Trotsky protested; 125,000,000 peasant proprietors would ultimately devour the Soviet state. Stalin saw this too. Hence Stalin's collectivization which eliminated private farming. Today, all Soviet peasants are collectivized. No Soviet peasant owns land, or a horse, or ox, or plow, or tractor, or any farm equipment. The state owns them. The state supplies seed and fertilizer and buys the crops. No peasant can decide to change from one collective to another. He is a serf and Stalin is his landlord, his feudal baron. Russian agriculture is more feudal than under Czarism; it is totally feudal.

The progression in the Russian villages was: feudalism mixed with some capitalism under the Czar; capitalism under Soviet control from 1917 to 1928; finally, the feudal collectivism of the present. Socialism was not suggested or attempted.

Similarly, Soviet industries operate on a feudal basis. The workingman cannot change his job at will. He is chained to his machine which belongs to the state. Bolshevism cultivates the fiction that the factories are the property of the workers. But since the workers are the property of the government the fiction convinces no one.

The Soviet state owns all factories, farm land, forests, oil fields, railroads, mines, public buildings, and apartment houses. It is the twentieth-century Behemoth.

Every Soviet citizen living inside the Soviet Union must have a passport. This registers him with the police. He cannot move from one city to the other without permission. The permission must be entered into his passport and no city or village will accept him without it.

In the choice of a profession, Soviet university students and other youth are subject to directives which the government may adopt. They are also subject to universal military conscription, and must participate in one of several "voluntary" military organizations.

It would be difficult to imagine a society in which the individual is more subservient to the state and the state more independent of the individual. This is Stalin's most monumental achievement. Ancient tyrannies and medieval autocracies lacked his technical instruments for ubiquitous suppression over vast territories.

Only under the present system could Stalin have become the supreme feudal lord. The survival of capitalism in Russia would have forced him to share power with the capitalists. Socialism would have enabled workers to run their factories and peasants to run their communes without the state, and therefore without the dictator. But superfeudalism makes all peasants, workingmen, technical personnel, and officials the servants of the state, and the serfs, consequently, of the man who is the state. Stalin has perfected Czarism.

As originally conceived, the Bolshevik government would be managed by everybody. It would be a soviet state. Each village and city would be governed by a soviet or council, popularly elected. Each county would have a soviet elected by the members of the local soviets and each province a soviet elected by the county soviets. The central soviet in Moscow would be elected by the provincial soviets.

Shortly after I first arrived in Soviet Russia in September, 1922, I asked the wife of an old judge what was the most important change wrought by the Bolshevik revolution. "The people talk more," she replied. The people talked more because they had more influence in politics and therefore more interest in politics.

The soviets, however, soon fell under the domination of their few Communist members. The Kremlin was forced to impose restrictive measures which would not have won a majority in the councils except under Communist pressure. The Communists tolerated no opposition in the soviets. The people grew afraid and talked less. (The anti-Soviet characters in recent Soviet novels are persons who argue.)

By the middle of the 1920's, the local, regional, and federal soviets were docile instruments of the Communist party. As early as 1924, Stalin urged the party "to revive the soviets, put them back on their feet." They were already dying.

Today, the soviets meet and "adopt" unanimous decisions—drafted in the Kremlin. The soviets are a red-ink rubber stamp. Sometimes, the newspapers print the proceedings of the national soviets. They are soporifically boring; the delegates repeat one another without apparent shame, and all of them repeat Stalin or *Pravda*. There is no debate, discussion, originality, variety, vitality, courage, or interest. The soviet system exists on paper only. Its power passed to the Communist party, which embraces a tiny percentage of the population.

The Soviet Union could have been a people's state or a party state, but not both. It became a party state. The Bolshevik party ruled. The soviets, through which the people might have ruled, are dead in all but name.

The fate of the soviets has been shared by the trade unions. In 1920 and 1921, Soviet public life was shaken by a vehement controversy on the purpose of trade unions. Trotsky, whose spectacular career as Red warlord may have influenced his thinking, proposed a plan for the military regimentation of workingmen. They would be the state's soldiers, or serfs, in factories. Lenin objected. The state, he said, might fall under the influence of the peasants or officeholders, forget that it was a workers' dictatorship, and become a dictatorship over the workers. Stalin took the same position.

Lenin's viewpoint prevailed. But today, Stalin has militarized the trade unions. Their function is to help the state raise output. Collective bargaining is nonexistent. Strikes are banned.

During the Second World War, Harry L. Hopkins, President Roosevelt's special envoy, told Stalin that certain shipments from America would be delayed because of strikes.

"Strikes?" Stalin asked, lifting his eyebrows. "Don't you have police?"

In Russia, the Communist party, backed by the police, seized control of the trade unions, and did not permit strikes. The cannibalistic party, which had swallowed the soviets, also swallowed the trade unions.

Then, perceptibly, the cannibalistic party was swallowed by the great cannibal: Stalin.

Before the 1917 revolution, and until 1929, there was at times more and at times less democracy in the Russian Communist party, but policy was always the result of discussion and votes. Various points of view were defended.

Stalin, however, was always quite indifferent to democracy in the party. As far back as January 17, 1924, in a speech, he ridiculed comrades who "made a fetish" of party democracy and elaborated in detail and with emphasis the many weighty factors operating and likely to operate against party democracy. This attitude bore fruit as Stalin's power waxed. Between 1918 and 1925, in all the difficult circumstances of foreign invasion, civil war, economic distress, and famine, the Russian Communist party met in annual congress to adopt the policies of the Soviet government. The annual congress was Mt. Sinai; it handed down the law. But in 1925, Stalin gripped the party machine. The next congress met in 1927, the next in 1930, the next in 1934, the next in 1939. Each time Stalin lengthened the interval by a year—systematically. Since 1939 there has been no party congress. The last few congresses were so short in duration and so large in membership that they resembled mass meetings rather than deliberative bodies. The Sixteenth Party Congress, for instance, which assembled on June 26, 1930, consisted of 1,268 delegates with voting power and 891 additional delegates with voice but no vote; in all, 2,159 delegates representing 1,260,874 party members and 711,609 candidates for membership. It could not transact business. It merely applauded Stalin.

The party has disappeared into Stalin's maw. Where there is one party it does not take long before there is no party. The so-called one-party system in Russia is, in fact, a personal dictatorship. The dictator dominates the party, the trade unions, the soviets, the government, the government factories, the government collectives, and wholesale and retail trade, which is also a government monopoly.

Originally, Soviet society resembled a pyramid. Its broad base was the soviets. A shelf higher were the trade unions. Narrower and higher still, the party. At the top of the pyramid was the Politbureau. Then Stalin gradually, methodically, turned this social pyramid upside down so that it stood on its point and all the power that had resided in the soviets, the trade unions, the party, and the Politbureau flowed down to Stalin. Drained of practical use, the pyramid shriveled into a column, the monolith of Stalinist dictatorship.

And above the entire Soviet political edifice sits Stalin, the little Red father, alone, afraid, a monarch without crown. "I am the state" satisfied the precapitalistic king and it satisfies the postcapitalistic, egocentric dictator. Stalin gets officially "suggested" presents from persons and groups in Russia and the empire, and he confers gifts. Peasants cannot approach him as they do the maharaja, but whatever they have, they are told, derives from his bounty.

Capitalism creates an impersonal relationship between employer and employee. Feudalism, ancient or Soviet, aspires to a personal relationship between employer and employee; "love" disguises exploitation. Socialism would have established a personal relationship without exploitation in communes and co-operatives. Stalin prefers his feudal eminence. He did not build socialism in one country, as he boasts. He built feudalism in one country.

Stalin is not subtle, not eloquent, not charming. He is no philosopher, no writer, no thinker. But he is a genius who knows how to harness and humble men. He has that in common with Hitler and Mussolini, that and boundless vanity. With this equipment he raised himself to the pinnacle. Stalin is the machine politician triumphant, the county boss on the throne of an empire. This has occasionally happened in a democracy. But under the Soviet dictatorship it has lasted a quarter of a century. It would have been impossible without a political doctrine which exalts the human mass and the all-powerful state. Stalin is the apotheosis of a system in which system matters most and man least.

Stalin is the machine age at its ugliest. He mechanizes politics and men. "Stalin," Man of Steel, is a fitting name for him. Steel is firm, cold, and hard but malleable. Steel is dead matter, yet it has vital attributes: it expands, contracts, and forms alloys. Steel is a hammer and steel is a spring. Above all, steel is the machine. The machine, designed to liberate man from poverty and drudgery, becomes man's master. It dictates. It enters the hearts and minds of men to enslave them. Equally, the machine state, too big to be controlled by its citizens, controls them. The people are then asked to worship the machine state and the man who runs it.

The dual danger of the machine and machine state hangs over the entire world. In the Russia of Stalin it is no longer a threat; it is a fact. The robotization of man and the mechanization of politics is the end product of Sovietism.

Stalin is dictator because his will, vigor, arrogance, intolerance, and belligerence make him a dictator by nature. But he needed a dictatorship to make him a dictator. If he lived in a democracy he might, with the same nature, have become a market manipulator, a gang leader, a political boss, a great builder, or a frustrated psychopath. In another era, he might have been a smuggler, poacher, pirate chief, hunter, or gold miner. Under the Soviet flag he is supreme tyrant. It is the Soviet feudal system that makes Stalin what he is, for it concentrates maximum power in the state and provides no checks and balances on him who runs it. What bigger boons could a power-lover ask?

Would Lenin or Trotsky have done likewise? In their theoretical justification of dictatorship and of the terror which perpetuates it, Lenin and Trotsky did not lag behind Stalin. But Lenin never enjoyed as much power as Stalin because the economic system was different; it was not yet Soviet-feudal. It was a milk-and-water solution of capitalism with the remnants of prerevolutionary liberties not yet liquidated.

Would Lenin or Trotsky have walked the same road after 1928? When so much power is concentrated in one person, when his bad dreams, bad moods, bad health, or pathological wishes can influence state decisions, it would be foolish to deny him a major role in history. Without Lenin the Bolshevik revolution might not have occurred in 1917 or ever; a Zinoviev or Kamenev might have missed the best opportunity. If Lenin had not died when he did—he died at fifty-four, and might have lived twenty more years—the Trotsky-Stalin feud might not have caused a split. Stalin needed complete police power to destroy Trotsky's influence in the Bolshevik party. In other circumstances, the fiercely personal dictatorship of Stalin might not have emerged. Power is a substitute for authority. Lenin had authority, and might have needed less power than Stalin. Time too is a vital factor in politics. Stalin feared the new capitalist class, but his measures against it were more hurried than is normal with him because Trotsky led the opposition to that rising class, and Stalin feared Trotsky.

At one party congress Lenin dissected Bukharin's policies and subjected them to withering condemnation. After the session he took Bukharin by the arm, called him "Bukhashka," and laughed.

They were the same friends as ever. Stalin lacks this gift. Some men win with wit and charm, others win by bullets.

Trotsky had a liking for regimentation. He, or Lenin, might have built feudalism too. But their tempo would have been different. The methods would have varied. Moreover, the bigger the man the less he worries about big men around him. Stalin has never been certain that his rivals did not want to displace him. Therefore he purges and humiliates. Lenin had so much prestige and ability that no rival appeared. Lenin could afford to nurse growth in others. Stalin does the opposite.

No one has compared Lenin with Hitler. Lenin tempered power with zeal for a new world. In Stalin the power grew and the ideals shrank and ultimately disappeared. Lenin was a fanatic in politics. Stalin is a mechanic in politics. Lenin believed. Stalin has passion but not fanaticism. His passion is for destruction, construction, and power, but not for improvements in human society or in the human being. Stalin has no vision of the perfect man; he craves the perfect robot. Lenin was not romantic in the German mystic, myth-loving sense, but he was inspired by a dream of the new society; he had his Utopia even though his means were sordid and violent and hence self-defeating. There is no romance in Stalin, no Utopia. His castle in the air is the biggest possible political powerhouse.

In Lenin, Russia was diluted by Europe and the twentieth century by the nineteenth. Stalin has some of Lenin in him but more of Hitler. Stalin is the type totalitarian of the modern age, the power-man. Nevertheless, it cannot be said of Stalin, as one could of Hitler, that he is "drunk with power." Stalin is sober, calculating, deliberate; "a perfectly co-ordinated machine, an intelligent machine," Harry L. Hopkins called him. The Man of Steel is a machine man, and he is the machine state, the state that has mechanized men in order to enthrone a new mechanical serfdom.

CHAPTER VI

How Stalin Treats the Men Around Him

Every dictator assumes that there is no person he cannot break. In Stalin's case, the assumption is correct. Given his power, the method is simple.

One morning in May, 1938, the photograph of Stanislav V. Kossior was removed from the outside wall of the apartment house in which I lived in Moscow. Kossior was a member of the supreme Politbureau and the Communist chief of the Ukraine, the granary and leading industrial area of the Soviet Union inhabited by about forty-two million persons. The enlarged photographs of Stalin, Kossior, and the other members of the Big Ten of the Kremlin were displayed on many apartment house walls and in most schools, offices, and factories. That morning in May, 1938, Kossior's picture was taken down from all walls. Nothing else happened. From that day to this no announcement has been made in Russia that Kossior was sick and died, or that he committed a crime and was shot or exiled or demoted or dismissed. No word has ever come from any Soviet source about Kossior's fate. He simply disappeared. He was the fifth or sixth most important Communist in Russia. Yet such is Stalin's contempt for his subjects, and such is their impotence, that he never felt impelled to tell them what happened to Kossior. In the same way, and in the same year, Vlas Y. Chubar, another member of the Politbureau, disappeared; in 1949, the same fate overtook Nikolai A. Voznesensky, of the same key body.

The power to shoot can be a rather important factor in politics. Foreigners occasionally underestimate it. In 1944, Stalin was eager to have the sympathy of Roman Catholics. He anticipated resistance in puppet Poland and thought popular support might be won by smiling on the Vatican. Stalin accordingly gave an audience to Father Orlemanski, a Catholic parish priest of Polish origin from

Springfield, Massachusetts, who, he vainly hoped, would sway Catholic opinion in Poland and Rome in favor of Russia. Stalin also wrote a conciliatory letter to the Pope. Apprised of the fact that the Holy Father had failed to answer Stalin's communication, President Roosevelt, early in 1945, took Edward J. Flynn, the Democratic party leader of the Borough of Bronx, New York, to Yalta. En route, Flynn visited Rome; later he met Stalin at Yalta and in the Moscow Kremlin. He also talked with Zhdanov, the Bolshevik boss of Leningrad.

After Mr. Flynn's return to New York I went to see him. Commenting on his trip he said, "I understand Stalin's problem; I have my own difficulties in the Bronx."

"But you can't shoot your opponents," I said.

Yet Stalin would not be a successful dictator if he were merely a policeman and an executioner. He is also a surgeon:

In 1944, Eric A. Johnston, then president of the United States Chamber of Commerce, had an interview with Joseph Stalin. The meeting was recorded and Mr. Johnston subsequently published the official text given him by Stalin's office.

Mr. Johnston was about to leave for a trip in the Ural Mountains industrial area and said, "I would like to ask permission to take four correspondents with me to the Urals."

"Why not?" said Stalin.

"Does that mean that I can take them?"

"Of course it does," Stalin declared.

"Well, thank you, Marshal Stalin," Johnston said. "But I don't know whether Mr. Molotov will approve. You see, his office has not yet approved my request."

Molotov, Foreign Minister at the time and prominently mentioned as Stalin's successor, was present at the interview. "I always approve of Marshal Stalin's decisions," Molotov exclaimed quickly.

Stalin, Johnston recalls, "cocked his head on one side." A broad grin animated his face. "Mr. Johnston," Stalin remarked, "you really didn't expect Mr. Molotov to disagree with me, did you?"

No, nobody would who knew Russia.

Was this conscious humiliation on Stalin's part? Or was it unconscious insensitivity? Either would be cruel. Mr. Johnston had witnessed an example of Stalin's surgery. The dictator used his knife to cut away a little more of the little that remained of Molotov's ego.

Stalin intimidates by killing and by cutting. The result is an underling who avoids too much popularity, lest Stalin resent the competition, and too much authority, lest Stalin suspect a dangerous ambition.

Marshal Zhukov commanded the Russian forces which saved Moscow from Nazi conquest in December, 1941. He took Berlin in 1945. Shortly after that historic event, General Dwight D. Eisenhower gave him a banquet in Frankfurt. *Army Talks,* official U.S.A. Army publication, and the New York *Herald Tribune* of June 18, 1945, reported the following conversation:

Zhukov: "We've got some of those German synthetic oil plants that we captured over in our territory. We have repaired them but we haven't been able to get them running yet. I understand you've got some running on your side. Could some of my experts come over and see how you got yours running?"
Eisenhower: "Sure, send 'em over. We'll show 'em how to do it."
Zhukov (in a surprised tone): "You mean you don't have to ask your government?"
Eisenhower: "Of course not. . . . Send 'em on over."

Russia's outstanding war hero was astonished at Eisenhower's independence in the small matter of admitting a few foreign engineers into his territory. Zhukov would have queried the Kremlin. He knew from experience that it was healthier not to take too much initiative. A Soviet officeholder must have no power except that deflected to him temporarily and explicitly by The Leader.

When the Second World War was concluded, Marshal Zhukov received invitations to lead ticker-tape victory parades in American cities. He would have been feted as the Russian who won the war. He did not go. Stalin won the war.

Instead, Zhukov was relegated to a relatively minor military post in the Odessa region where he had enough leisure to deflate himself by contemplation. Such demotions are sometimes first stops to the executioner's dungeon. The thought of this possibility could only make Zhukov thankful for remaining alive. His highest ambition was to exist.

Even Klementi Voroshilov, a member of the Politbureau, Commissar of Defense, and probably the most popular Soviet leader, knew his place. In the 1930's the Soviet Foreign Office requested him to pose for a foreign photographer who had arrived in the country to take pictures of the Bolshevik chiefs. "Has he photographed Stalin?" Voroshilov asked.

The Foreign Office man said no.

"Then I can't pose for him," Voroshilov said.

Stalin can have little respect for the surrounding toadies and pigmies who survive his whim for murder. They tell him dirty stories, laugh at his jokes, and applaud his deeds. He is too intelligent not to know they have no choice. They are too intelligent not to know that he understands their predicament. Stalin entertains his lieutenants and sups with his buddies. Sometimes the atmosphere is gay; he can be a pleasant host. But the gaiety must be haunted by ghosts. Among those who used to eat and drink in Stalin's Kremlin apartment late at night when he returned from a long day's work were Abel Yenukidze, secretary of the Soviet government, a tall, plump, blond, jovial Georgian who had been Stalin's friend since 1900, and Leo Karakhan, Assistant Commissar of Foreign Affairs, a handsome, suave, pleasure-loving Armenian. They belonged to Stalin's favored Caucasian company. Subsequently he ordered Yenukidze and Karakhan shot.

Sometimes Stalin gives much pain to the men around him. For instance: Constantine Oumansky, newly appointed Soviet ambassador in Washington, left for Moscow in the summer of 1939, carrying an important message to Stalin from President Roosevelt. There had been rumors of the impending Soviet-Nazi pact, and Roosevelt asked Oumansky to tell Stalin that "if his government joined up with Hitler, it was certain as night followed the day that as soon as Hitler conquered France he would turn on Russia." This prophecy, all the more remarkable because the world was still at peace, remained undelivered for at least ten weeks, until after the Soviet-Nazi pact had been signed. Stalin did not receive Oumansky.

Nobody of importance received Oumansky. He sat in his Moscow room and waited. The war commenced; Oumansky should have been back at his post, but no high official spoke to him. This smelled like doom. He expected to be purged. One day in October, 1939, Oumansky was instructed to appear in Stalin's office at 9 P.M. Andrei Gromyko, a minor official of the Soviet Foreign Ministry, was there too.

Early in the conversation, Stalin turned to Gromyko and said, "You are going to Washington. Work well, study the language. You will be the ambassador to the United States." This was Stalin's harsh way of telling Oumansky that he was in disfavor. On his way back to America with Gromyko, Oumansky told this story to a Soviet diplomat in Italy who now lives in the United States.

In receiving aides and little people, Stalin is often paternal, cordial, ingratiating. But lightning strikes when he is crossed. V. Molokov, a famous pilot whose daring exploits won him the highest distinction of Hero of the Soviet Union, was once called to Stalin. He reports the event in a Moscow publication. "I and my assistant, Comrade Kartushev," Molokov writes, "were summoned to the Kremlin. We were at that time on one of the airfields outside of Moscow. By the time they found us, by the time we arrived, much time had elapsed. In the Kremlin, we found Comrades Stalin, Molotov, and Voroshilov. They had been waiting two hours for us. I was quite frightened as I entered the office. Comrade Stalin eyed us intently, and said, 'Do you think we have nothing else to do? Where were you that it took you so long to come? And you call yourselves aviators.' "

Such pulverizing hammer blows, and the knowledge that he may deliver one at any moment, inhibit Stalin's visitors. Alexander Yakovlev, designer of the famous "YAK" fighter planes, went to see Stalin in 1944. He has described the interview in a Soviet book called *Meetings With Stalin*. He obviously hesitated to speak honestly to Stalin. "You need not look at the ceiling," Stalin admonished. "Nothing is written there. You better look straight at me and say what you think. That's all that is necessary."

This sally apparently intensified Yakovlev's nervousness; he earned another blunt reprimand. "Please say what you think. Don't try to say things that would please me," Stalin insisted.

On reaching Moscow as President Roosevelt's special representative in 1941, Harry L. Hopkins had a talk with another Yakovlev, a General of the Soviet artillery. He asked the general what was the weight of the heaviest Soviet tank. Yakovlev replied, "It is a good tank." He asked him whether Russia needed more tanks and antitank guns. "I am not empowered to say whether we do or do not need tanks or antitank guns," Yakovlev replied. But when Hopkins put these questions to Stalin he received an immediate, full and frank answer. "Nothing of real importance could be accomplished below the topmost level," comments Robert E. Sherwood in *Roosevelt and Hopkins*. W. Averell Harriman, who conferred repeatedly with Stalin during and after the war, formed the same impression. "There can be no doubt," he wrote, "that Stalin is the only man to deal with in foreign affairs. Dealing with others without previous instruction from Stalin about the matters under discussion was almost a waste of time."

Stalin's temperament and penalties have the effect of surrounding him with quaking Yes-men from whom he cannot extract the truth.

The only known No-man who miraculously survived—perhaps because Stalin secretly respects audacity—was Maxim M. Litvinov, Soviet Commissar of Foreign Affairs from 1930 to 1939. Litvinov was always tough and direct. Physically robust, mentally bright, sharp and resilient, he could bark and growl at assistants yet earn their affection. They called him "Papasha." He had been closely associated with Stalin in prerevolutionary work. He had intestinal courage. He obstructed the attempts of the secret police to infiltrate his department. He talked back in private to Stalin.

On May 3, 1939, Foreign Commissar Litvinov was asked to report to Stalin. He found Molotov there. Litvinov hated Molotov. Molotov is not his type. He had contempt for cringing sycophants.

Litvinov sat down at the table. Molotov began the conversation. The Soviet government, he said, intended to improve its relations with Hitler and, if possible, sign a pact with Nazi Germany. As a

Jew and as an avowed opponent of such a policy, Litvinov stood in the way.

Litvinov was angry. He asserted that a tie-up between Moscow and Hitler would spell disaster. He sketched the possibilities. He argued. He banged the table. Stalin sucked his pipe.

After listening for an hour without uttering a single word, Stalin put down his pipe and said, "Enough." Then thrusting a paper in Litvinov's direction, Stalin said, "Sign." It was Litvinov's letter of resignation. Litvinov signed.

Molotov succeeded Litvinov as Foreign Minister.

Litvinov retired to a bungalow in the woods outside Moscow. He played much bridge, learned to type, read poetry and fiction, and took long walks. He was completely isolated from Soviet politics.

Two years and seven weeks passed. Hitler invaded Russia. Some time later, the telephone in Litvinov's bungalow rang. It was an almost forgotten sound. Stalin invited Litvinov to his office and instructed him to deliver a radio address. He wanted the world to hear an authentic anti-Nazi voice from the Kremlin towers. Subsequently he used Litvinov as his English-language interpreter with high British and American officials.

One evening Stalin summoned Litvinov to the Kremlin. The dictator's first remark was, "Have you still got your dress suit?"

"I always keep my dress suit in mothballs," Litvinov replied.

"Take it out," Stalin ordered; "you are going to Washington as Ambassador." That ended the interview. Stalin needed a recognized anti-Nazi as his envoy to America and therefore took Litvinov out of the mothballs.

(In Washington and New York Litvinov described these episodes to two Americans whom he trusted.)

Litvinov was the exception. Resurrection is a rare phenomenon in Stalinist Russia. But as soon as Stalin could get rid of Litvinov he put him in mothballs again. Litvinov was not Stalin's leader type. In a private letter written on February 28, 1925, but not published until 1947, Stalin welcomed the eclipse of former "leaders"—the sarcastic quotes are his—like Lunacharsky, Krassin, Professor Pokrovsky, the historian, and other "literary folk" who had not shed their "social democratic baggage," who still, therefore, retained some culture and love of freedom. Stalin would not tolerate in his entourage any person with humanist or liberal tendencies or anyone who is not an imitation of his crude, rude, steely self. Stalin despises well-educated, contemplative, argumentative, introspective, soul-searching, idealistic men and women. There are none of them on the first or second leadership level. Gangster and boss types survive better than Hamlets or Einsteins. Stalin wants doers who do not think. A dictatorship is a state of war in which every citizen is a soldier whose duty is "to do or die" but not to reason.

Stalin is a good organizer and the subalterns and lieutenants around him have ability; otherwise he would not tolerate them. They do their jobs well within the limitations set by a dictatorship. But he has reduced them to the size of puppets. They specialize in the study of Stalin. They ape his taciturnity and gruffness. Some dress like him. They grovel before him. Stalin is the one and they are the zeros after it. He is the sun and they are the pale satellites to whom he gives light and life.

At Politbureau meetings Stalin rarely presides. Whenever he attends the weekly or semiweekly sessions he either sits and listens and doodles, or he walks round and round the conference table smoking cigarettes or a pipe. He rarely joins in the discussions. At some point, however, someone will say, "Comrade Stalin, what is your opinion?" And Stalin says, "I incline toward Comrade Malenkov's view," or, "I agree rather with Comrade Beria." That settles it. Stalin then writes out a resolution by hand—he never dictates—which defines the issue and the decision, and has a copy of it sent to each member of the Politbureau for signature or rejection. In this way, they are definitely committed. Stalin believes that formal documents are psychologically important.

If Stalin imposed his will on the Politbureau before discussion had taken place he would become the resented dictator; when he expresses his opinion after differences have emerged in debate he becomes the welcome arbitrator. He thrives on differences. An apocryphal story which circulated in Moscow illustrates his method:

One day Stalin summoned Molotov to his office. "How do you get on with Kaganovitch?" Stalin asked.

"Quite well," Molotov replied.

"But I hear that Kaganovitch has been telling everybody that you stammer," Stalin said.

"Well," Molotov stammered, "the fact is I do stammer."

"Yes," Stalin remarked, "but why should Kaganovitch be talking about it so much? He must have some purpose."

"That's true," Molotov commented, "I wonder what Kaganovitch is up to." Molotov leaves.

Stalin summons Kaganovitch. "How do you get on with Molotov?" Stalin asked.

"Quite well."

"Yes," Stalin said, "but I hear that Molotov has been saying that you are a Jew."

"Well," Kaganovitch replied, "I am a Jew."

"But why should Molotov be talking about it so much," Stalin demanded. "He must have some purpose."

"That's true," Kaganovitch agreed. "I wonder what Molotov is up to." Exit Kaganovitch.

Stalin rubbed his hands gleefully. "Now I can work," he said.

Stalin's coldly calculated manipulations of the men around him require aloofness. He isolates himself from his subordinates. He does not want them to be familiar with him. He does not want to have sympathy for them. He believes in the technique of the wall. The wall is the symbol of Oriental despotism and modern dictatorship. It also suits Stalin's temperament to be aloof and forbidding. The feudal prince in his castle, the feudal dictator in his Kremlin.

Sometimes he descends. Stalin once went to a party in somebody's Moscow suburban cottage. Ivan Papanin, the Polar explorer, wrote about it in the *Pravda* of December 18, 1939. "Comrade Stalin," he reports, "approached each one present with caressing attention. He came here not as The Leader, but as a comrade and friend. People tried to surround him with special attention. But Comrade Stalin does not like it when people cater to him, when he is set apart from the general mass. He himself caters to all, talks to everybody, pays special attention to everyone. That is what happened on this occasion. He went over to the gramophone, chose the records, and began to wind it up. He did not let anyone remain seated. He wanted everybody to dance. He brought over a lady to me and said, 'Dance.' " In the most relaxed moments he is still the commander.

At games he likes to win. He plays a Russian game called *Gorodki* which is comparable to tenpins. Two teams of two or three members each take positions about twenty-five feet apart behind rectangles a yard square in which they have made a figure out of six wooden pegs. The opposing teams in turn hurl sticks, usually two or more feet long and some two inches in thickness, at that figure and when all the pegs have been knocked out of the square the pegs are rearranged in an increasingly difficult figure. The skillful player knocks the figure out with one strike; otherwise the pegs are distributed throughout the square and each peg then requires a separate throw. The game is played out-of-doors on earth or sod. When Stalin plays this game at Sochi, the secret police picks men vacationing at sanatoriums near his villa to constitute the teams. After observing his partners and opponents, Stalin shifts the men around so that he has the winning team. This reflects not only a desire for victory. It is clever psychology. Without it, the men would play badly so that Stalin might win. But since they want to join Stalin's side, his choice of the best players for his team makes them play better.

Everything known about Mr. Stalin indicates a remarkable, formidable, frightening person driven by some insatiable desire toward an objective which eludes him. Despite his supremacy he seems unable to unbend. He is restless, tense, stony. Communists, ambassadors, and foreign statesmen who have seen him say, "A big man, but hard, cold."

I once asked a foreign diplomat who had conferred many times with Stalin whether he thought Stalin was unhappy. By way of reply he said that he had never seen any evidence of Stalin's warmth. At the Teheran Conference in November, 1943, he recalled, Stalin walked several yards toward Harry L. Hopkins to greet him, and the British and American delegates considered the event an unusual sign of friendliness, an indication, they believed, that Stalin had appreciated Hopkins' stamina and courage when, though ill, he made the long, hazardous air trip to Moscow to aid Russia shortly after the Hitler invasion. But this gesture to Hopkins did not become the prelude to a close relationship.

Stalin's impulsive gestures can be generous. On returning to Moscow after the end of the Second World War, U.S. Ambassador W. Averell Harriman went to talk with Stalin and saw in his office some photographs of the Moscow Victory Parade. Harriman expressed his admiration of the beautiful charger on which the commanding Soviet marshal had reviewed the parade.

"You can have the horse," Stalin exclaimed, "and I will give you another for your daughter."

Some time later, Harriman again conferred with Stalin and told him what excellent riding horses they were. "Do you want more?" Stalin asked eagerly. Harriman had difficulty rejecting a further gift. When the Ambassador left Russia, Stalin shipped both chargers for him to America. Yet Stalin's regal largess did not narrow the gap between the dictator and Harriman. Stalin keeps foreigners as well as Soviet citizens at a distance. Proximity might lead to intimacy, and intimacy to the discovery of something which he apparently wishes to hide.

CHAPTER VII

Stalin's Personal Life

Stalin apparently wishes to become Robot-in-Chief by dehumanizing himself. He is not only remote from his lieutenants and from the population; he keeps the facts of his life from the public. "It is difficult to write about Stalin," Abel Yenukidze, lifelong friend of Stalin, confessed in the *Pravda* of December 21, 1929. Why? Because "Stalin is woven into the entire thirty-year history of the Leninist party." His life is the life of the party, not of a person. All Yenukidze could say about the man he knew for twenty-nine years was that Stalin is the silent type and indifferent to material comforts.

In the same *Pravda* issue, Demyan Byedni, Soviet poet and friend of Stalin, makes it somewhat clearer why so little is known about Stalin. "I know: to write intimately of Stalin means to offer yourself up for self-sacrifice." That is how Byedni's article begins. "You will be barked at savagely by Stalin," the poet continues. "But I am reconciled to that in advance." At this point one expects the reminiscences to gush forth. Instead, Byedni recalls that he spoke at a meeting addressed by Lenin, and he talked about Lenin in a personal and comic vein and the audience howled with glee and Lenin laughed heartily too. Having thus taken Lenin as his shield against any future assaults by Stalin, the poet might have approached his task with a sense of security. But no. Tentatively, he offers a tribute: "You can betray Stalin. But you cannot fool him. No one can wind Stalin around his finger."

Stalin, he proceeds, called Lenin "a mountain eagle." This description, Byedni suggests, "is subconscious self-characterization." It was 1929 when a prominent writer could take such liberties. Further, Stalin once said that Lenin's "every phrase does not talk, it shoots." Whether this military figure of speech is also self-characterization Byedni did not dare to say. He was apparently afraid of

Stalin's bark. He decided to give up. The article, every item of which is mentioned in the above summary, ends abruptly with this story: Byedni was in the *Pravda* office in Petrograd in July 1917, with Stalin. The sailors on the island of Kronstadt, just outside the city, telephoned to ask whether they should carry their rifles in the coming political demonstration. "You should know best, comrades," Stalin replied. "But we scribblers, we always carry our weapon, our pencils. As for your weapons, you would know best, comrades." Byedni was amused. Stalin, he says in the article, had shown his "cunning." (Stalin had not told them to carry their rifles. That might have got him into trouble. Yet he showed clearly what his view was.)

This is the only personal story in the entire eight pages of the *Pravda* special issue on Stalin's fiftieth birthday. Everything else is political and couched in lifeless official Kremlin jargon.

Many book-length biographies of Stalin have been published in Russia without a single word about his wives or children. Stalin obviously wishes to convey the impression that he has no personal life. His life is politics, not emotions. His secretiveness in politics extends to his private affairs. It is the natural secretiveness of an animal that prowls at night, a secretiveness well adapted to a dictatorship which would wither under a searchlight of truth.

It is known, however—it could not remain secret—that in his forties, while he struggled with the oppositions, Stalin was sexually very promiscuous. In this role he was unsentimental and so practical as to repel his partners. Since then, a change seems to have intervened. In a country where lust links the Army with the ballet and the NKVD with beautiful women, no tongue of gossip has touched Stalin for more than twenty years. Pervasive hate would eagerly blow the smallest lick of scandal into a blackening flame. But none has appeared. The explanation may lie in greater sublimation or age or perfected concealment. In any case, rumor now leaves Stalin's private life coldly alone.

In youth and early manhood, Stalin did not have any warm home life. As a child and boy, his family life was darkened by poverty and his father's drunkenness and violence. If Joseph loved his mother there is no evidence of it. After he left Gori at the age of fifteen to attend the seminary, he never went back to live with her. He rarely wrote to her and rarely saw her. She told H. R. Knickerbocker, the famous American journalist, in Tiflis in 1930, that she had paid only one visit to her son in the Kremlin. "Soso," she said, "came to me once in 1921 and once three years ago." She added that he goes to Sochi every year. "I think he is there now," she remarked. Sochi, on the Caucasus Riviera, is an hour's airplane trip from Tiflis. Yet "Soso" did not telephone or send a letter or invite his mother to his private vacation villa.

After the two widely separated meetings with his mother in 1921 and 1927, Stalin called on her again in Tiflis on October 17, 1935. She described the visit to a correspondent whose report was printed in the Moscow *Pravda* of October 23, 1935. "He came unexpectedly, without warning," the old mother said about Stalin's first appearance in eight years. "The door opened—this one," she pointed, "and I see—it is he. He kissed me a long time. I kissed him too."

The brief visit became the text of many Soviet propaganda sermons for better treatment of parents.

Stalin's mother died in June, 1937. The fact was not mentioned in the Moscow press. Stalin sent a wreath.

Stalin's capacity for love and affection, limited by his nature, was further reduced by his disturbed existence as a revolutionist. Between April 5, 1902, the date of his first arrest, and March, 1917, the date of his last release, he spent eight years and five and a half months in Czarist jails and exile areas. Thus he was a prisoner during more than half of his life between the ages of twenty-two and thirty-seven. This would not conduce to a normal family life even in a person with greater talent for it than Stalin.

Having remained in jail and Siberia for one year and nine months after the first arrest, Stalin escaped on January 4, 1904, returned to Tiflis, and consummated his first marriage. His wife was Catherine Svanidze, a Georgian. She prayed to God while her husband preached atheism. He did not interfere with her religious observances. The marriage, according to the memoirs of friends, was a happy one. In 1906, a male child, named Jacob, was born to them. Within a year, Catherine died of tuberculosis. A boyhood chum of

Stalin who attended the funeral writes that Stalin, in a black mood, placed his right hand on his heart and pointing to the coffin, said, "This creature softened my stony heart. She is dead, and with her have died my last warm feelings for all human beings."

Jacob, the orphaned baby, was raised by Catherine's parents. As a teen-ager he stayed for several years with his father in the Moscow Kremlin where Stalin used to beat him for smoking. Later he lived apart from his father and preferred not to call attention to the relationship. At one period he worked on the railroad in Siberia, and it was perhaps as a humble railway mechanic that he served in the Second World War. The Nazis took him prisoner and, according to one report, he committed suicide in a German camp.

Arrested a second time on March 25, 1908, Stalin served one year and three months before contriving to escape. The next time his confinement lasted five and a half months from March 23, 1910, to September 6, 1911; the next time it was almost six months, from September 9, 1911, to February 29, 1912; the next time nearly five months, April 22, 1912, to September 1, 1912, and, finally, four years and a month from February 23, 1913, to March, 1917. Most of his detention was spent in Siberian villages where exiles were free to meet men and women and do very much as they pleased provided they stayed in the designated region. But in a man of Stalin's coldness, or inhibitions, this shuttling between freedom and exile militated against permanent emotional attachments.

The successful Bolshevik revolution ended Stalin's career as a transient prisoner of the Czar and gave him a permanent apartment in the Czar's Moscow Kremlin. In 1918, Stalin married a second time. His wife's name was Nadiezhda Sergeievna Alliluyev.

Nadiezhda's father Serge and her older sister Anna have written their memoirs. These books, published in Moscow in 1946, indicate that the Alliluyev family was Stalin's second family, indeed perhaps the only family with which he felt the slightest bond. The Alliluyevs were a closely knit, loving group. The father, originally a peasant from Central Russia, became a mechanic in the railroad repair shop in Tiflis and a locksmith in the electric power station at Baku. He married Olga Fedorenko, a sturdy Ukrainian woman who was born in Tiflis. Her knowledge of the Georgian language facilitated Stalin's relations with the family. She and Serge, a stately, serious, bearded man, had four children: two boys, Paul and Fedya; and two daughters, Anna and Nadiezhda.

The modest Alliluyev home, whether it was in Tiflis, or Baku, or, later, in St. Petersburg, served as a secret revolutionary center. Serge joined the Bolsheviks in early manhood, did illegal work, was jailed many times for short periods, and learned to know the men who played major roles in the Soviet regime.

As children, Anna and Nadiezhda would go to the residences of known revolutionary sympathizers to collect contributions for the Bolshevik party. With this money their mother bought food and clothing and the girls made the packages which were mailed to exiles in Siberia. Stalin was one of the recipients. When Stalin fled from Siberia to Tiflis in January, 1904, he came directly to the Alliluyev house to report.

Following his escapes in 1909 and 1911, Stalin again went to the Alliluyev home, both times in St. Petersburg. Anna, who admitted him when he knocked, unannounced, at their door on the second occasion, describes him as dressed in a black overcoat and soft hat and "very thin" and pale.

The Alliluyev home in St. Petersburg was likewise the terminus of Stalin's flight from exile in the winter of 1912. "We now know Stalin better," Anna writes. "We know that he can be simple and jolly and that, though usually silent and restrained, he can often laugh and joke in a youthful way and tell funny stories. He likes to notice the queer traits of people and imitate them in a way that makes people laugh."

That winter Stalin took Anna, aged fifteen, Nadiezhda, aged eleven, their brother Fedya, and their maid, for a fast ride in a horse sleigh. When Stalin reached his destination, he said, "Stop. I'm getting off here, and you go back home."

Stalin was illegally in St. Petersburg and had to elude the police. The night is made for arrests in Russia, and Stalin, knowing the police was on his trail and might search for him in the homes of known revolutionists or in cheap furnished rooms, stayed awake from dusk to dawn, walking the streets of the city in the company of Jacob Sverdlov, later the first President of Soviet Russia, with whom he had fled from Siberia. Usually they kept to the small winding lanes frequented by few nocturnal pedestrians. If they passed an open tea shop—a steaming room patronized by horse-cab drivers on the night shift—they would enter, order a pot of tea, and sip it for hours. Sometimes, between tumblers, they put their heads on the wet, oilcloth-covered table and slept.

When day broke, Stalin went to the Alliluyevs where Olga, the mother, would prepare his breakfast and send him off to sleep in the coal room, a tiny cubicle without a window next to the kitchen, where the family stored its fuel supplies. Though the narrow iron bedstead was hard, that was the quietest place in the apartment and also the safest if perchance the police violated its traditions and came by day.

In her memoirs, Anna comments on an occasion when she was together with Stalin and Sverdlov. "Sverdlov," she writes, "attracted people with his astonishing softness. He was always equally caressing and calmly cordial." She made no similar remark about her brother-in-law, the dictator.

The Czar's police caught up with Stalin on February 23, 1913, and transported him to the village of Kureyka, in the Turukhan district, beyond the Arctic Circle. From there he wrote a letter to Olga Alliluyev. It is the only wholly personal letter, without politics, he is known to have written. It is dated November 25, without a year. "Very, very thankful to you, much-respected Olga Evgenyevna," Stalin begins, "for your kind and pure feelings toward me. I will never forget your solicitous relationship to me. I await the moment when I will be liberated from exile and arrive in Petrograd to thank you, and also Serge, personally, for everything. Why, I have altogether only two more years here!

"I received the parcel. Thanks. I ask one thing—don't spend any more money on me. You need the money yourself." All he wanted was some picture postcards of the beautiful mountain scenery of Georgia. "Here everything is dull and frozen." In closing he sent "regards to the boys and the young ladies. I wish them the best."

The "young ladies" were Anna and his future wife, Nadiezhda, who was then fourteen or fifteen.

The signature reads: "Respectfully, Joseph."

Joseph made a great effort to write an affectionate letter but the product is formal and stilted.

War descended on the world in 1914. Revolution gripped Russia in March, 1917. When Stalin sped back from Siberia he went straight to the Alliluyevs and stayed with them and slept in the dining room where Papa Alliluyev also slept. Anna, Nadiezhda, and Olga occupied the family bedroom.

The Alliluyevs had to move, and looked for a new apartment. Stalin wanted to live with them. "Now, be sure," he urged, "definitely. A room for me too. Don't forget."

They did as he asked. They found an apartment of three rooms, bathroom, and kitchen. Mother and the two girls were to sleep in one room, the father and Fedya in the dining room (Paul, the other son, was a soldier at the front), and Stalin in the third.

But for some days Stalin did not occupy the room; he was too busy, and probably slept in the *Pravda* office. Its first Bolshevik occupant was Lenin. The Bolsheviks were bidding for power. The Kerensky government was alarmed; demands had been made for Lenin's arrest. Lenin went into hiding at the Alliluyev apartment. When he arrived he made a study of all entrances and exits and said to Olga, "Well, now just try to chase me out and I won't go. I like it here."

Stalin visited Lenin every day. The political situation grew more tense. The Kerensky government publicly invited the Bolshevik leaders to go to prison. Kamenev and Trotsky gave themselves up. Stalin opposed Lenin's surrender. They would lynch him in jail, he predicted. It was accordingly resolved to change Lenin's place of hiding. But to reach the new destination he needed a disguise. Olga, who was a war nurse, suggested that his head be bandaged. Lenin did not like the result. He said it would attract too much attention. "Wouldn't the best thing be to shave?" Lenin suggested.

Stalin shaved off Lenin's beard and mustache. Lenin then left with Stalin and Serge Alliluyev.

After that, Stalin spent the night occasionally in the Alliluyev home. Once the mother insisted that he get a new suit. He protested lack of time. She bought him one of the correct size. He asked her to sew in a warm lining. She also remodeled the jacket so he would not have to wear a collar and necktie. "He never liked wearing a collar and necktie," Anna writes.

Anna was helping out with secretarial work in Bolshevik headquarters. Nadiezhda was still in high school. In his few moments of leisure at home, Anna relates, Stalin enjoyed poking fun at people and giving them amusing nicknames. He caricatured friends and enemies.

Stalin was usually so tired he took a nap on returning to the apartment and only then asked for food. He would lie on his bed smoking his pipe and fall asleep. Once his blanket caught fire.

As the date of the revolution approached, Stalin came home less frequently. When he managed to visit the Alliluyevs he told the family about coming events. "Yes, everything is ready," he said on the eve of November 7, 1917. "Tomorrow we act. All city districts are in our hands. We will seize power."

Several days after the seizure of power, Stalin told them how the pro-Bolshevik Baltic sailors had captured the telephone exchange. "They march, like iron men," he declared. "The Junkers [Czarist guards] fired on them from the windows; the bullets cut down one after the other, but still they advanced; nobody wavered. Good boys, good boys: these are real Russians." Good, real "iron men."

Anna's memoirs end with the successful Bolshevik revolution. Her book, which appeared in 1946 in Moscow, was mercilessly attacked in the *Pravda* of May 14, 1947. "The freedom with which she writes about Lenin, Stalin, Kalinin, and other party leaders is not permissible," the *Pravda* article says.

Nor had Anna given sufficient importance to Stalin's part in preventing Lenin's voluntary surrender to the Kerensky government. Stalin, the article asserts, had saved Lenin's "precious life." The book was further condemned for its "invention of various episodes which in reality never happened and of which the party knows nothing." In the Bolshevik dialect this means that any episode not included in Stalin's sanctified history of the party had never taken place.

The *Pravda* article, which could not have been published without the personal censorship of Stalin, denounced his sister-in-law's book as "the trick of an adventuress" to get publicity and make money. It denied that Anna had ever been close to Stalin or any other party leader.

Anna's memoirs have been withdrawn from circulation in the Soviet Union. They gave too intimate a portrait of The Leader of whom there must be only graven images which are subject to retouching but no word pictures by an unsophisticated witness. How the book saw the light of day in the first place is a mystery. Anna probably delivered it to the publisher in 1945 when Stalin was so preoccupied with the war that it could not be shown to him. The publisher might well have assumed that Anna's recollections were harmless and friendly. But friendly or not, candid close-ups of the idol are taboo.

Of her little sister Nadiezhda, Anna wrote that she was "shy and proud," "alive and direct," played the piano, baked bread and cakes like an expert, and liked to keep house. Her father says in his book that she was born in Baku in September, 1901. She worked as Stalin's secretary when he became Commissar of Nationalities in 1917. In 1918, he married her. He was thirty-nine, she was seventeen.

The motives of such a marriage can be the subject of legitimate speculation or analysis. This much, at least, seems certain: Stalin is inarticulate and lacks the capacity or need to communicate. His first wife was a plain peasant, devout and with no education. Although Stalin was never as fervently antireligious as a good Bolshevik should be, there can have been no close intellectual contact or understanding between a man who was thoroughly immersed in politics and a woman to whom his revolutionary life was a blank.

Stalin's second wife was a child when he married her. He was a comrade of her father. She probably worshiped Stalin; he was the prominent leader and the co-worker of the great Lenin, and she had grown up in an atmosphere which gave glamour to underground Bolsheviks who went to Siberia, eluded the police, and overthrew governments. That may explain her action. But he was not seeking an equal with whom he could share deep experiences or doubts or discuss complicated political problems. As his junior by twenty-two years she would not make demands on any intimacy.

Nadiezhda Stalin developed into a pleasant-looking, handsome, tall woman. (She was much taller than her husband.) She studied textile engineering. She bore Stalin two children, a son, Vasili, a soccer fan, who rose to the rank of General in the Soviet Air Force, and Svetlana, a charming girl. When Winston Churchill visited Stalin's four-room Kremlin apartment in 1942, Svetlana appeared and "kissed her father dutifully." Churchill described her as a "handsome red-haired girl." She helped lay the table for a late supper.

On the evening of November 9, 1932, Marshal Voroshilov gave a party. Most of the Bolshevik leaders, including Stalin and his wife, attended. It was the year of the great famine and of tremendous political tensions in the country. In the discussions at the party, Mrs. Stalin made a few remarks which reflected her sympathy with the suffering population. When the Stalins returned to their apartment in the Kremlin, they apparently quarreled. She got into bed, pulled the blanket over her, and shot herself in the heart. This is the position in which she was found by the three doctors summoned by Stalin from the Kremlin hospital. She was thirty-one years old. The official announcement declared that she died during an emergency operation. The true facts about her suicide were ascertained from a person who cannot be named because he may still be alive in Russia.

Personal tragedies or personal celebrations are given scant attention in Bolshevik Russia. Russians were therefore surprised when Mrs. Stalin received a big public funeral in which massed trade unionists with banners, and many government officials marched behind the bier. The Prime Minister of Turkey, the Foreign Minister of Japan, and most of the ambassadors and ministers stationed in Moscow sent condolences which were published in the Soviet press. This was unprecedented. It was as though Stalin were atoning for something.

Stalin walked through the streets of Moscow at the head of the funeral procession. The secret police had cleared those streets of pedestrians and vehicular traffic; special agents were posted in all apartments along the route to keep people away from the windows.

Mrs. Stalin was not cremated. Cremation is normal Bolshevik practice. Nadiezhda's revolutionary family could not have objected on religious grounds. The objection came from Stalin. Did he fear that the burning of the body to ashes would uncover the bullet which had killed her? There were ways of liquidating everybody who might learn the secret. Or was there a psychological reason deeply embedded in some atavism? This primitive throwback may, along with the political factor, also explain Stalin's objection to the cremation of Lenin, his substitute father.

Over the grave of Nadiezhda in the Moscow cemetery, Stalin erected a monument consisting of a thin, graceful marble pedestal about three feet high surmounted by a bust in pale pink marble which is not a likeness but rather a portrait of idealized womanhood.

Since then Stalin has married a third time. His new wife, according to Moscow talk, is the sister of Lazar Kaganovitch, a member of the Politbureau and the last Jew to hold high Soviet office.

Stalin pampers Vasili and Svetlana, his two children by Nadiezhda. He wants their love. But they can hardly be ignorant of the story of their mother's suicide. A despot's family life is difficult. Unlimited power warps love. Besides, Stalin's mind dominates his heart. "I am a person who is not carried away," he once said. He does not give emotionally. What he cannot give he does not receive.

Stalin is a lonely man. Nobody can penetrate the steel cortex. He lives in air filtered free of emotions. He moves in air conditioned by fears and lies. Truth is the first casualty of tyranny. Friendship dies with it. Affection does not flourish in an atmosphere of falsehoods. Who would dare speak frankly to Stalin? Perhaps for a time, and gently, Maxim Gorki did.

The young Gorki in black blouse and furrowed brow was a symbol of the Russian people. He was rough-hewn and devoted to the millions in the lower depths, a kind of literary Lincoln. His talent as a writer, and the people's love, made him a towering figure. It flattered Stalin and helped him politically to bask in Gorki's company. Gorki had what Stalin lacked: culture, warmth, and authority with the masses. Stalin heaped honors on Gorki. Gorki may have submitted to the dictatorship's embrace in the hope of moderating its atrocities. For Stalin it was a satisfactory arrangement.

But soon Gorki's enthusiasm for the Soviet regime cooled. His relationship with Stalin cooled. In 1935, he wished to go abroad but was refused a passport. His death on June 18, 1936, is shrouded in mystery. At the Moscow trial his doctors, as defendants, attributed it to poisoning. Notoriously, however the defendants confessed to crimes committed not by themselves but by the regime.

Stalin has sacrificed friends and family to power. He has subordinated his own personality to the purposes of power. His personality is a mechanism geared to political needs.

The happiness of other persons does not appear to be one of Stalin's motivations. In a speech to the Executive Committee of the Third International on December 7, 1926, he discussed the goals of socialism. Although he, like all Communists, abhors Socialists because they are antirevolution and prodemocracy, the Soviet state still carries the much-abused name "Socialist." "What," Stalin accordingly asked, "is the economic purpose and economic base of socialism? Is it to create a 'Heavenly paradise' and general contentment on earth? No, it is not. That is a petty-bourgeois, middle-class conception of the economic purpose of socialism. To establish a Socialist economic base means to link agriculture with Socialist industry in one unified economic system, to subordinate agriculture to the leadership of Socialist industry, to establish smooth relations between town and country on the basis of the exchange of farm and factory products, to close and liquidate all channels with the help of which classes and, above all, capital are born, and to establish, finally, conditions of production and distribution that lead straight and direct to the annihilation of classes." This is the stuff of which Stalin's dreams are made.

Stalin sees society as a pile of wood blocks. His advertised life's aim is to rearrange them to fit a dogma which he once adopted. Will the new structure make mankind happy? That is irrelevant. Happiness is a middle-class ideal.

This attitude would inevitably impoverish Stalin's personal life. It may be, too, that he isolates himself from others as a protection from the unhappiness which, he has found, comes to him in any human relationship. Power, Stalin knows, repels friendship and love. Yet he prefers power.

CHAPTER VIII

The New Stalin Man

Power so grandiose as Stalin's could only be put to a grandiose, negative purpose. He has used it to recreate the Soviet individual in his own image.

Some fears, the fear of death for instance, are relieved by certainty. Fear in the Soviet Union is compounded by uncertainty. It misshapes the human being. With fear as the fire which softens, Stalin makes the big man small and the small man smaller and pours the reduced individual into a new mold.

The most important difference between a democracy and a dictatorship is the size of the individual. The difference, therefore, is one of degree. Both forms of society are confronted with similar problems. What distinguishes them is the manner in which they try to solve those problems. The central problem facing mankind today is the problem of power. Stalin personifies this problem. Specifically, the problem is: How can the modern individual maintain his inner peace and outer security, how can he remain free, honest, and himself in the face of the assaults being made upon him by the power of mighty governments, the power of mighty economic organizations, the power for evil that resides in cruel majorities and intolerant minorities, and the power now extractable from the atom?

The threat to individuals all over the world is great. Soviet man is the first to have succumbed.

Stalin did it by terror. But terror has by-products. The majority of the Soviet population have never been arrested on political charges. But few if any Soviet citizens have not known a person who has. The possibility weighs on all. News of early morning arrests is whispered, usually by housemaids, throughout the apartment house and down the street, and causes mournful head-shaking.

Loads of haggard men and women in freezing freight trains en route to concentration camps are a too palpable manifestation of cruelty to be forgotten or condoned. Stalin has failed to eliminate popular sympathy for his prisoners. But fear of implication prevents Russians from expressing their sympathy or helping the families of the victims.

The brutalities of the Soviet arouse indignation and repressed protest in part of the population. Stalin is too clever to neglect this phenomenon. Soviet propaganda attempts to counteract it. The propaganda theme is: Stalin loves all Soviet men, women, and children; everything he does is for their welfare; no more wonderful country exists on the planet than Russia; but some miscreants try to interfere with Stalin's endeavors and they must be punished else the people would suffer.

This propaganda does have some effect. But often it defeats itself, for it clashes with facts. A famous Soviet author, whom I knew well, fell from grace and was subjected to a barrage of bitter attacks. His works were proscribed. He was denounced as anti-Soviet. He was threatened with expulsion from the Communist party. The campaign of calumny undermined his health. Suddenly it stopped. Stalin knew the author and ordered him rehabilitated. I then said to the author, "You are a perfectly loyal, convinced Communist. Yet you were execrated as being just the reverse. Hereafter, when you read of similar charges against others, will you believe them?"

He looked at me, smiled, and did not answer. He obviously would not believe them.

Purges of the regime's spokesmen and of so many men who made the revolution have precipitated a crisis of faith in Russia. It is sometimes said that the Soviet system and the system in the "People's Democracies" of Eastern Europe, has imbued the people with a new faith. Or at least the intellectuals and writers are so imbued, one is told. But if they had such a faith, the regimes would have faith in them and not purge and censor them. Faith is an inner compulsion; it would make dictatorship superfluous. Faith generates its own fears and imposes its own penalties. It has no need of a secret police.

Communism once was a faith and an ideal. At that time the secret police did not molest Communists or average Soviet citizens. The Stalin cult has supplanted that faith. Even it would suffice for discipline. But Stalin doubts that the people have accepted the cult. They merely go through the motions required by it. Hence the terror. As the state departs from the ideal on which it was founded it destroys faith and substitutes force. Thereby it slowly begins to destroy itself.

Robbed of his faith, the new Stalin man becomes a cynic. Stalin is a model cynic. Before 1939, he courted England and France in the hope that they would abandon appeasement and aid Russia by resisting Nazi aggression. The moment England and France showed (in the spring of 1939) that they would resist Hitler, Stalin made a pact with him. Obliged in 1941, to fight Hitler, Stalin embraced the Western democracies. With Hitler defeated, Stalin had no more use for the Western democracies.

Stalin reached the peak of the Soviet pyramid over the bodies and backs of ex-colleagues. To crush Trotsky, he formed an alliance with Zinoviev and Kamenev. When Zinoviev and Kamenev shifted to Trotsky, Stalin entered into a block with Bukharin, Rykov, and Tomsky. Having destroyed Trotsky, Zinoviev, and Kamenev with the help of Bukharin, Rykov, and Tomsky, he executed Bukharin and Rykov. (Tomsky, so the report said, committed suicide before the police could take him.)

This is the easily recognized pattern of Stalin's strategy. The Leader's example is a potent force. Lesser executives follow it and convert the Soviet bureaucracy into a swamp of intrigue.

Every man's hand is against his comrade. There is no comradely feeling among the comrades. A fictitious denunciation will be hailed as "Bolshevik vigilance." Ofttimes an accusation is the equivalent of conviction, for in a dictatorship one is guilty until proven innocent. A smear sticks.

The battle for survival is desperate in Russia. Those who do not undermine others may be undermined themselves. Officials, professional people, and writers elbow their way forward at the expense of those who stand in the way. Did not Stalin do exactly that? To free a place for themselves on a higher rung they do not hesitate to pull somebody down to theirs or hurl him to the ground.

Success has its rewards. Stalin has made Russia thoroughly materialistic. He himself lives in simple luxury, and, though he probably never touches money, nothing he wants is denied him, including expensive foreign tobaccos and cognacs which he drinks "bottoms up." But his real compensation is power and adulation. Everybody else, however, must be content with a minimum of these. Instead they strive for money and privilege. The end of private capitalism in Russia has brought no relief from the pursuit of fleshpots. On the contrary; since the country is poor, despite its abundant endowment by nature, comforts and luxuries are relatively few and therefore much coveted.

The early revolutionary desire to reform the world by altering the relations between rich and poor has yielded to a passionate pursuit of worldly wealth. Equality is officially scorned in Russia as "a bourgeois virtue." There are very rich and very poor in the Soviet Union; in fact, the spread between rich and poor is greater than in America. Some Soviet citizens live in beautiful villas and apartments and others live in slums. Some enjoy luxury, others suffer want.

The regime makes no secret of the inequality it fosters. The favored upper class displays its wealth in streets, theaters, restaurants, and resorts. Inequality is the reward for service to an unpopular state.

This new aristocracy which, with dependents, probably numbers twenty million of the two hundred million inhabitants of Soviet Russia, consists of leading government officials, leading party functionaries, army officers, NKVD personnel, industrial managers, writers, artists, scientists, engineers, and a few workers who earn much money by setting high norms for others to emulate without wage increases. They are the climbing elite. They live extremely well by Soviet standards and fairly well by European standards.

Stalin allows them psychological rewards too. He is a student of the weaknesses of men. He remembers from his own past that he who is kicked likes to kick someone. Stalin has accordingly set up a nation-wide system of chain-kicking. The Red Army officer, exposed to the mother oaths and reprimands of his colonel, can beat and in an emergency shoot a private soldier. Each Soviet factory director, government trust chairman, and federal department chief is free to exercise absolute power over his subordinates. There are few prior checks and balances in the Russian totalitarian system. The factory director, for instance, is called "sole commander"; he hires and fires without trade union interference. He is undisputed despot to those below him. But he, in turn, humbly subserves his superior who is undisputed despot to those below *him.*

Stalin has bred a class of little Stalins.

The Soviet system is a combination of regimentation and anarchy. Since no appeal to law or moral values is possible, the supreme law is the exalted person. In the 1920's and 1930's, Stalin encouraged those with a grievance to write to him. He received thousands of letters of complaint and request and is said to have answered each one. Sometimes he took immediate action to satisfy a petitioner. Boris Pilniak, a gifted novelist, asked for a passport to go abroad and was twice refused. He wrote a note to Stalin and the same day received a reply in Stalin's own hand by courier promising to do what he could. Pilniak got the passport. (He has since been purged.) This method emphasizes Stalin's omnipotence and solicitude, but it also highlights Soviet lawlessness.

In his more limited field, the lesser Soviet official can, with a twitching eye on the watching Kremlin, also wallow in the anarchy of his personal regime. This opens up a vast field for back-stabbing, back-scratching, bribery, protectionism, and favoritism. Occasionally an official is fished out of the slough of corruption and held up for contumely and punishment. That denies security to the bureaucrats.

In a modern state, there is law because there is force. But where there is too much force there is no law. Too much force in the hands of individuals is banditry. Too much force applied by government is dictatorship. The Soviet dictatorship is political banditry. The law of Russia is the law of the frontier, the law of the jungle. The man with the biggest claw, the sharpest fang, the meanest mind, succeeds.

Obviously, therefore, Soviet living is dangerous living. Even the highest official or most favored author or most indispensable manager has no security, for security is an inner force which would diminish the might of the absolute ruler. In these circumstances, personal behavior responds chiefly to outside conditions and least of all to moral impulse. Expediency blots out ethical standards. "Is this good?" or, "Is this right?" are naïve questions, milestones on the road to suicide.

Studying the scene, Soviet youth grows up scorning ethics and ideals. The new Stalin man is hard-boiled. He admires Stalin, for Stalin has power. The Soviet Union is an acquisitive society. The supreme test is success. The indices of success are wealth and power.

Stalinism has evolved a set of unholy commandments: Shun the wrath of the god; it brings extinction. Avoid a perspective; it is unpatriotic. Relaxation is antisocial and detachment is taboo. Everybody must wear a harness; blinkers are required equipment. Have no philosophy of life of your own; philosophy is handed down by the Politbureau and the truth about genetics by Stalin. A nimble wit is preferable to wisdom. Adaptability is more precious than brains. A flexible knee is better than a stiff neck. The human chameleon has the key to survival. Keep in step with Stalin. Bow regularly at the shrine of Lenin in order to glorify Stalin. Read the *Pravda* every morning for its weather reports; the weather may have changed in the Kremlin. Grovel before superiors. Force inferiors to grovel before you.

These rules guide the daily life of the new Stalin man.

These rules are the Stalin man's attempt to adjust to the Soviet regime. To retain his sanity he must adjust. By absorbing the worst features of Stalinism the Soviet individual becomes less sensitive to its crimes. Unless he be a moral giant or saint, no man can, for years and in silence, resist the society under which he lives and to whose crimes he, as one of its employees, is an accessory. He must find a way of reconciling himself to it and even justifying it; otherwise he will eat out his heart for participating in it. By closing the outlet of safe, legitimate political opposition, Stalin exerts pressure on all Soviet individuals to accept the regime or risk losing their mental equilibrium. Resistance to evil is a safeguard against moral death. But resistance to Soviet evil means physical death. Few care to or dare to pay that price. The high cost of resistance and the comfort of adaptation put a premium on submission. Soviet man dies morally to live physically. Often the process of capitulation is so slow as to be imperceptible to the person undergoing it, and he would deny it if faced with the truth. But inside, the traumatic effect is no less painful.

However habitual the sycophancy, however automatic the public dishonesty of Soviet man, they continue to gnaw at his spiritual vitals. The strains of Soviet life create many mental disorders.

In May, 1938, I would sit on the courtyard balcony of our Moscow apartment taking the first sun of spring. A neighbor sat on a balcony opposite. His toothbrush, towel, and change of underwear were packed in a large kerchief. He was a middle-rank Soviet official waiting for the police. He wanted to be arrested soon. The tension of waiting had become unbearable. The NKVD's knock at three one morning came as a relief. In known cases, people have asked to be arrested when the strain became unbearable.

The NKVD, or MVD, the organization which implements Stalin's terror, is itself terrorized and subject to the heaviest, inhuman pressures. It is called upon to make arrests which its agents know are unjustifiable and to extract confessions which its secret-chamber investigators, or examining magistrates, know to be untrue. Here is an account of the nervous collapse of such a magistrate witnessed by one of the authors of a book published in New York in 1951 entitled *Russian Purge and the Extraction of Confession* by F. Beck, a German scientist once imprisoned in Russia, and W. Godin, a former Soviet university professor who escaped abroad.

"The interrogator," the account reads, "was a young lieutenant, obviously fairly new to the work, who sat at a desk, deputizing for the chief examining magistrate, while the prisoner had to stand. The endlessly repeated question "Who recruited you?" [into the alleged anti-Soviet organization] began to grow less frequent, and the stupefied prisoner suddenly saw the examining magistrate burst into a flood of tears. He allowed the prisoner to sit, gave him a drink of tea from his own glass, offered him a cigarette, and called for a relief. The interrogation then continued. Hardly any of the examining officials, perhaps only the simplest, fully believe in the prisoners' guilt."

Soviet Russia banished the supernatural but enthroned the unnatural, and it plays havoc with mortals.

A Soviet factory foreman of my acquaintance was exiled to Siberia. He left behind a daughter of twelve and a wife. What could the wife tell the girl? Tell her that Papa was anti-Soviet and a traitor? But the girl loved her father and knew him to be pro-Communist and loyal. Tell her that Stalin was unjust and that Papa was innocent? But the girl, like many Soviet children, respected Stalin. Besides, the girl might repeat to her schoolmates some of her mother's adverse comment about the government. The mother temporized and lied. The little girl lost her mind. Her conflict between Papa and Stalin was too great.

It is nonsense, of course, that the Bolsheviks wish to break up the family. Some of their theorists played with the thought in the early "romantic" period of the revolution, but those days are long forgotten. The family, however, is often the scene of a clash of loyalties. A girl of three and a half came home from school one day and announced to her father, "You are not my father any more."

"What do you mean I am not your father," he exclaimed, horrified.

"You are not my father any more," she reiterated. "Stalin is my father; he gives me everything I have." To reclaim the child, the father had to disprove Stalin's claim. The Soviet regime makes a mighty effort to capture the children of the land and where it succeeds unhappiness enters either for the parents or the children. Parents never know when they may lose their children by educational seduction. They often feign support of the regime in order not to alienate their offspring. Nerves may crack under this dichotomy.

An early interest in the politics of Soviet petroleum took me to the Baku and Grozni oil fields in 1924. Thereafter, since the Caucasus is so beautiful, I visited the fields once a year for many years. I gained the confidence of a number of Soviet engineers. One engineer at Baku said to me, "When I sink a new oil well I get skin eruptions. The well may be a gusher and then I receive a bonus, which is fine. But if it is a dry hole they will say I am a saboteur and send me to Siberia. It makes me nervous." Another engineer said exactly the same thing, only in his case the pathological phenomenon was heart palpitations.

The Soviet press stated in the 1920's that workingmen, who were promoted to positions of responsibility because the government did not trust trained technical managers, broke down under the unaccustomed burden; some were admitted to mental institutions.

The Soviet nation has inordinate health, for two reasons: the weaklings died off in the years of great physical hardships; the upper crust of Czarist days was destroyed and a new unspoiled, unexpended stratum of the population hailing from the steppes, mountains, and forests came to the fore. But it is not as healthy as it was.

The stresses of government service in town and village induce many sexual abnormalities, especially in important officials who have the greatest fears. Psychological disturbances, however, are not treated unless they become seriously pathological. The abnormal is normal in Russia and psychoanalysis is therefore taboo.

Among the most intolerable aspects of Soviet life is the insistence of the government on being present at all times. As the terror waxed in the 1930's, many Communists, including the highest, found relaxation in the old classics of Russian literature and in translations from foreign languages. But the Kremlin censured them. Why did they neglect Soviet writings? At the same time, a mad search developed for gramophone records of jazz music, which was frowned on by the authorities, and for Russian sentimental songs, especially those by Vertinsky, a Russian vocalist in exile, who makes Russians "swoon" with delight and who is Stalin's favorite too. People in all classes, workingmen as well as members of the Soviet bourgeoisie, took to drink, cards, sex, and drugs. These were attempts to get away from it all at least in the hours of leisure. Soviet man is rarely alone. Even the privacy of his home is invaded by the raucous voice of authority, and perhaps, unknowingly, by an informer. Escape is difficult. The Kremlin deliberately makes it difficult. The tension which is the essence of dictatorship would be dissipated if the government had citizens under its control only eight hours a day, six days a week.

The new Stalin man has the permanent company of Stalin. In the presence of Stalin one does not relax.

Stalin allows so few citizens to go abroad because there they would escape temporarily—and some have escaped permanently, by desertion—from his presence. Stalin wants his people to remain within earshot and rifle shot.

The Stalin man, of course, has his gaiety and enjoys physical pleasures. But oppressive espionage robs him of the deeper pleasure of unconstrained communication with his fellows and of the unfettered expression of his personality. Everyone watches his step; there is no room for spontaneity and abandon. Strain is written on all faces, the strain of constant self-control.

Youth, still unconscious of what awaits it and aware chiefly of material opportunities, may know temporary exhilaration. Adults feel the death hand of Stalin at their gullets—unless they have previously desensitized themselves by killing the inner man. Russia pays a high price for Stalin.

CHAPTER IX

Stalin Is Afraid

Under other absolutisms in history, the little man could keep out of harm's way by self-effacement or remoteness. In Stalin's Russia, every individual is dependent on the central government for his livelihood and existence. Through nationalized economy in town and country, through censorship and militarism, each worker, peasant, intellectual, and office worker is in direct, daily contact with the dictatorship.

The supreme Soviet fact is that there can be no escape for the big or little man from the arm and eye of the secret police and therefore no surcease from worry.

A nonvariable feature of the dank climate of Bolshevism is the heavy pressure area of terror covering the entire Soviet Union.

The Kirov episode is a study in the man-eating quality of the Soviet terror. On December 1, 1934, Serge Kirov, a member of the Politbureau and Leningrad leader, was shot dead by a young Communist named Nikolayev. Gossips said Kirov had shown interest in Nikolayev's girl.

Stalin immediately went by special train to Leningrad. He had a personal talk with Nikolayev. Nikolayev was executed together with all the members of his family. Shortly thereafter, 103 persons, allegedly members of the former nobility, who had been in jail for months, and in many cases years before Kirov's assassination, were taken out and executed. Concurrently, the top officials of the Leningrad secret police were purged for laxity. Later, Zinoviev and Kamenev, former intimate co-workers of Lenin and Stalin, were tried for plotting Kirov's death.

During the months following Kirov's killing, moreover, many tens of thousands of adults and children of Leningrad, who obviously could not have shot at or conspired against Kirov, were exiled to Siberia. For a long period, the richer residents of Moscow made trips to Leningrad to buy at bargain prices the furniture, linens, clothing, books, kitchen utensils, jewelry, etc., which the banished Leningraders had to sell in a hurry before trekking to the frozen deserts of Asia. These were random arrests. The Kremlin needed a planned number of victims to terrorize the nation. There was no way in which a fortuitously marked person could avoid punishment.

Soviet arrests are more closely related to policy than to crime. During many years, engineers were the most persecuted class in Russia. Presently Stalin made a speech extolling their services, and the arrests of engineers ceased. When the Soviet government plans a new huge industrial development in an uninhabited or sparsely inhabited area of Siberia or Central Asia it often arrests the necessary personnel and transports them to the new sites.

If an important official is purged his appointees and associates and usually his family are purged with him. The Kremlin's rule is: When in doubt, arrest.

A Soviet citizen may be arrested for the sins of others. He may be arrested for not having done something, for not informing on a colleague or neighbor, for instance. He may be arrested for something he did ten years ago when it was quite proper. He may go to a concentration camp for undertaking too much or too little. In each case, the citizen has no recourse to law, to a court, to a lawyer, to a trade union, or to friends. He is arrested and allowed no contact with family or advisers. He may be retained in prison for a year or more pending sentence, or quickly sentenced in secret by a collegium of three officers of the secret police and sent to Siberia or Turkestan. Only after the victim reaches the place where he is to serve his sentence are relatives allowed to communicate with him through innocuous letters or a food parcel.

Except for a few demonstration trials staged for propaganda purposes, political prosecutions are secret. And many things are political: the alleged mismanagement of a factory, absenteeism or lateness, alleged misappropriation of funds in a collective, a reported criticism of the government in private conversation, or an attitude of mind which displeases the authorities.

The NKVD, or MVD as the secret police is now called, has agents in every factory, school, farm, government office, apartment house, railway station, university, army unit, prison cell, newspaper, theater, etc. Their function is to snoop and inform. Nobody is sure who is a spy, and the spy does not know his colleague, and everybody suspects everybody else and the suspicions may be correct, for Soviet citizens are expected, under pain of punishment, to report any act or word which they think the secret police would like to know.

This universal system of finger-pointing is used to oust a rival, liberate a coveted apartment, or vent a personal grudge. In a country where you are guilty until you are proved innocent, an official receiving an informer's report is afraid to pigeonhole it without action. Kindness or hesitation could be "counterrevolution," and then the official might find himself in a crowded prison. Subsequently, he may go to a concentration camp.

The Soviet secret police maintains numerous concentration camps with millions of inmates. Some persons have escaped from these camps and gone abroad. I have spoken to a number of Russians who worked in the camps, were mobilized in the Red Army during the war, captured by Hitler, and preferred to stay in Germany when the war ended. Poles, Jews, Frenchmen, and others, released under outside pressure, have published reports and affidavits about the camps. Moreover, the Soviets and foreign Communists have admitted the existence of forced labor, only they argue that it is for the re-education of "politically unreliable elements."

Some, indeed, do "graduate" from the camps. But the "re-education" is wasted on that large percentage who die or are crippled from overwork and undernourishment in the frozen Arctic wilderness. Furthermore, a regime in its fourth decade, to which tremendous social and economic achievements have been loudly attributed, should not need to re-educate millions of its subjects in concentration camps. The achievements, the schools, the propaganda would be re-education enough.

Those millions may, from Stalin's point of view, require re-education. But concentration camps do not supply it. Concentration camps are a cold, slow-motion substitute for the gas chamber.

Concentration camps are only one feature of the Soviet system of compulsion which suggests that Stalin does not trust his people. Each word in every Soviet newspaper, magazine, book, radio broadcast, speech, poems, etc. is subjected to prior censorship. Soviet writers, composers, scientists, and politicians have had over thirty years of education through Soviet life. Yet it has not apparently sufficed to make them reliable and loyal.

Foreign Communists contend that the Soviet Union has a one-party system because there is no opposition in the country; everybody is satisfied with communism. Even if the Constitution did not proscribe a second party there would be none, it is argued, because all Soviet citizens are pro-Communist.

Then why the millions in the concentration camps? Why the dismissals, demotions, and purges reported in the Soviet press? Why the surveillance and censorship? Why impose dictatorship on a nation which is unanimously, enthusiastically for the existing political system? If everybody is pro-Communist, why the dictatorship? That it is a dictatorship is a Kremlin boast.

A government that is sure of its citizens' loyalty is a democracy. A government that doubts the loyalty of its citizens adopts the ways of a dictatorship.

Great Britain, Denmark, Sweden, Australia, France, and the United States are democracies because it is assumed that the majority of their people would not use violence to alter the social and economic bases of society. They may try to reform society by the ballot but not by force. "Ah," the Communists reply, "this is not real freedom. The ruling circles have everything under control." Why cannot Stalin give the Soviet people as much freedom as the people of England, America, and other democracies enjoy and also keep everything under control?

The only possible conclusion is that Stalin is afraid of his people.

In democracies, some newspapers praise the government, some criticize it. Some writers like the head of the government, some do not. If that much freedom were granted Soviet journalists they might not glorify Stalin. One historian might expose the falsifications which magnify Stalin's part in the revolution. One author or two or a hundred might mention a Stalin mistake. Such a pen-prick would explode Stalin's self-inflated balloon of infallibility and deflate his ego. Therefore writers must not have freedom.

In democracies, workingmen can strike. Stalin does not want his workingmen to strike. He is afraid they might if he granted them the right. Farmers might leave their collective farms.

Stalin has other fears. He is as afraid of assassination as the Czar and keeps as far from the public as the Czar. It is a long time since anyone has seen a photograph of Stalin mingling with a crowd. Stalin is so afraid that the public does not know when and by what train he travels to and from his vacation place in the Caucasus. The people do not know exactly where he lives in Moscow or where his country villa is located. For a number of years it was at Zubalova, outside the capital. He stayed there often and came into town to go to his office at about one in the afternoon, returning late at night, for he usually works late and even receives ambassadors at nine in the evening. After a while Moscovites knew the route he took; it was via Vozdvizhinka, up Arbat Avenue and then out into the country. Many other Soviet leaders, in their big limousines, followed the same route. Lest anybody watching on the street spot Stalin's car and learn its license number for future recognition, the front license plate was removed and then, so as not to make it conspicuous, all the front license plates in the Soviet Union were ordered removed.

In the early 1930's, I was sitting with M. Lapinsky-Mikhalsky, a prominent Soviet publicist, on a bench in Lafayette Square, opposite the White House in Washington, D. C. He had come to the United States on a confidential diplomatic mission and had interviewed important personages. As we sat there he kept looking at the people taking a short cut across the White House lawn. "Now that is democracy," Lapinsky remarked. Nobody could hurry across Stalin's front lawn or come near enough to see it. (A few years later Lapinsky was arrested in Moscow and disappeared forever. No one knew why; perhaps there was no exact reason. His culture, foreign experience, and understanding of democracy made him too dangerous in freedom.)

Stalin is afraid of people who have been abroad, of men who know too much, of orators who could stir the people's emotions, and of writers who might tell the truth.

Because Stalin is afraid of his people he needs the dictatorship to make the people afraid of him. The intensity of his fears explains the intensity of the terror. Fear whets his appetite for the power to crush those who might harm or disobey or expose him.

If Stalin had the charm to win he might dispense with some of his power to kill. But he is a poor speaker. His voice is colorless. He drinks water after every short paragraph and keeps pumping his forearm up and down for emphasis. Nor does he exude personal warmth. He cannot evoke devotion. He therefore depends on fear. He has it and he communicates it to others.

Stalin, who can bully everybody, is still as afraid as when the big boy bullied him in his childhood. Fear feeds on itself. The dictator abuses power and then fears the effects of his misdoing.

Stalin is right to be afraid. Many Soviet citizens hate him as the cause of their tribulations. Many would remove him if they could. His brutal acts breed frustrated enemies who abhor their tormentor.

CHAPTER X

Stalin's Blind Oxen

The revolver that kills, the terror that frightens, and the scalpel which cuts Soviet individuals down to convenient size are not Stalin's only instruments. He also has lies.

Stalin has a most astonishing attitude toward facts. In December, 1927, for instance, he addressed the Fifteenth Party Congress, the supreme policy-making body of the land. Reporting to it on world affairs, he cited a story in a London newspaper about a plan allegedly adopted by Sir Austen Chamberlain, the British Foreign Secretary. "I cannot guarantee the authenticity of this plan," Stalin began cautiously. "But there can be no doubt that its publication in the press is a symptom. This plan," he continued, "transfers the 'mandate' for Syria from France to Italy, grants Tangier to France in return for financial compensation to Spain, returns the Cameroons to Germany, exacts an undertaking from Italy not to 'intrigue' in the Balkans, etc., etc. All this under the flag of the struggle against the Soviets. As is known, no dirty deal is launched without relating the Soviets to it.

"But what is the real sense of this plan?" Stalin proceeds—and now he treats it as authentic. "The sense is to squeeze the French bourgeoisie out of Syria. Syria was always the gate to the East, to Mesopotamia, to Egypt, etc. From Syria harm could be done to England in the region of the Suez Canal and in Mesopotamia. And so Chamberlain, it seems, wishes to end this unpleasant situation. Obviously, the fact that this plan has appeared in the press cannot be called accidental."

Thus Stalin, presumably a serious statesman, erected a whole structure of deductions, for the guidance of his party, on one newspaper's tale about a plan which had no reality, which was not carried out, and which, in perspective, was a fantastic invention unworthy of the comments of a third-rate commentator.

In 1927, Sacco and Vanzetti were executed for a crime they did not commit. Throughout the United States and the world, loud protests were heard. How did Stalin interpret this? "I think," he said, "that the clearest proof of the growing crisis of capitalism, the clearest example of the spreading discontent and indignation of the working class is the events connected with the murder of Sacco and Vanzetti." Unable to understand human responses to an atrocity, Stalin distorted them into confirmation of his dogma.

Zinoviev had declared that the British Communist party was weaker. Stalin denied this. It was growing "from day to day." How did he know? Because the British Communist party was being attacked more than it had been. That is the only evidence Stalin gave. Actually, figures show that the British Communist party did not grow stronger. But what is truth when a lie could hurt Zinoviev more?

On March 1, 1927, Stalin, answering a question from the audience at a Moscow meeting of railway workers, said, "My reply: we will have no war either this spring or this fall." But writing in the Moscow *Pravda* of July 28, 1927, Stalin declared, "There can be no doubt that the basic, present problem is the question of a new imperialist war. This refers not to some general and vague 'danger' of a new war. This refers to a real, actual danger of a new war in general, and of a war against the Soviet Union in particular." Stalin's prediction of early war was echoed by Soviet propaganda. Just at that time, Georgi Chicherin, the Soviet Foreign Commissar, returned to Moscow from an extended study trip through Western Europe and reported that nobody was preparing to attack Russia. Bolshevik leaders told him to be quiet. The war-scare propaganda was needed to destroy Trotsky, they explained to Chicherin. Trotsky was being accused of making trouble at home while the capitalist enemy stood poised to invade the Soviet Union. What would he do, Trotsky was asked, if the West made war on Russia? In reply, Trotsky referred to Clemenceau who, when the Germans stood eighty kilometers from Paris, overthrew the French government and then conducted the defense of France with greater decisiveness. "And so," exclaimed Stalin triumphantly on August 1, 1927, "we see that when the enemy comes within eighty kilometers of the Kremlin this musical-comedy Clemenceau will not occupy himself with the defense of the Soviet Union but with the overthrow of the present party majority. And that he calls defense."

It was to trap Trotsky in this fashion that Stalin indulged in talk of imminent war.

Now Stalin had had it both ways: in March, 1927, there would be no war. Thus he calmed the public. In July, 1927, there would be war. Thus he smote Trotsky. But that did not satisfy Stalin. An ordinary person is content to have it both ways. Stalin wanted to have it three ways. In a speech on October 23, 1927, Stalin said, "And how many prophecies we have had about war! Zinoviev prophesied that we would be at war in the spring of this year. Then he prophesied that the war would commence, in all probability, in the autumn of this year. Yet now winter is coming and there is still no war. There you have the results of our peaceful policy." There you have three-way Stalin. It is impossible to know when Stalin is inconsistent and when he is lying.

In 1929, the "Right" opposition led by Rykov, Bukharin, and Tomsky demanded that the Soviet government import grain to feed its undernourished cities. Stalin's reply, in a speech delivered at a party conference in April, 1929, was a fantastic hodgepodge of irrelevancies, suspicions, distortions, and repetitions which provide a rare insight into the curious workings of his queer mind.

Rykov had told the party conference that foreign businessmen were offering large quantities of grain on credit to the Soviet trade agencies in Paris, Czechoslovakia, the United States, and Argentina. This would have been a normal transaction. The Soviet Union was short of grain. Foreign countries had surpluses. Foreign traders were therefore prepared to sell to Russia on credit. But Stalin said he did not believe it. "It would be strange to think," he declared, "that the capitalists of the West have suddenly come to pity us and want to give us several tens of millions of poods of grain almost for nothing or on long-term credit. That is nonsense, comrades."

The grain merchants, Stalin invented, are "intelligence agents of the capitalist world." "Their desire," he said, "is not so much to sell grain on credit as to ascertain whether our situation is really bad, whether our financial resources are really exhausted, whether our financial position is strong, and whether we will swallow the bait they throw us."

Therefore, Stalin announced, he and the Politbureau had decided to reject these foreign grain credits and "show all our enemies that we are strong and have no intention of succumbing to promises of gifts." Nobody had promised gifts. Stalin himself had spoken of credits. But "gifts" made the offer look more doubtful. By refusing the credits, Stalin repeated, Moscow had "smashed the gossip about 'the imminent collapse' of the Soviet government."

Yet in the very next sentence Stalin informed his audience that "the other day we had some preliminary negotiations with representatives of the German capitalists. They promised to give us a five hundred million credit and it looks as though they regard it as necessary to give us that credit in order to provide their industry with Soviet orders." For the same reason, Stalin added, British industrialists had offered considerable credits.

Thus when German and British industrialists offer Moscow large credits they are behaving legitimately; they want orders for their factories. But when grain merchants offer credits they are "intelligence agents" trying to spy out Soviet weaknesses.

Why did Stalin make this distinction between industrial credits and grain credits? Because he and the Politbureau had decided, in Stalin's words, "to get along without the import of grain and to save the foreign currency for the importation of factory equipment." They would try to get along without imported grain by taking more grain from the peasants, "maximum organization in the collection of grain" Stalin called it, and by forcing the cities to tighten their belts, or "maximum economy in the consumption of grain," to use Stalin's phraseology. This would be unpopular. People would support the Rykov demand for grain imports. Consequently foreign credits for imported grain had to be made to look as ugly and anti-Soviet as possible. Stalin hoped to achieve this end by saying that the grain imports were offered by foreign "intelligence agents." This was also designed to smear the "Right" which had advised the deal with those "intelligence agents."

On the other hand, since Stalin favored the importation of factory equipment, the German and British industrialists who promised credits for these imports were merely pursuing approved business tactics.

By these crude falsifications and twists Stalin dishonestly justified his own policy and undermined party antagonists. That made it good. "From the point of view of Communist morality," Radio Moscow said on August 20, 1950, "only those acts are moral which contribute to the building of a new Communist society." The judge of whether they do so is the man with most power. No standards exist.

In 1936, Stalin ordered the findings of the national census destroyed because they showed the loss of life in the 1932-33 famine. The truth was inconvenient.

"All the practical work of organizing the insurrection," Stalin wrote in the *Pravda* on November 7, 1918, the first anniversary of the Bolshevik insurrection, "was conducted under the immediate direction of Comrade Trotsky." But in Stalin's book, *History of the Communist Party of the Soviet Union (Bolsheviks)*, first published anonymously in 1938 and then under his name, Trotsky disappears altogether as an active organizer of the revolution; the little he did was in order "to disrupt and destroy." What Soviet citizen does not know, having been told so ten thousand times, that all the practical work of organizing the insurrection was conducted under the immediate direction of Comrade Stalin?

Politicians in democracies lie too. But they lie less brazenly and less frequently because they can be contradicted, criticized, and exposed. Stalin's lies enjoy immunity.

In the 1920's the successful Soviet playwright Alexander Afinogenov wrote a play entitled *The Lie* and submitted it to the theater. He told me what happened. For months he waited, with growing nervousness. "It is being read," the director said. "We haven't quite made up our minds," the manager declared. One morning Afino-

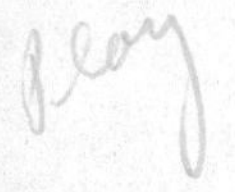

genov was pacing up and down his room wondering what to do when the telephone rang. Stalin's secretary was on the phone; "Comrade Stalin would like to see you." The censorship bureaucrats had lacked the courage to reject the manuscript of an important author like Afinogenov and so they had passed it up the hierarchical ladder until, since no one dared, it reached Stalin.

Stalin was very friendly. "You are our greatest playwright," Stalin commenced. "You are young and will be even more successful than you have been. I always enjoy your work. I enjoyed your play *The Lie*. It is a good script. But the people are not ready for it. Would you do me a favor and withdraw the manuscript for the time being?"

Afinogenov did Stalin the favor. "The time being" still continues. (Afinogenov was killed in 1941 in Moscow by a Nazi bomb.)

A Russian playwright named K. Finn wrote a play called *Honesty* which the Ermolova Theater in Moscow produced in 1951. But it was quickly closed after *Pravda* attacked it for "perverting the living truth" and "crudely vulgarizing the idea of criticism." This means that Finn, like Afinogenov before him, came perilously near being honest about the lie in Soviet life.

Stalin remains Censor-in-Chief. In the Moscow *Pravda* of December 21, 1949, Alexander S. Poskrobeshov, for many years Stalin's chief secretary, writes, "The authors of film scenarios ask Comrade Stalin to give his conclusions on their work. He acquaints himself assiduously with the scenarios and makes his observations." In Soviet Russian, "conclusions" means decisions. Stalin watches films and books and plays in order to check the flow of truth to the public. He prefers "Socialist realism" to truth. Socialist realism treats the future as though it already existed. This is a license for imaginative lies about coming events and the suppression of present facts.

Stalin could not allow film script writers or Afinogenov or anybody to reveal the truth behind the Soviet lie. Freedom of speech is freedom of honest speech. There is no freedom of speech in Russia except for Stalin. He tells the truth when he wishes and he lies when he wishes.

Stalin does not merely lie. He insists that others lie. A petty dictator would be content with his own freedom to lie. But Stalin is no petty dictator. He realizes that his freedom to lie would be imperiled if anybody told the truth.

Stalin wants to involve everybody in his acts. He wants expressions of agreement. Some do it out of sincere conviction. Others speak under compulsion. They speak like cracked records. They would rather not speak at all. But Stalin demands his pound of words. He demands untrue affirmations and contrived confessions. They humble the speaker. They hasten the process of moral disintegration.

Stripped of truthful words, Soviet citizens are powerless to defend themselves against Stalin's aggressions on their personalities. "Your words shall be my words," the helpless citizen proclaims. Words are the price of safety.

Democracy is, or should be, harmony. But dictatorship is unity. It speaks with one voice which shouts. It never whispers. The voice is the voice of Stalin.

A writer who craves fame or immunity or advancement quotes Stalin. Articles in newspapers and magazines often consist of skeletons, which are quotations from Stalin and Lenin, covered with thin meat and pale skin supplied by the author. Words from the Kremlin tower have displaced ideas.

Stalin knows that he would quickly lose his feudal mastery over bodies if he did not control minds. Minds are controlled by words. Words are the links in the chains worn by the Soviet mind. The Soviet nationalization of factories, forests, and land is as nothing compared with the nationalization of words.

In the abject service of the Soviet state, words undergo distortion. The words can offer no resistance. They go where Stalin drives them. Words are Stalin's blind oxen. He uses them to plow under men's brains.

The nationalization of words is the nationalization of minds. This leaves artists only one way of resisting the nationalization of their brains: silence. They abandon words. That exposes them to official threats. At the August, 1951, annual meeting in Moscow of the Association of Soviet Writers, Alexei Surkov, a poet, speaking on behalf of the association's directorate, said, "The circumstance that some important Soviet authors are in a state of prolonged creative idleness is very alarming. It is time to crush this shameful conspiracy of silence by writers who have not written anything for a long time."

Many of the best Soviet novelists and poets have not been published for years. Among them are Michael Sholokhov, author of the excellent novel, *And Quiet Flows the Don*; Leonid Leonov; Boris Pasternak, the best Russian poet, who has given up original work and translates Goethe and Shakespeare; Fedin; and A. Fadeyev.

The silent ones do write—for themselves and a few friends, or, as the Russian expression goes, "for the desk." Their manuscripts rest in their desk drawers because their honest words would not be published and they refuse to write dishonestly in order to be published.

The dilemma of the Soviet novelist is simple yet fatal. A novel gains interest by depicting conflict. Soviet novels, or plays, which must be political or risk condemnation as "divorced from reality," might show a conflict between a Communist and anti-Communist, or between a peasant who likes collectives and one who hates them. In portraying the anti-Communist or anticollectivist, the author would have to make him convincing, and this might be interpreted as reflecting the author's sympathies. The anti-Communist is accordingly depicted as a weak, repulsive, doomed character, and the conflict with the wise, sturdy, attractive, righteous Communist consequently never comes alive. If, on the other hand, the writer eschews a clash of characters and paints Soviet life as an Arcadia of agreement the result is dishwater dullness.

Stalin's monopoly of words eliminates honest discussion and good literature. It does more. It hampers moderation, compromise, and accommodation, and puts a premium on extremism and coercion. Where words are devalued by lies and smears the alternatives are uniformity and compulsion. Honest words are life's buffers. But a regime without free words must resort to the NKVD's revolver. The Kremlin's substitute for freedom of words is unquestioned dogma and undisputed police power. One is violence against the mind, the other against the body.

Stalin's ideal individual is a hollowed-out robot incapable of actions or responses except as they are piped through to him by the Kremlin power station. Stalin has failed to create this perfect automaton. In Soviet public life, to be sure, the robots dominate. Whenever Stalin utters a syllable or moves a finger they beat their cavernous breasts, cry "Hallelujah," and lower their faces to the feet of the Stalin idol. But in the secrecy of the individual mind, in the privacy of the family, some decency—and freedom of speech—survive. Every man guards the human spark, the more so since it is under fierce, unremitting attack. The spark is necessary for minimum self-esteem. Yet it must never be in evidence.

Self-preservation, the most highly developed trait of the new Stalin man, has stimulated the evolution of two sets of words. One is for himself and perhaps two or three others; the second is for public exhibition. To insure safety, he talks like a *Pravda* editorial or a November seventh manifesto. He suppresses the sigh and sings instead. He greets the blow that hurts. He praises Stalin who torments him. Soviet Russia has become the country of double-talk. This is the opposite of integrity. It is the disintegration of personality. It is schizophrenia on a national scale.

Stalin is aware of the prevalence of double-talk and double-mind. It serves his purpose. It induces loss of the self-respect. Fear has created a conformist who is conscious of his own debasement. The man with less self-respect is easier to rule. He bows his head in shame, and in that position the yoke falls naturally into place.

Self-disrespect is the cement of dictatorships.

The Soviet citizen who feels dishonored by his own acts is a better behaved prisoner in the country-wide jail.

"There is no freedom of speech in Russia" is thus the milder half of a depressing truth. It has the connotation of leaving people alone with their thoughts and honor but without certain rights. That would be too undynamic for Stalin. He goes further. He invades the individual and forces him to violate his conscience. Stalin's constant assaults on the spirit of Soviet man leave only the body, and that is powerless.

CHAPTER XI

Interview with Stalin

In fourteen years spent in Soviet Russia I saw Stalin innumerable times at Red Square parades, aviation displays, meetings, funerals, and the theater. In the theater or opera he sits far back in a box or behind a little curtain so that his presence is unknown to the general public. Once I saw Stalin on the jump seat of a large black limousine, alone with the driver, careening down Vozdvizhinka Street toward the Kremlin followed closely by a smaller car full of bodyguards with guns readied.

I saw Stalin at Kirov's funeral in December, 1934. He had gone to the Moscow hall where Kirov lay in state and kissed the dead man's lips. Later he walked into the Red Square as one of the pallbearers of the urn containing Kirov's ashes.

The assassination of Kirov had produced considerable nervousness in high quarters. A new special corps of guards, dressed in new uniforms without insignia, were spotted throughout the Red Square and stood shoulder to shoulder along Stalin's line of march between the grandstands and the massed army troops who filled the square. Henrik Yagoda, head of the GPU which had failed to protect Kirov in Leningrad, walked grimly a few feet from Stalin and never took his eyes off The Leader. Every precaution had been taken to prevent an attack on Stalin.

Normally at Red Square parades members of the Politbureau precede Stalin to the top of the Lenin Mausoleum and he then unostentatiously joins them. This funeral day, Stalin mounted the mausoleum first and alone. He walked up the marble steps, approached the parapet, put his hands on it, and, moving his head slowly from side to side, surveyed the scene. As one watched him from the grandstands nearest the Lenin tomb, Stalin's stance seemed to say, "Here I am. I am not afraid. Kirov has been killed.

But the situation is under control, my control." His demeanor convinced onlookers that this was so. A few minutes later the other leaders came up.

My best opportunity to study Stalin at close range was during a six-and-a-quarter-hour interview in his office outside the Kremlin. A group of Americans, among them Paul H. Douglas (later United States Senator); Stuart Chase, the author; Rexford Tugwell (later Governor of Puerto Rico); John Brophy and James Maurer, trade union leaders; and Jerome Davis, of the faculty of the Yale Divinity School, had been given an appointment with Stalin. They asked Mrs. Anne O'Hare McCormick of the *New York Times* and me to accompany them. It was September 9, 1927, a few weeks before Trotsky's fall. Stalin was already The Leader of Russia.

We entered Stalin's office at 1:00 P.M., and stayed until 7:15 P.M. During all those six and a quarter hours Stalin never left the room, never received a message and never sent out a message. There was no telephone in the office. He had so arranged his work that he could give undivided attention to the American visitors. This concentration is characteristic of Stalin's method as an organizer.

Twice during the long interview a typical Russian peasant woman in headkerchief brought in caviar, cheese, and sausage sandwiches, a large steaming samovar, sugar, slices of lemon, and glass tumblers for tea. She was the only person to enter the room and Stalin did not exchange a word with her. The eating did not interrupt the talking.

When we arrived Stalin gave each American a bone-crushing handshake and invited us to occupy smooth, curved-back chairs around the long table covered with green felt. It was here that the Politbureau met. Stalin wore a civilian khaki tunic buttoned up to the neck and khaki trousers which were stuffed into bright black boots that reached to just below his knees.

Stalin looks ordinary. Neither his face nor figure is distinguished. If he were not Stalin he would pass unnoticed in any Soviet street. He is five feet five inches tall, has drooping shoulders, sunken chest, a short thick neck, and large head. Both hands are big and strong. He moves lightly, like a mountaineer.

Stalin seated himself at the head of the table. I sat next to him on the left making pencil sketches of his face and notes on how he looked and what he said. I have kept the notes. I noticed the many deep circular pockmarks. His forehead is low and slopes backward. His hair and mustache were bushy and black. (He was then forty-eight.) His nose is long, the typical Georgian male nose. When Stalin smiled he showed short teeth, many of them blackened and gold-capped. He seldom smiles. He smiled when Harry Hopkins came to Moscow in 1941 as President Roosevelt's representative to offer Russia full military support. But Hopkins wrote that the smile was "cold, managed." The situation required a smile of gratitude and Stalin managed to manufacture one. He also smiled at the signing of the Nazi-Soviet pact; he shook hands with Nazi Foreign Minister Ribbentrop and smiled. It was a contrived grimace indicating to Hitler that he would collaborate. Stalin's smiles are political.

Stalin's face has no beauty. Neither is any feature beautiful. The colors are dull. His skin is sallow. The face reveals no trace of a spiritual quality. Its lines record no suffering. Nothing in it is delicate or luminous. It mirrors no rich emotional or mental life. It is not the face of a man inspired. It is the face of a man who schemes and traps, not the face of a sportsman or painter or poet.

My notes say that Stalin's eyes are "crafty." His eyes are gray-brown. They seldom open fully. Thick brows, heavy lids, and a moist film over the eyeballs seem designed to protect his eyes from inspection while he studies the person facing him. When he listens he does not look. When he speaks he stares at the visitor. He wants to know what impression he is making. He wants to know what the other person is thinking. "What is this fellow up to?" Stalin's eyes ask. They are the eyes of a hunter conscious of a dangerous prey that may spring on him, the eyes of a merchant who wonders whether this is the moment to conclude a bargain, the eyes of a man using his ears, eyes that feed material into a cerebral calculating machine. "It's not so easy to fool Comrade Stalin," Stalin wrote on July 9, 1929, in a personal letter not published until 1949. That is the warning conveyed by Stalin's eyes: "Don't try to fool Stalin."

For four hours Stalin, speaking Russian, holding his pipe and occasionally puffing on it, answered the questions which the American delegation had submitted to him in advance in writing. They reflected neither a desire to embarrass Stalin nor an intimate knowledge of Russian conditions. Several were theoretical. The first, about Lenin's contribution to the doctrines of Marx, permitted the dictator to wander for half an hour in the jungle of Marxist jargon and return without quarry. It merely showed that he had memorized a catechism which he used as a map. The performance was mental gymnastics. Stalin has little knowledge of or respect for theory. He uses Marx and Engels when they are convenient allies; in other circumstances he amends them. Marx and Engels, for instance, "concluded," in Stalin's words, "that a Socialist revolution could not be victorious in any one country." Since this conflicts with Soviet propaganda, Stalin declared, in a letter written on July 28, 1950, "that the old formula of Marx and Engels no longer corresponded to the new historic conditions." Very simple. Theory must prove Stalin right or it is bad theory.

The next question brought Stalin out of the Marxist woods into a clearing and revealed his ignorance. "Can it be said," the delegation asked, "that the Communist party controls the [Soviet] government?" "Everything depends," Stalin began, "on how you understand control. In capitalist countries control has a somewhat unique meaning. I know that quite a number of capitalist countries, notwithstanding the existence of 'democratic' parliaments, are controlled by big banks. The parliaments claim that they control the governments. But the fact is that the composition of the government is determined in advance, and their activities are controlled, by giant financial consortiums. Who does not know that in no capitalist country can a cabinet be formed against the wish of the big financial aces? All that is needed is to exert financial pressure—and the ministers fly out of their posts as though possessed. This is real control by banks over governments despite the would-be control by parliaments."

After this excursion away from the question, Mr. Stalin said, "Perhaps the delegation wanted to ask not about control but about the party's leadership of the government. If that is what the delegation wished to ask, then I reply, Yes, the party here does lead the government." The true answer would have been, Yes, the party controls the government as completely as anybody ever controlled anything. Stalin was simply trying to lead the delegation astray.

In fact, stripped of euphemisms and double-talk, Stalin himself admitted that the party controls the Soviet government. It "endeavors," he asserted, to have Communists appointed to all high government posts, and in "a great majority of cases, it succeeds." The party, furthermore, he declared, "examines the work of administrative departments, the work of government bodies, correcting their mistakes and deficiencies, which are inevitable. . . ." This, obviously, is control. But Stalin called it "leadership." Trained in the priesthood, expert in dogmatic argot, a diplomat when he wants to be, he employs scholasticisms to disguise hypocrisy.

The next question: "Since there is only one party in Russia, how do you know that the masses sympathize with communism?"

The Communist party, Stalin replied, could not have made the revolution and won the civil war without mass support. This was true. But Stalin moved on from this safe ground to say that the key role of Communists in the trade unions, the Young Communist League, and the soviets testified to the popularity of Communists. It actually testified to the existence of a dictatorship which imposed Communist control on those organizations. Stalin could not have it both ways: if the Communists are so popular, why dictatorship? No one said this, however.

Heckling did occur when Stalin dealt with the next question: Suppose a non-Communist group, which was pro-Soviet, advocated the scrapping of the Soviet monopoly of foreign trade; could it present candidates in an election and campaign for them?

The monopoly of foreign trade, Stalin replied, is an indispensable feature of the Soviet system. Only the bourgeoisie, "a negligible minority of the population," would advocate its elimination.

An American interrupted to remark that the monopoly of foreign trade was merely an example of the kind of issue around which a Soviet political group might be organized if the Communists were not the only legal political party.

The Bolsheviks, Stalin answered, deprived the bourgeoisie of their factories, railroads, banks, mines, etc., but it seems the delegation objects because the soviets went beyond that and deprived the bourgeoisie of their political rights too. "This, I think, is not altogether logical or, more accurately, is altogether illogical. On what basis do you demand magnanimity from the proletariat in relation to the bourgeoisie? Does the bourgeoisie of the West, which is in power, show the slightest magnanimity to the working class? . . . Whoever thinks of the possibility of restoring the political rights of the bourgeoisie should, if he wishes to be logical, go further and also raise the question of the return of factories and plants, the railroads and banks to the bourgeoisie."

Such argumentation would have won applause in a hand-picked Soviet audience. For was this not a spirited and logical defense of Communist policy? But an American pointed out that Stalin had not answered the question and was confusing the issue. Nobody had suggested the restitution of the bourgeoisie's rights. "The question is," the American insisted, "how can the opinions of the workers and peasants, as distinguished from the opinion of the Communist party, find legal expression?" A second American pressed the same point.

Stalin knew he had been caught and showed the good sense to surrender. "Very good," he said. "In other words, the question is not the restoration of the political rights of the bourgeoisie but a conflict of opinions within the working class and peasantry." Different opinions existed, he admitted, but they centered around improvement in the Soviet regime, not its overthrow, and that being the case, the monopoly of the Communist party found no opponents.

The next question followed logically: "Can you tell us, in brief, about the differences between you and Trotsky?" The implication was, Would not these differences warrant the formation of a second Soviet party? Here Stalin, who had spoken at great length on other subjects, refused to answer. He would not, he said, talk to non-Communist foreigners about party politics.

He did elaborate on the possibility of expanding Soviet trade with foreign countries. He believed in the coexistence of the capitalist and soviet systems of society. What about Moscow's support to outside

Communist parties? Did it, for instance, help the American Communist party? No, said Stalin, the American Communist party, being delicately sensitive, had never asked for help. "But what would happen," Stalin went on, "if the American Communist party turned to the Soviet Communist party for aid? I think that the Soviet Communist party would render it all possible assistance. And really, what would a Communist party, especially one that was in power, be worth if it refused aid to a Communist party in another country which lived under the capitalist yoke? I would say that such a Communist party was not worth a penny." This is an attractive sample of Stalin's bluntness.

At the end of four hours of interviewing Stalin, Dr. Jerome Davis, the leader of the delegation, finally wedged in his "Thank you, Mr. Stalin, for your kindness in giving us so much of your time." But Stalin was not finished. "No, no," he exclaimed, "I have answered your questions, now you must answer mine."

Stalin's questions were: "How do you account for the small number of American workers organized in trade unions?" "Is there a system of government insurance of workers in America?" "How do you explain the absence of a special mass workers' party in the United States?" "How do you explain that on the question of recognizing the U.S.S.R., the leaders of the American Federation of Labor are more reactionary than many bourgeois?" That was all. The questions and Stalin's remarks in the subsequent discussion, indicated that his purpose was propaganda rather than information.

Throughout the six and a quarter hours, Stalin showed a complete absence of nerves. His voice was calm. He was neither brilliant nor magnetic. He cannot wave the magic wand of personality to captivate or charm. He does not establish a personal relationship; he makes an impression. He made his impression in the interview the same way he built his political power: methodically, brick by brick. The impression is one of cold strength, iron will, and unsentimentality. His statements were sensible, solid, simple, and pedestrian. He lacks the capacity for witty epigram or terse phrase which lights up a whole field of thought. He plows long and deep. He wins by siege rather than by blitz. His weapon is the club, not the rapier.

What he lacks in brilliance, grace, inspiration, and personal electricity he makes up by hard work, persistent plodding, shrewdness, weight, and time. He is like a glacier, icy, slow-moving, massive, and irresistible. While Stalin lacks the penetration of Lenin and the grandiloquence of Trotsky, his intelligence, which has grown with his power and his access, therefore, to rich sources of information, is potent. He has a butcher-knife logic. It hacks away nonessential or inconvenient facts in order to get at useful meat. When the truth suits his needs he is also capable of giving correct assessments of world events. His analysis is hit-or-miss. Sometimes he misundertands major political developments. At other times his prevision is astounding. His attitude to the Western capitalist world is based on abstractions learned from a book and on selected misinformation. His relation to the Eastern feudal world is based on experience and observation.

In the course of the interview with the Americans, Stalin made a significant statement which is repeated to this day as current Soviet policy. Stalin told the Americans that as the "international revolution" developed, "two world centers will be formed: a socialist center attracting to itself the countries gravitating toward socialism, and a capitalist center attracting to itself the countries gravitating toward capitalism. The struggle of these two centers for the conquest of world economy," Stalin added, "will decide the fate of capitalism and socialism throughout the world, for the defeat of world capitalism means the victory of socialism in the arena of world economy."

Stalin sees Russia in the role of competitor of the advanced Western industrialized nations. The two worlds exist side by side and compete. They coexist until one ceases to exist. If Russia proves superior, the West will succumb. If the West proves superior, the Soviets will succumb.

There are two ways of winning a race. One is to move ahead as fast as possible, the other is to cripple the opponent. For twenty-five years, Stalin has been trying both methods.

CHAPTER XII

A Conspiracy

The 1920's were troubled times for Stalin, but his skill proved equal to his problems. As the decade grew older he became stronger. In 1927, Leon Trotsky, the enemy he most feared, fell from power. On October 1, 1928, the first Five Year Plan was inaugurated; with it commenced the rapid aggrandizement of the dictator's political monopoly. During an address in April, 1929, before the Communist party's Central Committee, Stalin's critics heckled him. It was probably the last time a Soviet citizen dared to heckle The Leader.

The April, 1929, speech, whose full text remained unpublished for twenty years, lasted seven hours. It was a continuous attack on the "Right" wing led by Rykov, Bukharin, and Tomsky. Stalin was moving in for the kill.

The banishment of Trotsky in January, 1928, sowed panic among Stalin's surviving opponents. The dictator could now concentrate his fire on the "Rightists." Political death threatened and they knew it. Stalin charged in his address that they had engaged in conspiracy.

They had indeed talked opposition politics in secret and searched for a way to overthrow Stalin. Gregory Sokolnikov, a former Finance Commissar, launched the move. At 9 A.M. on July 11, 1928, he rang the bell at Leo Kamenev's Moscow apartment. He called so early in the hope of eluding the eye of the GPU. He came without an appointment because he suspected that Kamenev's telephone was tapped.

Sokolnikov acted for Bukharin. They had agreed that if Sokolnikov did not return to Bukharin's home within an hour, Bukharin would appear at Kamenev's place.

Bukharin had sided with Stalin against Trotsky and Kamenev. Now he was condemning Stalin and courting Kamenev. Kamenev had been anti-Lenin, pro-Lenin, anti-Trotsky, pro-Trotsky, pro-

Stalin, and anti-Stalin. Stalin had stood with Bukharin and Kamenev against Trotsky, and with Bukharin against Kamenev. Now he was against Bukharin. Therefore, Bukharin sought an alliance with Kamenev.

Stalin is an ideological corkscrew. His enemies, however, were scarcely less sinuous in their loyalties.

Bukharin, Sokolnikov, and Kamenev talked for almost two hours. When his unheralded guests departed, Kamenev wrote a memorandum on their visit. Several of Kamenev's friends made copies of this document and within a few days one of these copies reached me in Moscow. I made notes.

In the preliminary tête-à-tête, Sokolnikov told Kamenev that Bukharin was through with Stalin. Stalin, he said, had adopted the "Left," Trotskyist line of persecuting the peasants and fostering the rapid growth of industry. Stalin, therefore, Sokolnikov predicted, would soon try to patch up his relations with Kamenev and Zinoviev; but they would do better to side with Bukharin.

At this point, Bukharin arrived. He was extremely nervous and spoke for forty-five minutes without stopping. Stalin's policies, he said, were undermining the Soviet government. He had not talked with Stalin for several weeks although they met in the Politbureau. Recent sessions of the Politbureau had been stormy; members called one another "liar" and "scoundrel." Stalin, Bukharin declared, had no principles; he merely wished to control everybody. "You cannot put a single document into Stalin's hands," Bukharin declared, "without him using it against you." Bukharin thought Stalin would soon try to remove him from the important post of *Pravda* editor.

Bukharin wanted to engineer the return of Kamenev and Zinoviev to the Politbureau. If they did not unite against Stalin he would arouse the peasantry against the government by his policy of squeezing too much grain out of the villages at low prices in order to finance industry. The result would be civil war.

Though Stalin was philosophically illiterate, Bukharin continued, he fancied himself a theoretician. He tried, before a meeting of the Politbureau several weeks ago, to curry favor with Bukharin. "Bukhashka," Stalin addressed him affectionately, "Bukhashka, dear, you and I are Himalayas. The others are pigmies."

"Stalin," Bukharin declared, "has no scruples. He is an opponent of the Genghis Khan variety, loving revenge, and expert in knifing in the back. He will destroy us all," Bukharin exclaimed. Bukharin was a young, stormy petrel, a joyous scholar and artist, a sensitive mimosa-person.

"What are your forces?" Kamenev asked soberly.

The answer was disappointing.

Nothing came of this "conspiracy," as Stalin called it publicly. It was too late. By the end of 1929, Stalin was undisputed dictator, and both the "Right" and "Left" had lost most of their influence. Against any opposition, Stalin could invoke the ingrained Bolshevik horror of disunity and dissidence. Whenever necessary, moreover, he could arrive arm-in-arm with Lenin who had rejected him. "Thus spake Lenin," Stalin told a conference. "Maybe the opposition doesn't agree with Lenin? Just let them say so openly." That silenced all debate.

Stalin rose to supremacy over the dead bodies of the "Right" and "Left" oppositions thanks in part to his talent as a Machiavellian tactician. He can sit on the fence or between two stools or on two stools at once. He is a flexible experimenter, an opportunistic empiricist. His acts clash with his words. "We want no foot of foreign territory but we shall not relinquish an inch of our own," Stalin said in June, 1930. Since then he has annexed not a foot but thousands of square miles of foreign territory. In 1930, Stalin probably did not intend to seize foreign territory; he had no opportunity. When the opportunity came he seized it.

Soviet Russia is said to have a planned economy. The idea of a plan is to chart production in advance so that the government knows how much raw material, fuel, manpower, etc., is required. But the moment a Soviet plan is adopted the Kremlin propaganda machine begins to call for a speed-up with a view to the overfulfillment of the plan. I once asked Ivan Smilga, chief of the federal Planning Commission, whether the overfulfillment of a plan did not really disrupt it. "Of course," he replied.

Overfulfillment involves supplementary raw materials, labor, electricity, etc., not according to a precise, previously drafted plan but in accordance with what happens to be the degree of the speed-up. And the degree will vary in different parts of different industries. A Stalin plan, whether at home or abroad, is nothing more than a tentative, minimum target. It is not a blueprint for a smooth, predictable operation. The operation will back and fill, zig and zag. It will respond to the forces arraigned against it and behind it. Stalin moves by trial and error, not according to a plan and not according to a theory. By this uninhibited strategy he defeated his enemies from Trotsky down. In 1929, as a result, Stalin was King Bolshevik. The party controversy rolled on for a few more months, but its outcome was certain; Stalin could not lose.

When the secret police watches everybody, including its own officials, all members of the Politbureau, and Stalin, the chances of a successful conspiracy are small. If two trusting friends shared their anti-Stalin views and talked to a third person about overthrowing Stalin, the third person would inevitably suspect a trap. He would have to assume that they had been ordered by the NKVD to talk to him in order to test his loyalty. "If I do not report this conversation," he would say to himself, "the police will conclude that I am anti-Stalin." He accordingly makes the report. That is the end of the conspiracy.

Terror protects a police state in normal peacetime.

CHAPTER XIII

Stalin Faces West

Having secured his position at home, Stalin undertook a gentle reversal of the Soviet Union's foreign policy. His talk about imminent capitalist aggression notwithstanding, Stalin knew that the West did not intend to attack Russia. Nor, judging by his actions, did he take seriously his own diatribes against Bukharin who maintained that capitalism would stabilize itself and ward off revolution.

No revolution impended in Asia or Europe. Maxim Litvinov, Chicherin's Undersecretary in the Soviet Foreign Commissariat, had long held this view. He once told me that he despaired of the world revolution the moment the armistice of the First World War was signed on November 11, 1918, for peace meant stabilization. But many Bolsheviks were less realistic. Trotsky had staked his career on the spread of revolution; he saw the salvation of an isolated Communist Russia in the fall of one and preferably more capitalist regimes. Stalin likewise recognized the necessity of redressing the unequal balance between the solitary Soviet Union and the rest of the planet. The industrialization of Russia would, in his view, contribute to that end by making her stronger. Revolution abroad would have the same effect, and Stalin was ready to welcome any such windfall. But the foreign policy developed under Stalin by Foreign Commissar Georgi Chicherin resembled Czarist foreign policy more closely than it did a revolutionary foreign policy.

Chicherin, who held office from 1918 to 1930, was a strange genius with a high-pitched voice, painfully sensitive, and a gifted pianist. His only book, a treatise on Mozart, was read by a few persons in manuscript but never published. He descended from a noble family related to the Czars. His father was an official in the Czarist foreign ministry and in early manhood he himself worked as a minor clerk in the same department. He spoke French, German, English, and Italian fluently. His culture was fantastically inclusive, and his knowledge encyclopedic. The exquisite drafting of his diplomatic correspondence as Soviet Foreign Commissar is still remembered by connoisseurs. He detested Stalin and said so in private conversation. Yet this Bolshevik, who disliked any mention of his royal blood, and Stalin, the non-Russian, jointly evolved a foreign policy reminiscent of the traditional policy of the Russian monarchy. Its axis was hostility to Great Britain.

The Czars, fearing a British advance toward Russia's soft, non-Russian underbelly in the Caucasus and Central Asia, wished to expand beyond those areas. Hence the monarchy's imperialist designs on Constantinople and the Turkish Straits, on Persia, Afghanistan, and, at times, India. From London and New Delhi this naturally looked like aggressive penetration into the British world.

The result was a stubborn Anglo-Russian antagonism.

To be sure, "the bear that walks like a man" and the lion that dominated so much of Asia did lie down together after they had shared the Persian lamb in 1907. That enabled them to join arms in the First World War against the Germanic coalition which barred Russia's way into the Balkans. But Russia's hostility toward England remained and carried over into the Bolshevik period.

On seizing power, Lenin denounced and renounced Russia's imperialist aspirations in the Near East and Central Asia and, instead, offered friendship to Turkey, Persia, and Afghanistan. He tried to draw those countries into the Russian orbit by courtship rather than conquest.

Stalin, however, held back. In 1920, he sent Russian troops from Georgia into the Persian province of Ghilan and annexed it under the guise of sovietization. He was likewise lukewarm toward Moscow's 1921 military alliance with Turkey. He behaved like a Czarist Russian nationalist.

Lenin reprimanded Stalin for his aggression in Persia, and when coolness to Turkey was no longer practicable, Stalin gave Chicherin a free hand in wooing those two countries and Afghanistan with a view to weakening their ties with England. Stalin lost no opportunity to spur the disintegration of the British empire. Chicherin predicted its liquidation.

Just as Britain had barred Russian expansion in the Near and Middle East so Japan blocked the Czar in the Far East. Britain and Japan were therefore equally unpopular in the court of Nicholas II. Stalin's Kremlin was no less impartial. He and Chicherin aimed to create a strong China which would resist not only Japan but Britain too. They expected American assistance.

The United States was just beginning to loom on Russia's horizon as a great power. Soviet Moscow considered it a potentially friendly power. Stalin wanted American help against Japan and England.

No territorial disputes or commercial rivalry separated America from Russia. President Woodrow Wilson had supported the territorial integrity of Soviet Russia, and Secretary of State Charles Evans Hughes as well as Wilson opposed Japanese penetration in Siberia. The United States considered Russia a necessary counter weight to the growing strength of Japan and did not want to see Russia weakened. Stalin considered America a counterweight to Japan.

Stalin and Chicherin also regarded the United States as a possible ally against England. Unchanging rivalry and even war between England and the United States were basic in the doctrinaire thinking of Lenin, Trotsky, and Stalin. Logically, therefore, the anti-British Bolsheviks leaned toward friendship with the United States. Moscow always tried to put the most favorable interpretation on American acts. Soviet writers and leaders described the 1918-20 American military intervention in Bolshevik Russia as negligible. In fact, when Stalin, in a speech on January 26, 1924, referred to foreign interference he mentioned only "the armed intervention of England and France." (In his *History of the Communist Party of the Soviet Union (Bolsheviks)*, published in 1938, Stalin likewise minimized the part played by the United States in the anti-Soviet intervention.) America was a capitalist nation and the Kremlin should have loathed it. But Stalin's motivations were not Marxist. He pictured America as a balance against Japan in the Pacific and against Britain in the Near and Middle East. He accordingly desired good relations with the United States and was disappointed not to achieve them.

(The Second World War completely altered this situation. For all practical purposes, America has become Japan blocking Russian expansion in Asia; witness Korea. For all practical purposes, America has become England blocking Russian expansion in Turkey, Greece, Iran, and so forth. The United States consequently inherited the traditional hostility which Russia had focused on Japan and Britain.)

Unable to build a bridge to America, Chicherin and Stalin used Germany as the pivot of their foreign policy. Many Bolsheviks had known Germany as revolutionary exiles from Czarism and as students of Marx, Engels, Kautsky, Bebel, and other German socialist theoreticians. A far larger proportion of them spoke German than English or French. The Bolsheviks, and Russians in general, were impressed, indeed often awed, by Prussian military prowess and German efficiency. When the Soviet leaders thought of Europe they thought first of Germany, and they congratulated themselves on having established close ties with Germany as early as 1922 when England and France were hostile and America indifferent. Chicherin cultivated these ties with the passion that characterized him and he simultaneously endeavored to obstruct a German reconciliation with London and Paris lest it cool Germany's interest in Soviet Russia.

In pursuance of this pro-German orientation, Chicherin backed Germany against Poland, France, and England, and Lithuania against Poland. Germany, Lithuania, Turkey, Persia, Afghanistan, and China were the Chicherin-Stalin solar system. It was a limited sphere.

In 1930, Stalin brusquely dismissed Chicherin who had been ailing for a long time. Chicherin learned of his dismissal from the newspapers. Maxim M. Litvinov succeeded him.

Litvinov had lived in England as an exile for fourteen years. His wife was British. He repeatedly said in private that he never saw the sense of antagonizing a great power like England for the sake of Persia or Afghanistan or even China. He was a fervent Bolshevik,

Catherine Djugashvili, mother of Stalin

Sc

Police photographs of Stalin (1910)

So

Lenin and Stalin at Gorky, near Moscow (1922)

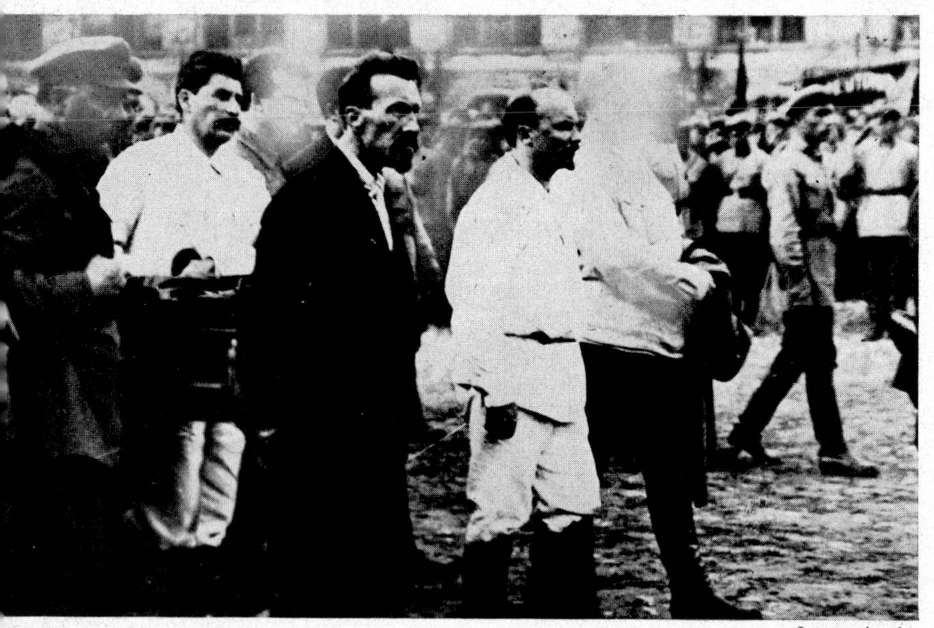

International

Funeral of Dzerzhinsky (1926). Voroshilov (wearing cap), Stalin, Rykov, Bukharin and Yenukidze

Keystone

Stalin's second wife, Nadiezhda Alliluyev, who committed suicide in 1932

Keys

Trotsky (with beard, saluting) reviewing troops in 1920. Second from right is Leo Kamenev who was shot in 1926

So

At the Bolshoy Theater in Moscow on Nov. 6, 1937, celebrating the twentieth anniversary of the revolution. Left to right: G. Dimitrov, Kaganovitch, Stalin, Molotov, Mikoyan, Shvernik, and Svetlana, Stalin's daughter

Acme

Stalin and Ribbentrop shaking hands after signing the Soviet-German treaty and agreeing on partition of Poland in 1939

Sovf

Three views of Stalin in 1945 during his speech branding Japan an aggressor

Churchill, Averell Harriman, Stalin, Molotov during the war

European

The Teheran Conference: in back of Stalin, Roosevelt, and Churchill are (left to right): Harry Hopkins, Molotov, Harriman, Churchill's daughter Sarah, and Anthony Eden

Sovfoto

The Yalta Conference: in back (left to right): Eden, Edward Stettinius, Molotov, Harriman

Sovfoto

A painting of Stalin as Generalissimo

Keysto

A photograph of Stalin at the same tim

Ac

The Potsdam Conference: Attlee, Truman, and Stalin

probably the last of the idealistic Bolshevik Mohicans. In foreign affairs, however, he behaved like a cold realist. He was the businessman in diplomacy. And he was a Westerner.

Stalin was an Easterner. "I too am an Asiatic," he exclaimed to a Japanese journalist who came for an interview. But Asia had neither revolution nor trade to offer. England and America, on the other hand, were proposing large credits for the purchase of machine tools which, the Kremlin discovered to its surprise, were superior to many German products. Litvinov, the Jew, moreover, felt no sympathy for Germany; Hitler's star was rising.

Persons acquainted with the Soviet Commissariat of Foreign Affairs accepted as an axiom that if Chicherin said "Yes" Litvinov would say "No" to the same question, and if Chicherin said "No" Litvinov would take the affirmative. Yet for many years Stalin kept both of them in the Foreign Office. Stalin's reward was a ready-made Foreign Minister and a ready-made foreign policy when he decided, toward the end of 1929, to turn away from Asia, Germany, and Chicherin, and seek closer ties with England and the West generally. Yet being astutely Stalin he never burned the bridge back to Asia and Germany.

World revolution was in the doldrums. Russia was industrializing rapidly. Britain and France were stronger than Germany. Stalin chose the West.

In 1930, a *de facto* truce existed between the capitalist and Communist worlds. No doubt, Stalin still thought in terms of the conflict between them and the ultimate triumph of his world. But at the moment, he could not crush capitalism, neither could capitalism crush Russia. Except for scattered debris, the organized party factions that had opposed Stalin at home were dead, and he no longer needed to pay political tribute to the idol of world revolution. Stalin consequently wooed the foreign forces he wished to destroy. There is no evidence that this pained his political conscience.

Litvinov had fought hard to convince Stalin that the Soviet government must reverse its foreign policy. Litvinov was courageous. He dared talk back to Stalin. Stalin yielded to him. Circumstances favored Litvinov's argument: in 1931, Japan occupied Manchuria;

Germany moved toward militarism. Stalin feared an attack from two sides. Litvinov sought security for Russia by collective action with England and France, and if possible the United States.

The prize Stalin and Litvinov coveted most was American diplomatic recognition. When recognition finally came in 1933 through an agreement negotiated by Litvinov with President Roosevelt in the White House, Stalin uttered two words and they went out over the ticker as orders to all Russia. Stalin said, "*Ne Razkhlebatsa*" which can be translated, "Don't display excessive glee." He knew that editorial writers would be inclined to throw their hats in the air and their restraint to the winds and rejoice over the friendly relations with the most capitalistic of all nations. Stalin was reminding them that Russia was a great power, and a Soviet country, and must not congratulate herself too obviously.

CHAPTER XIV

Dr. Freud Wonders about Stalin

Sigmund Freud, in a book entitled *Civilization and Its Discontents,* wondered what Stalin would do after 1929. "It is understandable," Dr. Freud wrote, "that the attempt to build up a new communistic culture in Russia finds its psychological backing in the persecution of the bourgeoisie. Only one cannot help wondering," Freud added, "what the Soviets will undertake once they finish exterminating their bourgeoisie." Stalin already knew the answer. He would, with added zest, exterminate Communists.

The nearer an opponent stands to Stalin the greater Stalin's antagonism. His hatred of Socialists exceeds his hatred of capitalists, and as between right-wing and left-wing Socialists he has said he abominates the latter more. Stalin's fiercest ire, however, is for his own party comrades. He has killed a larger number of Communists than any other person in the world. A dissident Communist infuriates Stalin more than a distant capitalist, and brother Georgians get shorter shrift than Russians.

The Freudian dilemma, therefore, did not trouble Stalin. After liquidating the old bourgeoisie he would liquidate Bolsheviks and simultaneously he would liquidate the new Soviet bourgeoisie, the children of his own policies. A dictator never wants for victims. If necessary he breeds them in order to devour them.

The need of further bloodshed may have eluded the casual observer, for Stalin's position in Soviet politics was impregnable. He could not be overthrown. The alternative giants had been deprived of their power inside the party. But the party still had power with which Stalin was obliged to reckon.

The Russian Communist party was a remarkable political instrument. Conceived and bred by Lenin to seize and wield power with professional proficiency and fanatical intensity, it concentrated all the power of the state within itself. The party was the dynamo of the Soviet government. Lenin led the party and often bent it to his will. But sometimes it voted him down. In any case, he operated through it and only through it. The party, consequently, was accustomed to rule.

Stalin thinned the blood of the party with hundreds of thousands of new recruits who accepted membership as an honor and opportunity for advancement. They were not leaders. They were content to follow The Leader. Some of these Stalin elevated to higher rank. But much of the party still consisted of the prerevolutionary old guard and of those who joined it in the flush of idealism born of the 1917 insurrection. Many members were steeped in the Leninist spirit of incorruptibility, evangelism, and purity of revolutionary purpose. The Communist party leadership of the Red Army, for instance, of the secret police, and of other sensitive government departments was still firmly entrenched, and Stalin had not dared to tamper with it. The rationed ruthlessness of his purges and Machiavellian manipulations had depressed and deflated the party. Yet some independence and belligerence remained. Despite the blows to their faith and hopes, many top-rank Communists still believed in communism.

These people constituted Stalin's problem. They bowed to his supremacy but not to the extent of their own extinction. He could rule for them, not without them. The question was: Would Russia become a personal despotism instead of a party dictatorship dominated by one man? The life of the party hung on the subtle difference between the two. A party which retained the right to make decisions, even if most of the decisions were to the taste of the dictator or made by him, would still be an irksome limitation on a despot and might some day, in a crisis, oust him.

By 1930, the bourgeoisie of city and village had been exterminated as a class. Stalin's party rivals were defeated men. But when he surveyed the battlefield on which he had won this dark victory he discerned the party. The party was the battlefield and arsenal; it supplied the men and weapons and grew the laurels. Stalin had reduced the party to a myth, but he feared the myth, for the myth of the party's power had once corresponded to reality—and could again.

Stalin now undertook to kill the party beyond resurrection. This was a mammoth task; it required a transformation of Soviet life, for the party was Soviet politics.

There was only one way to do this: abolish politics.

Stalin has done exactly that. It is the ultimate in politics. The Soviet Union is today a nonpolitical state.

Resentful of the exhausting political struggle whereby he had forged to the top, and never secure enough within himself to be certain that the trouble would not recur, Stalin resolved to put an end to political battles by putting an end to politics.

Politics is the process of establishing a government, formulating its policies, guiding their execution, and replacing it. The process had become superfluous in the Soviet Union. Stalin was the irreplaceable master who adopted his own policies. He needed no party to make them or unmake him. He needed only a body of managers to carry out his policies. Government in Stalin's Russia is a problem in management.

The steps taken over a number of years by Stalin, the miracle organizer, to destroy the party organization are clearly demarcated:

1. Discussions inside the party, once fully reported, with adequate attention to opposition speeches, by the Soviet press, ceased in 1930.

2. The glorification of Stalin as the engineer of all the Soviet Union's successes was enormously intensified and the party, in consequence, seemed less important.

3. Formal "cleansings" of the party occurred in 1934, 1935, and 1936. At least a million members were dismissed from the ranks and replaced by men and women devoid of the Bolshevik spirit and ignorant of the party's traditions. Most of the expelled members had been guilty of independent thinking or independent acts. The new ones were easily regimented.

4. The Young Communist League or Komsomol, the junior branch of the party, hatchery of Communists, was purged several times in the 1930's and its members told, in so many words, to keep

out of politics. Youthful idealism was a commodity for which Stalin had no use.

5. In May, 1935, Stalin disbanded the Society of Old Bolsheviks, the Old Guard who had served under Lenin before the revolution. They knew the past. They were the party heritage, the party memory, the party conscience. They were the party's soul and therefore an inconvenience to a dictator intent on killing its body.

6. To mangle the body, Stalin merged the Communist party with the Soviet government. This constituted one of the most fateful changes in Soviet history.

The Bolshevik party had always been over, yet outside the Soviet government. The government obeyed the party, but the party did not become enmeshed in day-to-day administration. The government was the policeman-administrator. The party was the government's political mentor and motor.

The party gave the orders. Their execution, when faulty, did not compromise the party. The party kept its distance and could accordingly criticize, condemn, and correct.

Many party officials, to be sure, were also government executives. Overlapping was frequent. But Politbureau members like Zinoviev and Bukharin had never been part of the government. In the early years Stalin held two government posts: Commissar of Nationalities, and Commissar of Workers and Peasants Inspection whose work Lenin bluntly attacked in a newspaper article. Since 1923, however, Stalin had no government appointment. He preferred the twilight of the party's Secretary-Generalship where his deeds were subject to least scrutiny.

Gradually, Stalin made the overlapping between government bureaucrat and party officer well-nigh complete. Important and lesser party leaders were burdened with myriad executive tasks. Their responsibility for administration increased as their participation in policy-making vanished. Communists ceased to be politicians and became office workers.

Of top-rank Bolsheviks, Stalin alone remained outside the government. He could thus condemn the government's mistakes while refusing blame for them. He was the check and balance on the government, he alone. With the passing of years, his hunger for recognition as father of all things Soviet led him to co-sign important decrees with the head of the government; presumably the government lacked the necessary prestige without Stalin's name. But Stalin merely signed the decree. The execution rested on others whom he could attack for errors or failures.

By the middle of the 1930's, party tasks were thoroughly intertwined with government tasks. The earlier separation of functions had yielded to total identification. Lenin and Bukharin had warned against such a fusion. So, actually, had Stalin. In a speech in 1926 he gave the very best reason for not doing what he himself subsequently did. The opposition, he declared, urged that the party become the government, and that the party, instead of the government, carry out the dictatorship of the proletariat. Stalin objected vehemently. "Dictatorship in the exact sense of the word," he said in his 1926 speech, "is government resting on violence, for without elements of violence there is no dictatorship in the exact sense of the word. Can the party be a government resting on violence toward its class, toward the majority of the working class? Clearly, it cannot. For in that event it would be a dictatorship not over the bourgeoisie but a dictatorship over the working class."

Stalin then went on to explain just how the Soviet system became what it is today: a dictatorship over the working class. "The [Communist] party," he said, "is the teacher, the guide, the leader of its class, but not a government based on violence toward the majority of the working class. Otherwise there would be no sense in talking about the method of persuasion as the chief method of a proletarian party among the working class. Otherwise there would be no sense in saying that the party must convince the broad masses of the proletariat of the wisdom of its policies and that only by so doing can the party consider itself a truly mass party capable of leading the proletariat in battle. Otherwise the party would have to replace the method of persuasion with orders and threats to the proletariat, which is absurd and which is completely incompatible with the Marxist understanding of the dictatorship of the proletariat."

So long as the Soviet government, under orders from the Communist party, exterminated the bourgeoisie while the party itself remained "the teacher, the guide, the leader" of the working class, it would claim to be the agent of the dictatorship of the proletariat. But when, in Stalin's own words, the party abandoned persuasion and began to use "orders and threats" to get more production out of the factory workers and peasants, when, moreover, Stalin availed himself of government violence to win controversies in the party, the party ceased to be a political party and assumed the role of policeman and hangman of its own members. As Stalin had foreseen, it now made "no sense talking about the method of persuasion as the chief method of a proletarian party among the working class." The NKVD was the archpersuader.

The next steps were inevitable. In 1935, for the first time, Stalin was able to obtain approval from the Politbureau for the shooting of a group of secondary party leaders, and in 1936, Zinoviev and Kamenev, past pillars of the party, were sentenced to death. A teacher and guide does not shoot men. Shooting is not persuasion. The party had abandoned the weapons which made it a party and assumed the weapons employed, as Stalin explained, by a violent dictatorship. This, Stalin himself said, is incompatible with the Marxist concept of the dictatorship of the proletariat. It is, he noted, a dictatorship over the proletariat.

The merging of the party with the state marked the triumph of Stalin's personal terror and soon culminated in the Moscow trials and murderous purges of 1936, 1937, and 1938. The merging of the party with the state sounded the death knell of all remnants of freedom in the party and in the country.

Stalin had solved Dr. Freud's conundrum. The party was slated for extermination.

The party was Lenin's child. After Lenin's death Stalin embraced it and crushed it. The child has joined Lenin in the mausoleum; it too is an embalmed, deified corpse. From the top of the mausoleum, Stalin rules in the name of Lenin and of the party. "Stalin is Lenin today," Bolshevik propaganda asserts. The son has become the father. "The peoples of the Soviet Union, the entire Red Army and Fleet, call Stalin their father and friend," Klementi Voroshilov, War Commissar, wrote on Stalin's sixtieth birthday.

Stalin looked at his handiwork and saw that it was good. Anastasi Mikoyan, a member of the Politbureau, writing on the same sixtieth anniversary, quotes Stalin as saying in sadness, "Ah, what a pity that Lenin is not alive. He lived and worked in a difficult period. If he could see now what a road we have traversed, what we have achieved! Lenin would be pleased." This shows Stalin pitying Lenin for achieving so little. Stalin achieved more: the extermination of the revolution.

In 1938, Stalin's *History of the Communist Party of the Soviet Union (Bolsheviks)* was published in Moscow. It is in the nature of the party's epitaph. On the last page of the volume, Stalin revealingly quotes an excursion he made in March, 1937, into Greek mythology. "In the mythology of the ancient Greeks," he said, "there was a celebrated hero, Anteus, who, so the legend goes, was the son of Poseidon, god of the seas, and Gaea, goddess of the earth. Anteus was very much attached to the mother who had given birth to him, suckled him, and reared him. There was not a hero whom this Anteus did not vanquish. He was regarded as an invincible hero. Wherein lay his strength? It lay in the fact that every time he was hard pressed in a fight with an adversary he would touch the earth, the mother who had given birth to him and suckled him, and that gave him new strength. Yet he had a vulnerable spot—the danger of being detached from the earth in some way or other. His enemies were aware of this weakness and watched for him. One day an enemy appeared who took advantage of this vulnerable spot and vanquished Anteus. This was Hercules. How did Hercules vanquish Anteus? He lifted him from the earth, kept him suspended in the air, prevented him from touching the earth, and throttled him."

The moral of the myth, Stalin explained, was that as long as the Bolsheviks "maintain their connection with their mother, the masses, who gave them birth, suckled them, and reared them," they would be invincible. That is precisely what the party no longer did. Hercules—Stalin had lifted it away from the masses, far above the masses, made it a dictatorship over the masses, and throttled it. Then he replaced it with an elite which, by its very character, lacked any connection with the masses.

The Bolshevik party was the first Soviet ruling class. It implemented the dictatorship of the proletariat. But the dictatorship soon acquired so much power that it could ignore the class in whose name it ruled. Nazi Germany witnessed the same metamorphosis. Hitler took office on behalf of the industrialists and middle class. Before long he was strong enough to defy them and dictate to the entire nation.

Equipped with the latest technology, a modern dictatorship is so almighty, the citizen so puny, that it becomes a free-wheeling monster concerned merely with finding, using, and recompensing the servants who, like automatons, do its bidding.

CHAPTER XV

The New Managers

Stalin worked with both hands. While liquidating the party, which was a political ruling class, he performed a masterful, slow process of creating a new managerial ruling class that had no pretensions to power, control, or criticism and did not aspire to play a historic role. It merely wanted good pay.

With advancing industrialization and with the mechanization of collectivized agriculture, the country was dependent on the loyal collaboration and good will of the engineering class, the technical intelligentsia. But the Stalin regime had always had an anti-intellectual bias. Part of Stalin's antagonism to Trotsky, Bukharin, Rakovsky, Zinoviev, Kamenev, Ossinsky, and other big-brain Bolsheviks was due to the fact that they were intellectuals.

Answering the charge in Lenin's last testament that he was rude, Stalin said publicly, "Yes, I am rude." Rudeness, impoliteness, rough language, no neckties for men, and a man's cap for women constituted, during long Soviet years, the rope by which the intellectual let himself down to the level of the workers and peasants. Stalin did not need to descend. That was an element in his political strength.

By their conduct, dress, and education, the intelligentsia became associated, in the eyes of the proletariat, with the hostile bourgeoisie. And many intellectuals were hostile to the Bolshevik revolution. Often, they maintained an attitude of scoffing neutrality while the Bolsheviks fought for survival.

When the Russian intellectual looked around him in the early years of the revolution, he saw that he had lost his old world and could not fit into the new. He abhorred the methods, manners, and dogmas of the Bolsheviks and frequently hated himself for being forced by material necessity to become their mercenary. The Kremlin rubbed salt into his wounds. The engineer on an important building project was not trusted and found himself working under an inexperienced Communist watchdog. Lawyers were scorned as "capitalist vermin." A new graduate who professed Marxism displaced a veteran, prerevolutionary scholar at the university. Grammar school teachers were persecuted by rowdy, spying pupils.

The Bolsheviks could have won the sympathies of the intelligentsia if they had tried. But the Bolsheviks did the very reverse, and when Stalin's struggle against the oppositions reached its zenith, intellectuals were subjected to persistent persecution. In the Shakti trial in June, 1928, and the trial of Professor Ramzin and his seven co-defendants in December, 1930, prominent Soviet engineers, inventors, and industrial specialists were accused of plotting with foreign spies to overthrow the government. This induced a pogrom atmosphere. Thousands of engineers were imprisoned. Their chief crime was that they were engineers; the word "engineer" was synonymous with counterrevolutionary. The man hunt on technicians became so ferocious that finally Sergo Ordjonekidze, Stalin's friend and chairman of the Supreme Economic Council, went to Stalin and reported that it would be impossible for him to continue his work unless the seizure of engineers stopped. The terror struck down not only old engineers inherited from the Czarist period but young Soviet graduates as well. Nineteen thirty was the intelligentsia's blackest year since 1917.

Suddenly, the sun began to shine again for the intellectuals and technicians; Stalin made a speech. Delivered on June 23, 1931, it acquired the unofficial title of the Magna Charta of the intelligentsia. "The problem is not to discourage these comrades," Stalin said sweetly. Washing his hands, as usual, of past sins, he declared that "specialist-baiting has always been considered and continues to be a harmful and shameful manifestation." The regime, he ordered, must court the intelligentsia and cater to their welfare.

Stalin's words were translated into law. A government decree of August 1, 1931, granted engineers and technical personnel equal status with factory workingmen in obtaining rationed food and clothing, apartments, and accommodations in rest homes and sanatoria. Their income taxes would be reduced. For study at home they could claim an extra room from the house committee which allocated living space. Children of the technical intelligentsia would be accepted in schools on equal terms with those of factory workingmen. These were tangible, valuable boons.

Stalin can be regally lavish in entertaining visitors or making gifts to favored persons. He will shower anybody he needs with privileges and benefits. At such times he likes to appear in the role of miracle-worker, changing black to white. Stalin now became the angel of the specialists. Non-Communist technical men were promoted to the highest positions of trust in their fields. Scores of engineers were awarded the Order of Lenin and other decorations. Special clubs, libraries, and well-stocked restaurants were opened for technical personnel. Government offices were instructed to pay heed to any complaint or request from an engineer. Many engineers were released from exile and jail. Salaries of specialists were raised steeply. The GPU was purged of those who had, on orders from the Kremlin, hounded the technicians. Now the secret police required a specific warrant, signed by a high official in one of the industrial departments of the government, before it could arrest engineers. They were Stalin's darlings. Having purged them and cowed them, and brought them as low as possible, he took them to his bosom and expected gratitude. He got it, for they were immensely relieved by their new prosperity and their opportunity to participate in the exciting process of nation-wide reconstruction.

Stalin had turned his attention to the problem of management. All over Russia gigantic industrial enterprises and whole cities were rising. In fulfillment of the first Five Year Plan, hydroelectric power dams, tractor factories, metallurgical plants, railway spurs, etc. mushroomed everywhere. The Soviet Union was like a beehive, an ant-hill. Everybody worked. A sense of elation swept the country which contrasted sharply with the depression in many foreign nations. The Kremlin boasted of unprecedented economic progress. "Bolshevism is overtaking capitalism," Moscow proclaimed. Hope was renewed. The people, at last, saw the prospect of dividends in the shape of better living.

But looking closely, Stalin saw the deficiencies. The tractor factory at Stalingrad, one of the new Soviet industrial giants, was opened in July, 1930. Moscow was jubilant: 25,000 tractors a year. Actually, the opening was premature. Many of the machine tools had not yet arrived from abroad. Management was miserably inadequate. The workers had little experience. Raw materials and parts were not available. The result: instead of 2,000 or more tractors a month, the Stalingrad tractor plant produced exactly nothing for ten weeks, and then began creeping forward at the snail's pace of two or three tractors a week. This was not unnatural in a new factory in a country undergoing industrialization. But a year later, in June, 1931, the Stalingrad works was still operating disappointingly. In the first twenty days of that month it turned out 1,249 tractors. The daily yield was 42 on June 19, 62 on June 20, 75 on June 21, 65 on June 22, and 71 on June 23. This was below plan; production zigzagged irregularly.

The Moscow *Pravda* of June 25, 1931, published an editorial entitled "We Must Work Differently and Manage Differently." It flayed Communist factory directors for bureaucracy and "paper leadership." "Excessively large industrial units," it urged, "must be broken up into smaller fractions." Even more striking, the editorial demanded that "collective management must give way to individual management." No more management by committee. *Pravda*, which speaks from the highest battlement of the Kremlin, told party factory bosses to cater to experts and engineers.

"In the reconstruction period, technology decides everything," Stalin told an industrial conference on February 4, 1931. Not politics, as hitherto, but technology. This became a slogan hung on tens of thousands of walls. It was the party's funeral crepe.

Many Communist directors of factory and presidents of industrial trusts were caught in the dragnet of the purges. Frequently, inefficiency at work supplemented the usual charge of sympathy for Trotsky or Kamenev or Bukharin. Their places were filled by non-Communist specialists and engineers who could be trusted to do a better technical job and who, having never been in politics, were free of suspicion.

In the 1920's, the Communist was trusted and the engineer was suspect. In the 1930's, the Communist was suspect and the engineer was trusted.

The substitution of non-Communists for Communists proceeded slowly but steadily. Years passed. The great purge of 1936 to 1938 was in the offing, but perhaps already in Stalin's mind. In May, 1935, at a banquet for Red Army officers, Stalin made a most momentous statement. Toasting those present, he said, "To the health of all Bolsheviks, members of the party, and those outside the party. Yes, those outside the party. Those who belong to the party are only a minority. Those outside the party are the majority. But among those outside the party are there not real Bolsheviks?"

Theretofore "Bolshevik" meant a card-holding member of the Communist party of the Soviet Union. But by this pronouncement Stalin said that nonmembers could be Bolsheviks too and just as good, just as loyal, just as responsible, as party members. He effaced the difference between Bolsheviks and non-Bolsheviks, and placed an equal sign between them. Indeed, in practice the Bolshevik member often had a minus sign in front of his name because of his political past, whereas the nonparty Bolshevik had a plus sign because he had no political past.

The Bolshevik minority had ruled Russia. Now Stalin stressed the importance of the majority which stood outside the party. Turning away from the party, which had pretensions to power, he made an obeisance to the people, the majority. The party had lost its paramountcy.

Two days after he drank that famous toast to the Army officers, Stalin addressed the graduating class of the Red Army Academy. In February, 1931, he had stated that "technology decides everything." Now, four years later, he made a discovery. "Technology without human beings who have mastered technology is dead," he announced. He had discovered the human being! "We must finally understand," he pontificated, "that of all precious capital in the world, the most precious capital, the most decisive capital is human beings, cadres. We must understand that, in our present condition, cadres decide everything. If we have good and plentiful cadres in industry, in agriculture, in transport, in the Army, our country will be invincible. If we have no such cadres we will limp with both legs."

Cadres are not rank-and-file men and women, they are trained staff, officers of the Army, managers in industry, the chosen upper class, the elite. These now decided everything in Soviet Russia. Stalin was their benefactor. He had given them this status. Some were Communists. Most were non-Communists. But communism mattered less than efficiency. The nonpolitical machine age had arrived.

The party, of course, remains. But when people now refer to acts of the party they mean the work of the secret police or of other government departments. The party has no power to do or to criticize. Robbed of its political function, the party is today the priesthood of a church that has forgotten its religion and adopted the cult of lama worship. The High Lama is Joseph V. Stalin. The Bolshevik Brahmins make known the will of the Kremlin god and do his bidding in every town and hamlet. They glorify his name, bow to his idol, sing his praises in the temples, and recite the ancient Marxist scripts which are now an occult abracadabra even for the priests, let alone for the people. Party members are the ministers of the state religion which has many names that recall the dead past: socialism, communism, Marxism, Leninism. But these isms are only for export to innocents abroad, for missions to the heathen in darkest capitalist nations. The Soviet reality is Stalinist feudalism, a church without soul or faith, a fossilized, institutionalized religion. For good form, many managers have joined the church, the new nonpolitical managers have invaded the shell that remains of the former political ruling class, the party.

In Stalin's theocratic state there are no orators. Of what use would they be? There are no political heroes. There is only one. There are no thinkers. They might think something wrong. There are no political scientists, there are only hacks intent on proving Stalin right. There are no historians, there are only falsifiers of history. There are no educators, only school administrators. The heroes of Russia are aviators, high-output workingmen, engineers, technicians. The Soviet system is a theocracy in form and a technocracy in content.

Stalin's acts show that he holds a low opinion of the human animal. His appeal is to base motives. He treats the government cadres or bureaucrats, the industrial cadres or technocrats, and the armed services officers' class as mercenaries who work for rich material benefits. They are his Praetorian Guard. They save him from men devoted to a cause and inspired by ideals.

Stalin's additional compensation to the mercenaries is status. The new upper class is endlessly stratified into numerous castes. Instead of equal comrades in a party or equal citizens in a country, Stalin has established strict hierarchical gradations with barriers, titles, and differentiated pay and privileges. Factories have two, sometimes three or four restaurants; the worst is for workers, the best in food, spaciousness, service, and privacy is for the director and his immediate subordinates. In the remote Soviet past, officers and soldiers in the Red Army wore uniforms of the same material and were equal except in their duties. Today, the officers are decked in epaulets, braids, fine clothing, and all the accouterments of a caste army, occupy the best apartments, and impose strictest discipline on shabby privates who no longer may mingle with officers. Officers have clubs, messes, and entertainment barracks to which soldiers have no access. Until 1934, Red Army and Navy officers were designated by their tasks: Commander of Battalion, Commander of Brigade, and so forth. "Colonel" and "General" were synonymous with counterrevolution. But when Stalin introduced the counterrevolution its titles returned.

Everyone knows his or her rung on the long Soviet social ladder. Promotions and demotions are numerous, but caste molds are beginning to harden. This is especially true since the introduction of paid tuition in colleges, in violation of the Stalin Constitution of 1936. Higher education is now available to the children of the upper class and to some scholarship winners, but the offspring of workers and peasants are usually routed into technical schools which train them to be foremen, locomotive drivers, and skilled mechanics.

The restriction of higher education to those who can afford it tends in a poor country like Russia to make the castes hereditary. Nepotism has the same effect. The son of an Army officer will be favored in becoming an Army officer, and high officials of the secret police are likely to introduce their offspring into the same service. Children of top-rank managers are advanced more quickly than others; this is an obeisance to their fathers.

The managers are rewarded with money and status and some security from arrest. It is the price Stalin is ready to pay for their services and loyalty. Since theirs is the best of all possible worlds in the Soviet Union they are probably reconciled.

The Soviet caste system, like all caste systems, provides for a sharply specialized division of labor. The factory director does not soil his hands and the workingman does not direct. The manager manages but abstains from politics. The political caste is a small club consisting of Stalin and the few he admits into it because he is, alas, only human and needs assistants.

Actually, that club is too big for Stalin. In Russia, he is a caste to himself. At the Yalta Conference in 1945, Stalin said that the Big Three (Roosevelt, Churchill, and he) were "an extremely exclusive club"; to join, he declared, one had to have five million soldiers. He wished to keep France out; she could not pay the initiation fee. That is the ultimate in caste exclusiveness—necessarily accompanied by the practice of untouchability.

CHAPTER XVI

The Strange Decade

The decade from 1930 to 1940 impressed the world as the most puzzling in Soviet history and gave Stalin the reputation of being an enigma and a riddle. At times it seemed that his left hand did not know what his right hand was doing or, at least, that one had lost its habitual cunning.

The strangest aspect of the period was the apparent contradiction between two sets of acts (1) the harsh purges and prefabricated Moscow trials of 1936, 1937, and 1938 which constituted a massacre, unprecedented in world annals, of brains and talent; (2) a number of measures, of which the 1936 Stalin Constitution was the best known, tending toward a moderation of the dictatorship and suggesting a Stalin flirtation with the people.

Yet in the perspective of time it is clear that the apparent conflict was actually the design. Stalin's left and right hands were consciously engaged in two separate and opposite operations. The purges liquidated the party as a ruling class, while the Constitution and companion innovations were a sop to the surrogate ruling class of technocrats and bureaucrats and to the collectivized but still obstreperous peasantry. Far from clashing, the two sets of acts were complementary. The first made the second necessary.

The task of administering a gigantic country by compulsion is a formidable one. Exceedingly rapid industrial expansion increased Stalin's difficulty and created a necessity for new incentives.

The first Five Year Plan was launched in October, 1928, on resources accumulated in the seven years of the New Economic Policy. Part of these resources came from taxing private-capitalist Nepmen and private-capitalist peasants who had been enriching themselves. The other part was earned by the Soviet state in its own industrial establishments and from the sale of vodka. In a letter dated March

20, 1927, but first published in 1948, Stalin defended the government monopoly of the manufacture and sale of vodka, and, admitting that the potent drink was an evil, told how Lenin, who had originally opposed the monopoly, agreed to it after foreign countries had refused Russia a loan in 1922. Without the official vodka monopoly, Stalin explained, the Soviets would have lacked the money for the development of the nation's economy. "If, for the sake of the victory of the proletariat and peasantry," he wrote, "we must soil ourselves with a little filth we are ready even for this extreme measure in the interest of our cause."

By 1931, however, the reserves accumulated before 1928 were exhausted and the capitalist sources had been choked off. Returning to Russia after an absence abroad, I said in the Baltimore *Sun* of July 13, 1932, "My first impression on reaching Moscow is that supplies of food and clothing are more meager than they were six months ago. The second impression is the inordinate amount of construction." The nation could no longer pay for that construction out of savings. It had to pay by tightening its belt and wearing old, patched trousers.

Soviet Russia's standard of living, higher in 1928 than ever before or since, shot sharply downward, and in the winter of 1932-33 came the famine which took several million lives.

The famine was the grisly result of a tug-of-war between Stalin's obstinacy and peasant recalcitrance. In order to feed the cities, Stalin insisted on larger state grain collections than the peasants would tolerate, so they declined to harvest. In the Ukraine just before the famine I saw crops standing and rotting in the fields. "Grain procurements in East Kazakstan," read a report to the Moscow *Pravda*, "are proceeding in an atmosphere of bitter class war." Translated into plain language, this meant that the Army and secret police were seizing grain against peasant objection. "There is grain in the North Caucasus," said another dispatch, "but it is hidden from the government in pits." *Pravda* called this "sabotage." It was. It was the peasant's instinctive urge to keep the bread for which he had labored long and hard. It was also an intuitive-ideological battle, the last, waged by the farmer against feudalism. The Kuban, a grain-rich territory near the Black Sea, actually rose in revolt. This was revealed during one of the subsequent Moscow trials.

Stalin countered the countryside's resistance in characteristic fashion. First, he took measures which even for him were unusually draconic. Millions of peasants were transplanted to distant regions. Whole villages in the Ukraine, the North Caucasus, and other areas were depopulated. This ruthlessness clarified the alternative: enter the collective farms or go to Siberia.

A weaker arm might have broken under the strain of driving over a hundred million peasants into a system of cultivation and a new form of society which was repugnant to them. Stalin held the wheel firmly. It was the supreme test of his political career, as crucial as the Second World War. He won because he did not shrink from the cruel cost in human suffering.

On the evening of November 6, 1932, the annual meeting celebrating the 1917 revolution was held in the Moscow Opera House. Stalin had not said a word in public since June 23, 1931. The country was in crisis, yet the only person who could give a lead or offer a hope had remained silent for almost a year and a half. That is Stalin's technique. When conditions are bad he prefers to be forgotten; he does not want the population to think of its woes and of him at the same time. Stalin attended the Opera House meeting. He was expected to speak. He did not speak. War Commissar Klementi Voroshilov received more applause on that occasion than Stalin.

In this context, seventy-two hours later, after a political argument with her husband, Stalin's wife committed suicide. The nation was in a black mood.

It must now have occurred to Stalin that despite progress in industrial construction, the material results of the revolution were disappointingly small. Meat would be in short supply for many years. Bread would be a problem for many years. Consumers' goods would be scarce for many years. To the average Soviet man and woman Bolshevism was an economic failure. A popular anecdote which circulated widely in Russia indicates general sentiment: two workingmen, in their own airplanes, met in the air. "Whither?" asked one. "I'm off to Kiev to buy a pound of butter," came the reply. "Where are you going?" asked the second. "I'm en route to Odessa to look for a pair of socks," said the first. Machinery, airplanes, but not enough food or clothing.

The country was too poor to provide everybody with a satisfactory living standard. Since Stalin could not give adequate good to the greatest number he would give the greatest good to an adequate number, to those who manned the key posts, the technocrats and bureaucrats of the new Soviet ruling class, the "cadres." Their contentment lends stability to Stalin's despotism.

Stalin's worst headache, however, was the peasants. He realized that if he did not mollify the villages there would be more sabotage and another famine. In January, 1933, accordingly, Stalin abolished the grain procurements whereby the government collector, often backed by police, invaded peasant barns and took as much as he wanted; or the collector came once and carted off a share of the crop, and appeared several weeks later for a second helping. Instead of procurement, Stalin introduced the grain tax, which the peasant had wanted in the first place. But by 1934, most Soviet peasants had been pushed into collectives where the unhappiness and inefficiency were great. In 1935, consequently, peasants in collectives were granted the right to cultivate an acre or less around their cottages as a private farm and to sell its produce privately. This was a temporary capitalist concession to sweeten the bitter pill of the new Soviet feudalism.

Stalin relented because the tension was so high. But the peasants continued to dislike the collectives into which they had been dragooned, and their taxes, either direct or in form of high prices for scarce goods, remained excessive. Somebody had to pay in reduced consumption and harder work for industrialization and government blunders. The workers paid and the peasants paid. Only the new ruling class lived well; new shops, with lavish displays and heavily laden shelves, were opened for them. On the other hand, the grocery stores patronized by the ordinary mass citizen displayed tantalizingly realistic and mouth-watering imitations in wood of hams and sausage.

In the circumstances, Stalin had to devise substitute incentives. They could not be material incentives because he had no materials to give. They had to be nonsubstantive or largely nonsubstantive.

One of these was the new 1936 Constitution.

In the early 1930's, a group of leaders, including Bukharin, Kirov, Radek, Gorki, and Arnold Soltz, a member of the pivotal Central Control Committee, had been preaching "proletarian humanism." "We are not accustomed to value the human being sufficiently," Soltz complained in the Moscow *Izvestia* in 1932. For an interlude, and intermittently, this group had Stalin's ear. Trotsky, watching from afar with the keen eye of a fallen hero, noted the banquets where Stalin was photographed with workingmen and women around him and a laughing child in his lap, and commented, "His sick ego had to have this balm." "It is clear," Trotsky observed, "that something frightful is being hatched." And he expressed apprehension over Stalin's "access of kindness and decency."

Something frightful *was* being hatched for the Communist party, but the "access of kindness and decency," whether simulated or sincere, and perhaps it was both, did not represent Stalin's attempt to camouflage the frightfulness. When the frightfulness came it was deliberately unadorned and stark. The banquets—Stalin's Georgian soul loves them—gave him the illusion of being generous. The photographs were for history and publicity. The entire performance was a facet of the coquetry with the masses, fanfare for the unveiling of the Constitution.

Bukharin, active though out of power, and Karl Radek, unkempt, ugly, witty, Puck-like publicist and the sauciest cynic in Stalindom, wrote most of the Constitution under The Leader's "wise guidance."

The "Stalin Constitution" contains an inspiring bill of rights—with no provision for implementation. It prescribes a system of government which had no reality, for Stalin's power remained uncurbed. It grants a monopoly of political action to the Communist party which Stalin had crippled and was about to kill.

The Constitution makes the vote of a peasant equal to that of a workingman; a paper crumb thrown to the villages. Previously a worker's ballot had the value of five peasant votes. But all votes, workers' and peasants', were for elections to the soviets, and the soviets had long since lost their political function.

Prior to the publication of the Constitution, Stalin spoke to Roy Howard, president of the Scripps-Howard papers of America, about "lists of candidates" and a "very keen electoral struggle" between them. But in the elections of December 12, 1937, the first under the new Constitution, there was one list and no struggle. Ninety-four million electors were entitled to vote. Of these, 96.8 per cent actually voted. The single list won 98.6 per cent of the votes. Such near-unanimity is democratically abnormal; in fact, it is humanly impossible without forgery or force. Stalin called it "a remarkable victory." It was remarkable.

A 98.6 per cent vote means that the government used compulsion; or, if it did not, it means that with so much public support there is no need of a dictatorship.

The Constitution legalized direct inheritance; this had considerable value for the new Soviet bourgeoisie which owned government bonds, homes, and other forms of personal wealth. It also enfranchised priests, for the first time since 1917. This concession to the peasants and religious townfolk inaugurated a series of changes which years later led to the establishment of the Greek Orthodox Church as an arm of the state, with the NKVD appointing the clergy and printing the synod's literature. Stalin, who had urged "a cautious relationship even to the superstitions of the peasant" was never passionately antireligious. He subordinates ideology to expediency. His first concern is to ease the task of governing.

However minor the concrete benefits of the Constitution, Stalin's desire to exalt the document into a charter of freedom was a tangible gain. Every weapon and trick of propaganda came into play to stress the Constitution's epochal importance. It was hailed as a radical departure from the past. Much of this was deceit. Yet it showed that the Kremlin knew what the people wanted. Russia truly rejoiced over the Constitution. The joy created an illusion of the Constitution's reality. People began to talk more freely, and that, together with the economic improvement in 1935 and the first half of 1936, produced an atmosphere of hope and relaxation.

Personnel changes in the GPU encouraged the belief that more democracy was around the corner. Next to Stalin's office, the secret police is the most important department of the Soviet system. In its first incarnation, as the Cheka or Extraordinary Commission, the secret police pursued, persecuted, and punished the enemies of Bolshevism during the early period of civil war and foreign intervention. When peace came, the Cheka became the GPU or State Political Directorate. It still hunted armed and unarmed persons suspected of being active against the Bolshevik government; but its chief victims in the 1920's were the new capitalist elements and the intellectuals and specialists. Beginning 1924, Stalin also used it to spy on, intrigue against, and arrest party oppositionists.

Stalin's June 23, 1931, "Magna Charta" speech to the engineers and the professionals inaugurated a new phase. Only remnants of the Nepmen and kulaks remained in city and village. The GPU's former intellectual quarry would now become the new ruling class, the pampered "cadres." Stalin, furthermore, was planning vengeance on the troublesome old ruling class, the party. This necessitated a new broom; the GPU had to be reorganized.

Due to the prolonged illness of Vyacheslav Menzhinsky, the head of the GPU, its actual chief for many years had been a short, lean former pharmacist with a Hitler mustache named Henrik Yagoda, who officially was Menzhinsky's first assistant. Yagoda knew too many secrets, and Stalin does not like people who know too much. Yagoda knew all about Stalin's maneuvers against the Trotskyists and "Rightists." He had carried out some of Stalin's shadiest acts. This gave him power. A man with power in such a powerful organization as the GPU is an inconvenience to a dictator. Stalin decided to get rid of Yagoda.

It proved difficult. In 1931, Stalin demoted Yagoda to second assistant of the GPU chief and placed Ivan Akulov over him as first assistant. Akulov was a milder person who believed in "revolutionary legality" rather than wholesale, unwarranted arrests.

Yagoda, however, refused to co-operate. He sulked in his suburban Moscow villa. This continued for four months until Stalin reinstated Yagoda as first assistant and sent Akulov down to the relatively unimportant post of Communist party secretary in the Donetz coal basin. The Soviet press published these changes.

Stalin had been defeated. The GPU was apparently strong enough to defy The Leader. In 1931, conditions in the country were unsettled, the collectives were new and full of boiling resentment, and Stalin did not dare purge Yagoda.

Patient as usual when he lacks sufficient strength, Stalin waited two years. On June 20, 1933, he brought Akulov back from the Donetz coal basin and created a special post for him as Federal Prosecutor or Attorney General. The decree which did so stated that he would exercise "supervision . . . over the legality and propriety of the acts of the GPU." Akulov could stay any sentence passed secretly by the GPU. He would have access to GPU secret files. He could reinvestigate any closed case.

Stalin wanted Akulov to curb Yagoda.

Akulov's headquarters in Moscow was beleaguered night and day by relatives of imprisoned citizens. Thousands of exiles returned from Siberia. Akulov commuted a number of death sentences. The population responded favorably and the campaign of Stalin glorification was intensified.

In January, 1934, several of the judicial functions which the GPU exercised secretly were transferred to open, civil courts and the GPU was renamed the Commissariat of Internal Affairs (NKVD). This was the third incarnation of the secret police. Though shorn, it continued mighty and terrible.

But the new Commissariat had no commissar. Normally, a new commissar would have been named at the time of the creation of the commissariat. But for six months no commissar was named, and Yagoda remained in control. A fierce struggle raged behind the scenes to oust him, but Stalin, though dictator to the country and master of the party, still had to reckon with the will of Yagoda. In July, 1934, Yagoda was named Commissar of Internal Affairs. Yagoda had won again.

Kirov's assassination, ascribed to the NKVD's negligence, weakened its prestige. The sudden flaring of the terror after the murder of Kirov did not stop the trend toward more freedom for specialists and bureaucrats. Communists were tried more often, but the average citizen enjoyed greater peace. Economic conditions improved—and 1935 saw the drafting of the Constitution. Children were taught to chant, "Thanks, Comrade Stalin, for a happy childhood."

Stalin pulled a velvet glove over his right hand. Communists were told to be nice to their parents, their divorced wives, and their children. Citizens were instructed to offer their seats to older people in streetcars. The necktie was enfranchised. Beauty parlors multiplied, and lipstick, perfume, permanents, and paint became fashionable. Officials were reprimanded for omitting the daily shave. Army officers were required to learn ballroom dancing. At the end of 1935, the ban on the Christmas tree was lifted.

All these things had been scorned as "bourgeois," "middle class," "decadent." Now the Kremlin boasted of them as unique Socialist achievements manifesting the regime's tender concern for the masses.

Stalin himself, however, did not rate too highly the value of the tawdry foibles and limited liberties he could give the country. He knew that only some powerful emotional upsurge would counteract the coldness toward the Soviet system resulting from widespread material hardships and peasant discontent. Stalin accordingly introduced a popular incentive destined to transform the character of the Soviet regime and seriously embarrass Russia's relations with the world. He introduced nationalism.

CHAPTER XVII

Stalin, the Russian

The strange 1930's became stranger still when Stalin, the Georgian, made Russian nationalism the major nonmaterial incentive designed to rally an unresponsive people around the Kremlin banner.

From the moment, in January, 1933, when Adolf Hitler came into office, Stalin watched him closely. Dictators learn from one another. The Italian embassy in Moscow had permanent instructions from Mussolini to send him any material which might throw light on Stalin's methods. Mussolini took a correspondence course with Stalin. And Stalin, a much more advanced student, took a university extension course with Hitler. I once asked Karl Radek, who directed the international-affairs branch in Stalin's headquarters, whether Stalin read only the newspaper accounts of Hitler's speeches. "No," Radek replied, "we translate the full text into Russian for Stalin and he reads them carefully."

Stalin observed, with envy possibly, the enthusiasm evoked by Hitler's hysterical, fanatical appeals to German nationalism and patriotism. At the Teheran Conference in 1943, according to an official United States record quoted in *Roosevelt and Hopkins,* by Robert E. Sherwood, Stalin said he "did not share the view of the President that Hitler was mentally unbalanced and emphasized that only a very able man could accomplish what Hitler had done in solidifying the German people. . . ." Stalin wanted to solidify the Soviet people. At different stages of his political career, Stalin enjoyed the support, at variable temperatures, of some of the people. But he never had the pleasure of being on the same emotional wave length with all the people. He recognized the enormous political advantage such identification would give him.

It would also bring him a personal satisfaction. Power tasted sweet to Stalin. But could he not have the icing of popularity as well?

Cake, after a time, lacks savor without that icing. Stalin did not like being merely "The Boss." Among themselves, and even in talking to outsiders, Soviet officials referred to Stalin, without ill will, as "Hozyayin," The Boss. But in the mid-thirties, Radek, who beat the biggest drum in the campaign of Stalinatry, said to me, "The name 'Hozyayin' is bad. He ought to be called 'Starik.' " Starik means Old Man, which connotes tenderness. "Boss" has a harsh ring.

The moment was sure to come in Stalin's life when he would want to be cast in the role of father of his people. Stalin was not satisfied with being advertised as The Leader; he wanted the people to accept him as The Leader. The effort to pile-drive Stalin into the hearts of the nation mounted steeply. But sometimes his cruelties severed the tenuous strands of sympathy between him and the country. On January 27, 1936, for instance, Stalin was photographed in the Kremlin embracing six-year-old Gelea Markizov, a beautiful Buryat-Mongolian girl with a sweet, round face, smiling cheery eyes, and a head of thick black hair which fell in bangs over her forehead. She had brought him a bouquet of flowers, and he had picked her up and smiled, and she put her arms around his neck. This photograph appeared in many newspapers and was reproduced on millions of posters—evidence of Stalin's love of children. Also in the photograph, smiling broadly, is the secretary of the Buryat-Mongolian Communist party, Comrade Erbanov. The Moscow *Pravda* of September 7 and 18, 1937, denounced Erbanov for un-Communist activities, and the *Pravda* of September 22, 1937, accused Erbanov and Markizov, the little girl's father, of "despicable deeds." Subsequently, Erbanov and Markizov were shot on Stalin's order. Of course, all the posters had to be pulled down. But the *Pravda* of September 23, 1937, printed a large, first-page photograph of Stalin with two boys in sailor suits—more evidence of his affection for children. The effort to make Stalin the father of all Soviet children continued. But it was subject to setbacks by the terror, and it could not make him the Father of the Nation.

To be the Father of the Nation there had to be a nation, and the revolution had not created a nation. Quite the contrary. The Soviet government waged war on certain classes. That divided the nation.

The revolution broke with the past and with tradition. That disrupted the continuity of the nation's life.

Stalin decided to end the class war. He told Roy Howard untruthfully on March 1, 1936, that "there are no classes" in Russia; "the dividing line between classes has been obliterated." Since the government would suspend the class war on the peasantry and managers, everybody could be united into one group, the nation. Stalin had chosen nationalism.

Stalin likewise decided to lean Bolshevism on Russian history. As a first step, figures from Russia's past, whom the early Bolsheviks had reviled and discarded, were lifted out of the dustbin of history and redecorated as Soviet idols. Among them was a thirteenth-century feudal prince named Alexander Nevsky who fought the Teutonic knights; Ivan the Terrible, Peter the Great, and Catherine the Great, the crowned parents of Russian imperialism; General Suvorov who led Russian armies against revolutions in Western Europe; and Prince Kutuzov who grappled with Napoleon on the plains of Russia. These now became the nationalist heroes of Soviet Russia. Russia had had other heroes; Pugachev and Stenka Riazin, for instance, who led unhappy insurgent peasants against the Czars. But Stalin had no more use for rebels, least of all for rebels who reminded the collectivized farmers of Russia's tradition of insurrection. The Kremlin drew a blanket of oblivion over Pugachev, Stenka Riazin, and other nonconformists, and, instead, clutched reactionary monks, Czars, princes, and generals to its undiscriminating bosom.

Stalin could either uphold the revolution and break with the nationalist past or break with the revolution and return to that past. He returned to the past and broke with the revolution. To prove it he destroyed the party of revolution, the Bolshevik party.

Cell by cell, and fiber by fiber, the tissues of the Soviet regime were changing. If Lenin were not visible in his glass case one might have said that he turned in his grave. But Lenin's words could be turned upside down to give sanction to anything Stalin did. Besides, Stalin's concern was not with Lenin but with his own position as The Great Red Father. The prerequisite was nationalism.

The campaign for nationalism, which began in 1934 as a faint squeak from the Kremlin, now became a deafening, incessant roar. With the intensity characteristic of communism, the Soviet propaganda machine shrieked and hammered on one theme: every Soviet citizen must be a nationalistic patriot. Communists had always considered patriotism the last refuge of capitalist scoundrels. Not nationalism but internationalism, or cosmopolitanism, was the Bolshevik credo. The Bolsheviks condemned nationalism as the source of militarism, imperialism, and wars. They contended that the worker had no fatherland. Consonant with the theory of class war and internationalism, a British worker and a French worker were brothers, and enemies alike of British and French capitalists. The Communist masthead motto was, "Workers of the World Unite" against the capitalists of all nations.

The shift from internationalism to nationalism was prepared by Stalin during his controversy with Trotsky in the 1920's. Trotsky maintained that communism could not succeed in Russia alone; the revolution must spread to other countries. "Socialism in one country," Stalin replied. Trotsky depended on the Communists of the West to save communism in Russia. Stalin took the opposite view: Russia could survive without world revolution. This position stemmed from his anti-Western, anti-European attitude. As early as August 19, 1917, Stalin wrote in a newspaper editorial, "Once upon a time it was said in Russia that the light of socialism came from the West. And that was correct. For there, in the West, we studied revolution and socialism." But things changed. In 1906, the West helped the Czar with a loan. "In that connection," Stalin continued, "it was noted that the West exported not only socialism to Russia but also reaction in the shape of billions." Since then, Stalin declared, there had been further retrogression; in 1917, "the West exported to Russia not so much socialism and liberation as slavery and counterrevolution."

Rejection of the West is not new in modern Russian history; it runs like a red thread through Russian culture. The influence of the East, reflected in and deepened by Russia's conversion to the Greek Orthodox church of Byzantium in 989, was further intensified by the Tartar conquests in Central Russia and the Ukraine and the consequent isolation of those areas from Western civilization for two centuries (the middle of the thirteenth to the middle of the fifteenth century) during which, to make relations worse, the West in the shape of the Poles and the Lithuanians was in constant conflict with Moscovy. The extension of Russia's domain toward Asia by Ivan the Terrible, who reigned from 1547 until his death in 1584, and by others strengthened the ties with the East.

Peter the Great, born June 9, 1672, died February 8, 1725, tried to open a window to the West. He borrowed British and Dutch construction techniques though he used serfs as builders. Russian intellectuals from the eighteenth century to the latest era of Stalinism cultivated intimate contacts with the West, and Russia's civilization as seen in her literature, painting, music, and science, is profoundly Western.

At the same time, her Eastern soul protested and sought independence from Europe. The Easterners or Slavophiles upheld the doctrine of Russian superiority over the West. The Russian attitude toward Europe has always been a mixture of humble obeisance and haughty disdain. As respectful pupil, Russia yearned to learn from the West; as arrogant mistress she denied her need of Western culture and envisaged its eclipse with equanimity or delight.

The Stalinists, like the Czarist Slavophiles, proclaim that they have the true faith destined to conquer the decadent West. Simultaneously, they are afraid that this may not be so. Until the conquest, therefore, they choose to isolate themselves lest Western civilization win too much influence over Russia.

To the young Stalin, the West was something unfamiliar and unpleasant, remote and mighty. It gave him Marxism to which he paid formal allegiance. But the European Marxists, he held, had betrayed the faith. And in any case they were of no help to his Soviet state.

Western hostility to the new Soviet government ripened Stalin's aversion to the West. Whenever necessity required it, he would of course cultivate relations with Western governments. He also kept the Third International or Comintern alive, but more, as he often indicated, for the help it could render Russia than out of an interest in Western revolution. The Western revolutionaries had let Russia down; there had been no revolution. Internationalism, accordingly, was not a great asset to Russia. Perhaps nationalism would be.

By 1934 and 1935, Stalin's preoccupation was not revolution but war. He sincerely feared an attack by Nazi Germany in league, perhaps, with militaristic Japan. He could not have been sure of the loyalty of the Soviet people. Nationalism was expected to stiffen their loyalty. The peasant, for instance, and the intellectual, might not fight for the perpetuation of Bolshevism, which many of them abhorred, but they might fight for their country. Stalin's aim, now, was to identify Bolshevism with Russia. Hence his acceptance of the heroes of the past.

Sometimes, Stalin achieved this identification by a clever statement of his goals. Thus, addressing the first Conference of Industrial Managers on February 4, 1931, and appealing to his audience of engineers to serve the nation, Stalin said, "Incidentally, the history of old Russia is one unbroken record of the beatings she suffered for falling behind, for her backwardness. She was beaten by the Mongol khans. She was beaten by the Turkish beys. She was beaten by the Swedish feudal lords. She was beaten by the Polish and Lithuanian gentry. She was beaten by the British and French capitalists. She was beaten by the Japanese barons. All beat her—because of her backwardness. . . . We are fifty or a hundred years behind the advanced countries. We must make good this discrepancy in ten years. Either we do it, or they crush us. . . ."

In later years it became unpatriotic to recall the military disasters of old Russia; the assumption was that Russia had always been great. But when Stalin spoke to the engineers in 1931 his own nationalistic propaganda had not yet enslaved him, and he could point out an impressive truth. Without Bolshevik construction, he was saying, Russia would succumb to foreign domination. In fact, President Kalinin said that without the Bolshevik revolution of 1917, Russia would have fallen prey to Western imperialism. This was a bid for the intellectual's reconciliation to the revolution for patriotic, Russian reasons.

But to be saved, Russia had to advance a century in a decade. In different words, Stalin said the same thing when he had told the American group which interviewed him on September 9, 1927, that communism was competing with capitalism; unless communism's power increased, Russia would succumb to foreign capitalism. Thus Stalin intertwined the nationalistic motive with the world-communism motive so that the two are indistinguishable. To try to disentangle them has no political value though it may delight the swordsmen who specialize in splitting thin ideological hairs. In Stalin's mind, internationalism has always been synonymous with nationalism. "An internationalist," he said in a speech on August 1, 1927, "is one who unconditionally, unwaveringly, without conditions is ready to defend the Soviet Union, for the Soviet Union is the base of the world revolutionary movement, and it is impossible to protect and to advance that revolutionary movement without protecting the Soviet Union." Stalin equated internationalism with national defense, and his position, as he explained it, was a justifiable one. A revolutionist was bound to defend the homeland of the first successful proletarian revolution as long as he regarded the Soviet Union as a revolutionary country.

But in 1934, Stalin went beyond national defense. He introduced a racist nationalism. He introduced Russian nationalism. He restored the nationalism of the Czars.

The Soviet Union is a multinational state. In 1939, according to official statistics, it had a population of 170 million of whom only 99 million, or 58 per cent, were Russians. The remaining 71 million were divided among over a hundred national minorities. Sixteen per cent of the total population were Ukrainians, 3 per cent were White-Russians inhabiting an area near the Polish frontier, and some nationalities, like the Georgians, Armenians, and Tadjiks, numbered about 2 per cent of the total.

Under the Czar, the Russians played the dominant role throughout the country, whereas the minorities were persecuted by the Russians and fought among themselves. The Bolshevik revolution, however, made all races equal; none was superior and none inferior. This may have irked the Russians, accustomed to their superior status, but it made for racial harmony.

Now Stalin was encouraging Russian nationalism and emphasizing the glories of Russia's past. That past had not been a happy one for the non-Russian national minorities whom the monarchy oppressed and Russified.

Of the national minorities, the Georgians were among the worst sufferers. They were oppressed and Russified and they rebelled and then underwent further oppression and Russification. Yet Stalin, the Georgian, never shared the anti-Russian sentiments of his people. He always felt pro-Russian. He remained insensitive to persecution and did not resent Russian domination. In fact he called himself "a Russian Bolshevik," although "Bolshevik" would have been enough, and in his report to the Sixteenth Party Congress on June 27, 1930, he proclaimed that the Russians were superior culturally to the Ukrainians and White-Russians and far superior to the Georgians, Armenians, Kirghizi, Turkomens, etc. Stalin is impressed by superiority. He prefers the big and the strong. He scolded Demyan Byedni, the poet, in a letter written December 12, 1930 (and first published in 1951), for criticizing the national characteristics of the Russians, and declared that "the revolutionary workers of all countries unanimously applaud the Soviet working class, and first of all, the *Russian* working class. . . ."

Napoleon, the Corsican, became the imperial Frenchman, and Hitler, the Austrian, became the imperial German. But their case is no parallel to Stalin's. A Corsican is related in blood and language to a Frenchman, and so is an Austrian to a German. The Georgian language, however, is as different from Russian as English is from Arabic, and the Georgians belong to a totally different race. Stalin simply saw the wisdom of cultivating one hundred million technically and culturally advanced Russians. Because he was a Georgian, whom they regarded as an interloper, his courtship of the Russians was all the more expedient. Without the loyalty and support of the Russians, who constituted the majority of the population, the Soviet Union could not win a war. Nor could it have a proficient, faithful ruling class of cadres. Nor could Stalin become the father of his country. He could not glorify Russia's past while denying Russians the same paramount role which they had played in that past. Personal vanity and ambition, combined with political opportunism, induced Stalin to adopt Russian nationalism as a prop for the Soviet regime.

In the strange 1930's, Stalin erected a new Soviet system. One of its pillars was the managerial class. Another was the Russians. Both implied inequality; the managers were made superior to other groups and the Russians were made superior to other nationalities. Stalin believes in inequality and seeks to derive every possible advantage from it.

In the 1930's, his power being adequate to his purpose, Stalin shifted gears and went into reverse. He looked to the past instead of the future. The revolution became counterrevolution. Soviet internationalism became racist nationalism. Soviet capitalism changed to Stalinist feudalism. The working class went to the bottom and the managers to the top. The Communists went to the death house and the concentration camps. Stalin went to the peak of the Soviet pyramid.

CHAPTER XVIII

Blood Flows and Heads Roll

The true, internationalist Communists, Stalin anticipated, would resent his betrayal of the revolution and their replacement by the new ruling class which had no ideals and no politics. They could not oppose him openly; Stalin had had enough opposition in the twenties and would allow no dissent now. But they might curse him in their hearts, and, being a fearful person, he may have thought that they would plot against him.

Stalin probably realized that nationalism and managerial unpolitics constituted a far-reaching counterrevolution and expected that the revulsion against it would be equally far-reaching. Whether he believed that revulsion would translate itself into revolt is a matter for conjecture. "Socialist realism" in literature is Stalin's invention. It requires a writer to describe as fact that which is still future. The brain which evolved this mental trickery might also trick itself into assuming that somebody who ought to plot was actually plotting.

It is equally possible that as a good organizer Stalin did not think a policy should be implemented by persons to whom it was repugnant. In the interests of "efficiency" he therefore decided to liquidate all who were revolutionary enough to dislike his counterrevolution.

Stalin now introduced what might be called "protective death." To save Soviet citizens from acts that were sure to get them into trouble Stalin would shoot them before they did anything. The bigger the massacre and the greater the number of prominent victims the more plausible the official explanations would sound. "Where there is so much smoke," people were likely to say, "there must be some fire." The fire was all in the death cellars of the NKVD. The lucky ones were content with a long sentence to Siberia.

The time had come for Stalin to sweep out the old-style leaders with fighting pasts who came to Bolshevism through an interest in people and freedom. These men and women were experienced enough to perceive how great was Stalin's departure from Marx and communism. A new generation of Gromykos, Maliks, Malenkovs, Yezhovs, Zhdanovs, etc., had been trained to hard-boiled insensitivity in the Stalin finishing school. He preferred them to the generation that knew him when he was a second-rank intriguer who played shadow to the Lenin mountain.

A new era had dawned which was building a bridge to Czarism. The Lenin period was the gulf to be bridged and the quicker its survivors disappeared the sooner Stalinist national-feudalism would be linked with Czarist obscurantism.

A pogrom on the men of the past would accord with Stalin's avowed strategy of never leaving nuclei of resistance behind him. This was all the more urgent in view of the international situation. With Hitler in power a world war seemed more likely. Suppose Russia was drawn in. Suppose Russia lost. Would Stalin, like Nicholas, lose his life? Would the potential oppositionists of today rise against him tomorrow?

The Great Purge of 1936 to 1938 was related to Hitler in another way. The Nazis came into office in January, 1933, and began immediately to perpetrate atrocities against Jews and others, including Communists. Decent people throughout the world protested. But Moscow did not protest. On the contrary, after complete neutralism for a year, during which many staunch, anti-Nazi Bolsheviks chafed and told me of their chagrin, Stalin made Hitler an offer of friendship. Reporting to the Seventeenth Bolshevik Party Congress on January 26, 1934, Stalin said, "Some German politicians say that the Soviet Union is now orienting itself on France and Poland, that it has changed from an opponent to a proponent of the Treaty of Versailles, that this change is explained by the establishment of the Fascist regime in Germany. That is not true. Of course, we are far from enthusiastic about the Fascist regime in Germany. But the point is not fascism, if only because fascism, in Italy for instance, did not interfere with the establishment of the best relations with that country. . . .We were not oriented on Germany and we are not now oriented on Poland and France. We were oriented in the past and are oriented now on the Soviet Union and only on the Soviet Union. And if the interests of the Soviet Union demand the establishment of closer relations with one country or another not interested in breaking the peace, we will do so without hesitation."

Hitler did not react favorably to Stalin's proposal. Nor did some Soviet Communists. But Stalin knew the inconstancy of governments in foreign affairs. An improvement of Soviet-Nazi relations might still be attained. On that day he wanted no heckling from idealistic anti-Fascists.

After Stalin's attempt to befriend Hitler had been rebuffed, the Soviet press joined the world protest against Nazi barbarism. What could be more natural in the circumstances, given Stalin's well-known technique, than to accuse his marked victims of plotting to do what he had failed to do: make an alliance with Hitler?

That is what happened.

In Stalin's 1936-1938 man hunt the prey that interested him most was the Communists at the head of the Army and the secret police, for these were the two organizations that might, because of their armed power, give him most trouble in an emergency. The military chiefs of the Red Army were all Communists from early manhood. Trotsky had appointed them during the civil war, and Stalin had retained and promoted them. They were popular with the country, especially with the youth.

The head of the Red Army was Marshal Michael N. Tukhachevsky, handsome, intellectually brilliant, and a military genius. In 1920, at the age of twenty-seven, he, already a General, commanded the Red Army which marched into Poland. That victorious advance gave him tremendous prestige in Europe and Russia; many looked on him as a new Napoleon.

Pilsudski's Polish Army had invaded Russia and taken Kiev on May 8, 1920. The Bolshevik forces struck back and drove the Poles from Soviet soil. The question now was, Should the Red Army follow them into Poland? Trotsky said No. Radek and Rykov agreed with him. They were afraid of arousing Polish nationalism. Lenin, Zinoviev, Kamenev, and Stalin said Yes. They hoped to arouse a

Polish revolution. The invasion was ordered. Tukhachevsky commanded the main Russian army of 150,000 men on the fields of Smolensk, where Napoleon once crushed the Czar's last bulwark on the road to Moscow. He struck early in July. Success was immediate. From July 4 to July 20 Tukhachevsky moved forward into Poland at the rate of thirteen miles a day. The Poles were completely demoralized and scattered in the direction of Warsaw. Pilsudski, describing Tukhachevsky's drive in a subsequent book entitled *1920*, called it "a terrible kaleidoscope." "The [Polish] government trembled," Pilsudski writes. Its Prime Minister rushed to London and Paris for help. If Russia conquered Poland, all Europe, then still prostrate after the First World War, would have lain open to the Red Army. The history of the world might have been changed.

With undiminished haste, Tukhachevsky approached Warsaw and stood before the gates of the city. The Kremlin sent three top Communists, Dzerzhinsky, Markhlevsky, and Kon, to form a new Polish government. They were operating in a wood twenty kilometers from Warsaw. On August 16, Tukhachevsky reached the Vistula.

A second Soviet army, mostly cavalry, under General Budenny and Voroshilov had invaded Poland further south. Stalin accompanied it as political commander. It had cut deep into Polish territory and was poised to capture Lemberg (Lvov) the capital of East Galicia.

Tukhachevsky had extended his line. The French had come to Pilsudski's aid with superior strategy. Tukhachevsky called for reinforcements. Moscow ordered Budenny to abandon his drive on Lemberg and march to Tukhachevsky's assistance. For three days Budenny did not answer Moscow's messages and then he shifted directions so haltingly that Pilsudski was able to fall on Tukhachevsky's flank, break his line, and force the Russian army to retreat. Soviet military experts, later analyzing the disaster, declared that had Budenny come up in time, the Polish counterattack would have been strategically unworkable. It is known that Tukhachevsky, Trotsky, and others laid the blame on Stalin who, Trotsky says, wanted the glory of capturing East Galicia. Pilsudski himself writes, "Our situation seemed to me utterly hopeless. I saw the only bright spot on the dark horizon in Budenny's failure to launch his attack on my rear."

Apart from the fact, then, that Marshal Tukhachevsky was the beloved leader of the Red Army in 1937, and therefore a potential peril to the dictator, Stalin bore a grudge against him and assumed, no doubt, that Tukhachevsky bore a grudge against him. On June 12, 1937, the Soviet press announced that Tukhachevsky had been shot for participating in a "military-Fascist organization" connected with a foreign power, presumably Germany. With him, seven other generals, all commanders of armies, were shot, and an eighth, General Gamarnik, committed suicide when the police came to arrest him.

The official bulletin revealing the executions said that Tukhachevsky and his comrades had confessed. But nobody knows whether they confessed. Nobody knows whether the secret military trial mentioned in the communiqué ever took place. Of the special court of eight high military men which allegedly sentenced the generals, three were subsequently shot for treason, and the others are silent. In all the years since the event, neither the Soviet government nor anyone has published any proof of the guilt of Tukhachevsky and his fellows. Former United States Ambassador Joseph E. Davies says in his book, *Mission to Moscow*, that Soviet "Ambassador Troyanovsky assures me it had to be done to protect ourselves against Germany—and that someday the outside world will know 'their side.'" The outside world is waiting. If Stalin had the evidence he would have divulged it long ago, for he knows the skepticism with which this and other accusations are received at home and abroad. Any hesitation owing to a desire not to offend Hitler, with whom Tukhachevsky allegedly conspired, should have ended in 1941 or at the latest in 1945 with the death of the Nazi and his government. Still Moscow maintains its guilty silence.

It is not in Stalin's nature to cut off a head and leave the body dangling. The entire leadership of the Red Army was purged when Tukhachevsky and his eight comrades were purged. Big new houses in Moscow, each containing hundreds of apartments reserved for high military officers, were emptied of their old residents by the purge and reoccupied by fresh appointees. The same substitution was noted in other cities. All the Red Army officers who served with so much devotion in Loyalist Spain were brought home and shot. It has been stated that thirty thousand officers died in the Tukhachevsky purge.

The purge of the powerful NKVD was equally drastic and murderous. Henrik Yagoda, the master of the secret police, had been entered into Stalin's little black murder book for failing to bow to the dictator. Yagoda and his staff and thousands of their subordinates were now purged.

Yagoda was succeeded by Nicholas Yezhov, a Stalin henchman in the party machine. Yezhov was five feet tall; the country had never heard of him. But his appointment on September 27, 1936, as chief of the NKVD, ushered in a period popularly known in Russia as the "Yezhovstchina" which was the biggest blood bath in Soviet history. It included the Tukhachevsky purge of June, 1937, the Moscow trial of Sokolnikov, Radek, and fifteen others in January, 1937, the trial of Yagoda, Rykov, Bukharin, Krestinsky, Rakovsky and others in March, 1938, and the death, without trial, of countless top-rank, second-rank, third-rank and fourth-rank officials. Of the twenty-seven (Stalin plus twenty-six) outstanding Bolsheviks who drafted the 1936 Constitution, fifteen had been shot by 1938. Eleven of Litvinov's ambassadors were shot, and a thirteenth, Feodor Raskolnikov, who made a brilliantly heroic record during the civil war, committed suicide in Nice. Universities saw their entire faculties vanish. Many hundreds of foreign Communists who had found asylum in Russia were executed. Thousands of journalists, novelists, poets, playwrights, theater managers, actors, sculptors, and painters were purged. Pages and pages could be filled with the mere surnames of nationally famous Communists who were killed during the Yezhovstchina. With each prominent party member went at least a score of his associates, friends, and relatives. Many cabinet members in the federal governments and in the smaller regional republics were purged; their staffs, often numbering thousands, were purged with them. "Eventually," write Beck and Godin who were arrested at this time, "there was practically no one in the Soviet Union who did not have at least one relative or close friend in prison."

"During the Yezhov period," Beck and Godin say in their book, *The Russian Purge*, "people used to say, 'He's not a party member and he's not a Jew, so why has he been arrested?' " Stalin was liquidating the Communist party to make way for the new managerial ruling class, and he was liquidating the Jews because racist nationalism always brings anti-Semitism in its wake.

In the middle of 1939, after less than three years as Stalin's long bloody arm, Nicholas Yezhov himself was purged. In the usual gentle, Stalin installment-plan manner (murder in two easy steps), Yezhov first received a minor appointment as Commissar of Water Transportation, and shortly thereafter he disappeared forever into the bottomless void to which he had consigned so many. His name is a curse in Russia. Mourning mothers, widows, children, fathers, brothers, sisters, and friends remember him as the little man who was the biggest butcher in Russian history.

The executions, the bulging prisons, the crowded concentration camps are a recurring, harrowing nightmare. More than flesh died, more than men and women were buried in the earth or in cells. An epoch of history was buried with them. A culture was crippled. The torrents of blood that flowed in the Yezhov purge swept the last remnants of ideals and illusions out of Soviet life.

Yezhov was succeeded by Lavrenti Beria, a Georgian. On assuming the post of secret-police director he restored some prison privileges, like books, which Yezhov had abolished, and released thousands of prisoners arrested by Yezhov. He did not resurrect the dead. The Soviet press reported that a number of NKVD officials were punished for extorting confessions by torture. Some of them were tried publicly.

The dismissal of Yezhov, and the penalizing of a handful of investigating magistrates who were obeying instructions, was Stalin's oft-used technique of attempting to deflect guilt from himself by directing all eyes and animosities toward a subordinate. It also created the impression that the tortures were "excesses" rather than the rule.

The Yezhov purge made the confessions a national and international enigma which has two aspects: (1) why did the Soviet government want confessions it knew to be false? (2) why did the prisoners confess?

The usual procedure in Soviet prisons is to confront a prisoner with a statement prepared by the investigating magistrate. It is a first-person confession which the prisoner is asked to sign. In it he admits being a traitor and counterrevolutionary, guilty under Paragraph so-and-so of Article so-and-so of the Criminal Code. Sometimes, the document lists the names of persons whom the prisoner recruited for a counterrevolutionary organization which plotted to overthrow the Soviet government and surrender Soviet territory to Germany or/and Japan. Prisoners have been known to sign such confessions when they had not even heard of the names of those whom they allegedly recruited and when they were themselves innocent. They signed because they had, in the large common cells occupied, sometimes, by dozens of prisoners, seen men and women come back from encounters with the investigating magistrates bleeding, limping, crippled, hysterical, with, at times, blackened eyes, smashed lips, broken ribs, broken spirits. Magistrates used their fists, or chair legs, or sharp rulers, or other objects for beatings. I talked to one former prisoner of Stalin, now in Germany, who had tobacco stuffed into his throat with a penholder and who got nicotine poisoning and heart injuries as a result.

On occasions the torture is more refined. Prisoners are kept awake, and standing under interrogation, for forty-eight and more hours by several investigators working in shifts. They are kept in cells floodlit with bright lights or prevented from sleeping for many days and nights and, when their will has been crushed, subjected to questioning and confronted with NKVD-made confessions. Prisoners with strong personalities hold out for a week or two or even more. Some never confess and the secret police despairs of extorting a confession. Most confess.

Persons who confess may be shot or banished to Siberia. But cases are known in which prisoners who admitted to the most serious political crimes were released a few months later. Thousands of

Soviet citizens who confessed and were released, later served in the Red Army, were captured by Hitler, and, when the war ended, preferred not to return home. I have talked at length with several score of Russian displaced persons in Germany who suffered varied tortures in Soviet jails. The whole matter of torture, not only in Russian prisons but in the prisons of Russia's satellites in Eastern Europe, is now too well-documented to be doubted.

However, some confessed without torture. The leading Bolsheviks, close co-workers of Stalin, who appeared as defendants in the famous Moscow trials were apparently not tortured. If they had been tortured they could have blurted out the fact on the witness stand or they would have shown signs of it. Their confessions are more puzzling. All in all, there were about fifty of them compared to hundreds of thousands punished without confessing or after confessing.

Trotsky, with all his inevitable bitterness and prejudice against Stalin, was nevertheless the man who knew the Soviet system from the inside better than any Russian exile abroad, and he also knew intimately most of the Soviet leaders who confessed at the trials. Writing in Mexico in 1940, Trotsky asserted that "for the promise of a pardon, Yagoda assumed at the trial personal guilt for crimes rumor had ascribed to Stalin. Of course, the promise was not kept: Yagoda was executed." In my book, *Men and Politics*, written before I could have read this Trotsky explanation, I came to the same conclusion: the defendants had been promised their lives in return for confessions. They were also promised that their families would not be harmed.

Why should these top Bolsheviks, who knew Stalin's character, have believed the promise? The answer is, first, that in Soviet history other prominent persons sentenced to death in public had been pardoned in secret and allowed to live out their lives in obscurity in Siberia; secondly, the difference between certain death the next minute and a one per cent chance of life is as big as the entire universe, and men reduced to complete cynicism and disillusionment by Stalin's counterrevolution would take that chance because hope persists as long as life. It is very difficult for a person who does not wish to commit suicide to actually sentence himself to death, especially since he would die heroically only for the record which would be distorted in his disfavor by Stalin.

The leaders who confessed made their confessions sufficiently fantastic and added enough subtle remarks at the trials to evoke doubt in the mind of the discriminating public and of the future historian. With the masses, however, Stalin used the confessions as "proof" that traitors and spies were responsible for all the shortcomings of his administration. The trials really rest on Stalin's fundamental disrespect for people and his belief that they will swallow any lie presented with adequate vehemence.

The x-ray-eyed secret Soviet police, with agents everywhere always, never discovered a single little item of evidence to produce at the trials in corroboration of the alleged far-flung conspiracies involving many hundreds of people. The sentences were based solely on confessions. Obviously, therefore, Stalin needed the confessions to make the trials, and he needed the trials to exhibit his scapegoats.

It is more difficult to explain why the Soviet government should have wanted to obtain confessions by torture from lesser citizens in prison who could have been sentenced to death or concentration camp without confessions.

There is a plausible explanation. At various times in the history of the Soviet Union, the Communist party was "cleansed." The cleansing took place at public meetings of the small party units called "cells" and consisted of breast-beatings, mutual accusations, and fervid avowals of loyalty. In each periodic cleansing, some members were expelled from the party. This was regarded as necessary to the health of the organization; it kept members "vigilant" was the saying. Each cell was given a quota of the number to be expelled, and if, after all the public hearings, enough members had not been found to fill the quota, the cell went back to work and, cleansing with greater vigor, expelled some more.

In the same way, city, town, and village branches of the NKVD were given quotas of citizens to be arrested as spies and counterrevolutionaries. They had to fill the quota or expose themselves to dismissal and punishment. Without the discovery and arrest of "enemies of the people" in each locality the confessions and trials in Moscow would have been less real, for the leaders arrested in the capital were accused of heading spy networks covering the entire country and since nobody had any proof of this statement and never produced any proof of it, confessions were necessary from little people in the provinces to confirm those of the big people in the Moscow jails.

Stalin was eliminating the political ruling class, the party, and it had members in every town and hamlet. Therefore the purge had to reach into each one of them. Therefore the arrests and confessions in each one of them. If people did not confess, the NKVD in Kharkov or Dagestan could not report to Kremlin headquarters that it had carried out or even zealously exceeded the quota assigned to it. The confessions were a protection for Soviet officials; they knew their bosses. They knew that Stalin might order them to push peasants into collective farms one day, and the next day accuse them of "dizziness with success," of collectivizing forcibly. For reinsurance against future policy shifts, every arrest and penalty should be backed by a confession; that makes it legal. Stalin, like Hitler, believes in "legality," that is, in underpinning every arbitrary act with a legal fiction. Dictators like to commit people and their subordinates by signatures, public utterances, and confessions.

Stalin worships bigness. In Soviet industry, quality is often sacrificed to a statistically large output, and the highest Soviet ambition, in inanimate things, is size. Bigger is better. The Kremlin went on the assumption that whereas a little purge might invite doubt a colossal purge would be convincing. "More, more" best expresses Soviet ideology and practice. In the purge of 1936 to 1938, the Soviet cannibals had as much as they could stomach.

CHAPTER XIX

Hitler and Stalin

In Stalin's lifetime, Czarist Russia had fought two major wars: the Russo-Japanese War of 1904-1905, and the First World War. Both produced revolutions. A second world war might do the same. The Great Purge removed the potential opposition to Stalin in a possible political crisis arising out of war. It also beheaded the Army, disorganized all government departments, and discouraged the people. In that condition, Russia could not go to war.

In any case, Stalin's temperament, which mingles passion with caution, would incline him to abstain from war until it is safe, and profitable, to participate. He made some interesting remarks on this point in a speech delivered January 19, 1925, and first published in 1947. Humanistic Bolsheviks had urged a reduction in the size of the Red Army and its conversion into a peacetime militia. Stalin opposed the move and advocated, instead, a larger military budget. "In a few years," he declared, war might come and Russia must prepare. He assumed, he said, that revolutions might occur in the West. "But it would be very difficult for them to survive," and Russia should therefore arm.

"This does not mean," Stalin warned, "that in these circumstances we must definitely attack anybody. That is not true. If anybody has any such slight notion—it is incorrect. Our banner remains the banner of peace." The Soviet government, Stalin was saying, would not march to the support of a foreign revolution. "But," he continued, "if war comes we will not be able to sit by with folded arms—we will have to enter. But we will enter after everybody else. And we will enter in order to throw the decisive weight into the scales, the weight that would tip the scales." The implication is that Stalin's choice of sides would depend on which way the battle was going.

No leader plans in 1925 what he will do in 1939. But the mind which says in 1925 that Russia will stay out of war as long as possible in order to strike in the last phase when both sides are nearing exhaustion is the kind of mind that would negotiate the Soviet-Nazi pact of August 23, 1939. That document was designed to keep Russia passive until Stalin chose the most advantageous moment for action. This suited his psychology and gave Russia a respite from the disruptive purge.

While Stalin purged and the West appeased, Hitler armed. Germany found the situation most agreeable. She took Austria and a part of Czechoslovakia.

But when the Nazi tiger swallowed the rump of Czechoslovakia the West, in painful panic, abandoned the attempt to tame carnivores with red meat. British Prime Minister Chamberlain, who wore striped trousers at the funeral of Czechoslovakia on March 15, 1939, donned a soldier's uniform on September 1, 1939, and declared war on Germany. The sudden change in Chamberlain's attitude came, under public pressure, in the latter half of March, 1939.

Stalin saw his opportunity. Hitler's rejection of Stalin's 1934 bid for better relations deprived Moscow of its bargaining position: it could only woo France and England who were less bellicose than Germany and therefore less dangerous to Russia. The purpose of Stalin's pro-Western policy between 1934 and 1939 (including his support of the Spanish Loyalists and the "Popular Front") was to wean England and France from appeasement, weld a strong anti-German alliance, possibly with America, and thus provide greater security for Russia.

He failed. It was the seizure of Czechoslovakia that killed appeasement in Britain. England and Germany now faced one another in anger. Thereupon Stalin quickly occupied his favorite position at the fulcrum of the seesaw, in the center between the antagonists, where he could sway this way and that until the time came for him to enter the war "after everybody else."

In this preferred posture, Stalin naturally invited advances from both sides. In a speech in Moscow on March 10, 1939, Stalin verbally invited both sides by inference to make competing proposals. During the summer of 1939, the Kremlin negotiated with France and England on the one hand and Germany on the other. The talks with the West were open, with Germany secret.

When Stalin dismissed Litvinov in May, 1939, he sent a confidential person-to-person telegram to the heads of Soviet embassies and legations abroad. He had never communicated with them directly. The telegram, the contents of which were disclosed to me years later by one of the recipients, attributed Litvinov's dismissal to his refusal to work harmoniously with Prime Minister Molotov. Stalin placed all his individual prestige behind this message, and there must have been a very special reason for it. He may have feared that Soviet diplomats who were loyal to Litvinov might desert. But more likely he wished them to believe and disseminate the explanation of Litvinov's departure for personal reasons lest somebody guess that the removal of the foreign minister foreshadowed a new foreign policy built around an understanding with Hitler. It was important to Stalin that the negotiations with Germany, which were about to begin, remain secret. If Stalin had wanted an agreement with the West he would have negotiated openly with Hitler. That would have put pressure on the West to give Russia a better bargain. Instead, Stalin negotiated openly with the West. That put pressure on Hitler to give Russia a better bargain.

A careful study of the Soviet-Nazi pact documents found in the German Foreign Office archives by the American and British troops advancing into Germany in 1945 and published by the State Department reveals that Stalin never intended to come to an agreement with the West. He preferred the pact with Hitler because it launched Soviet Russia on her career of imperialism.

The Soviet-Nazi pact of August 23, 1939, and the supplementary agreements of September, 1939, made Moscow a present of the eastern half of Poland and of Bessarabia and enabled Stalin to wedge into the Baltic countries.

The Baltic countries had been part of Czarist Russia. Lenin recognized their secession and independence in 1918. In reconquering them Stalin satisfied the Russian nationalism which he had nurtured since 1934.

The annexation of Eastern Poland was likewise designed to strengthen Russian nationalism by binding the Ukraine more closely to Russia. Eastern Poland included approximately seven million Ukrainians; Bessarabia and Moldavia, which Russia annexed in 1940, held additional Ukrainians. By bringing them into the Soviet Union Stalin hoped to win the good will of the forty-two million Soviet Ukrainians who had not always been happy under Moscovite rule. The Ukrainian Communist party was purged several times in the 1920's and 1930's for "bourgeois nationalism," that is, for resenting Russian domination. Now Stalin could say to the Soviet Ukrainians, in effect—and this was actually the burden of Kremlin propaganda: Moscow had brought all the Ukrainians of Europe under its flag, why, then, should you secede from Russia?

Nationalism must always be fed; its favorite dish is territory. Nationalism thus breeds imperialism. Russian nationalism's first feeding, as planned by Stalin, was to consist of two courses: Eastern Poland and the Baltics. He felt he had to have them. He asked the British and French for the same areas in the summer of 1939. The British and French did not have them to give, nor would it have been democratic to give them. Hitler had no such scruples. He let Stalin take them.

If Stalin had joined the West he would have won no food for Russian nationalism and he would have had to enter the war immediately. But Hitler gave him territory and time. That is what Stalin wanted.

The pact was regarded as a triumph of Stalin's hard-boiled diplomacy. In retrospect, however, the indications are that the Russian dictator did not understand the Second World War. In the beginning he thought it would start and end with the conquest of Poland. To judge by the public statements of Hitler, Goering, and of Soviet spokesmen, Russia and Germany expected at least a temporary peace after they had partitioned Poland. Indeed, Soviet diplomats worked for that peace. These hopes were father to the thought in Stalin's brain that when Poland fell, England and

France, reconciled to the accomplished fact and too weak for a trial of strength with Germany, would revert to appeasement. He did not know England. He judged others by himself.

When Hitler locked horns with France and England, Stalin increased his shipments of strategic materials to Germany. In 1938, for instance, Russia sold Germany 33,154 tons of oil: in 1940, 700,000 tons.

Stalin also stoked the fires of Communist propaganda against the West. "It was not Germany who attacked France and England," he wrote in the *Pravda* of November 30, 1940, "but France and England who attacked Germany, thus assuming responsibility for the present war." (Later, during the period of collaboration between the West and Russia, he naturally said just the opposite.) Taking their cue from Stalin, the British and American Communists, suddenly assuming the false face of pacifism, interfered with the defense effort, while the Communists of France stabbed her as she fell.

In these and all other ways Stalin tried, during the twenty-two months between the pact with Hitler and Hitler's invasion of Russia, to give Germany evidence of his good faith. Anti-Fascist and anti-German propaganda and education were discontinued inside Russia. Anti-Nazi films like Friedrich Wolf's *Professor Mamlock*, and Serge Eisenstein's anti-German *Alexander Nevsky* were no longer shown. As a gesture to please Hitler, Moscow recognized Rashid Ali, the pro-Nazi, anti-British rebel of Iraq. In April, 1941, after the Soviet government had signed a nonaggression treaty with Japan, Germany's ally, Stalin went to the railway station to see off the Japanese Foreign Minister, Matsuoka. Stalin had never done such a thing. Henry C. Cassidy, Associated Press correspondent who was present at the station, wrote that Stalin kissed Matsuoka good-by. Then Stalin wound his way among the specially invited foreign diplomats on the station platform, found Colonel Hans Krebs, the Assistant Nazi Military Attaché in Moscow, shook hands with him, and said, "We shall be friends."

These were messages to Hitler. Stalin was promising to behave. On May 6, 1941, Stalin removed Molotov and appointed himself

Prime Minister. That served as an indication, to anybody who had a doubt, that Stalin was in complete control and would personally take all steps necessary to carry out the policy of friendship with Germany.

From the day the pact was signed, Stalin lost no opportunity to reassure Hitler. On his sixtieth birthday, December 21, 1939, Stalin received congratulations from Hitler and Nazi Foreign Minister Ribbentrop. Replying to Ribbentrop, Stalin wired, "The friendship of the peoples of Germany and of the Soviet Union, cemented in blood, has every reason to be lasting and firm." (The blood was presumably Polish.) Stalin thus encouraged Hitler to strike at the West. The Soviet-Nazi pact, the *Pravda* wrote on August 23, 1940, "has guaranteed Germany undisturbed security in the East." In other words, Hitler need not fear hostile action by Russia; he could safely continue his war against Britain. Perhaps Hitler would finally destroy the British Empire and open the road to Russian expansion in Central Asia and the Near East.

Stalin believed that once Hitler had tangled with England he would not desist until he won. Litvinov is authority for this statement of Stalin's miscalculation. On December 13, 1941, shortly after he had arrived in Washington as the new Soviet Ambassador and six months after Hitler's attack on Russia, Litvinov, apologizing for Stalin's view—his own had been more intelligent—said to reporters, "My Government did receive warnings as to the treacherous intentions of Hitler with regard to the Soviet Union, but it did not take them seriously and this not because it believed in the sacredness of Hitler's signature, or did not believe him capable of violating the treaties he signed, and the oft-repeated solemn promises he made, but because it considered that it would have been madness on his part to undertake war in the East against such a powerful land as ours, before finishing off his war in the West."

Why should Stalin have thought Hitler incapable of madness? And was it madness? Hitler could not cross the English Channel. He lacked sea and air superiority. More and more American aid was coming to England in the form of supplies and in direct collaboration. If Hitler could not smash England he had to try to smash Russia or risk the possibility of a two-front war at some future date.

Litvinov had spoken of Russia as "a powerful land." But the Great Purge, especially the purge of the military, the fact that Stalin had signed the pact with Germany, and the poor performance of the Russian Army in the war against Finland in 1939-1940, created the impression that Russia was not powerful. This helped shape Hitler's decision to leave off attacking England and turn on the Soviets. If he could defeat Russia in a few months—"within eight weeks," Ribbentrop told Ciano—he would then assail England again with no peril in his rear and Russia's grain, oil, metals, machines, and manpower at his command.

The purge led to the pact and the pact led to the war on Finland and all three led to a low opinion of Russia's military strength. That led to Hitler's invasion of Russia. Stalin outsmarted himself. His diplomacy proved not quite so clever as he had expected. Instead of entering the war "after everybody else" and deciding the issue with a minimum of effort, Russia was deprived by Hitler of the power of decision and forced to wage a four-year war which in human beings lost and lands devastated was the most expensive she had ever fought. No enemy had ever taken such a heavy toll of Russian lives. No enemy had ever penetrated so far into Russian territory. For fifteen years, at tremendous cost to the people, Stalin had been preparing the country for war. Yet when war came it found the Soviet system too disorganized to pursue the best national strategy. Russia could not have fought well in 1939. At lunch in the White House on May 30, 1942, Soviet Foreign Minister Molotov gave President Roosevelt, Secretary of State Hull, General George C. Marshall, Admiral Ernest J. King, Harry L. Hopkins, James Forrestal, Senator Connally, and other guests a summary of the military situation in Russia. The Germans, he said, had been driving into the Kerch Peninsula in the Crimea. "This drive," he conceded, "had resulted unfavorably for the Russians. The Soviets had originally possessed superiority of forces in the Eastern Crimea, but had used this superiority ineffectively because of the inefficiency of the local commander, General Kozlov, who had proved weak and had not, as a matter of fact, taken part in previous operations against the invading forces. . . . As far as personalities went," Molotov explained, "the Soviets had found that inexperienced officers and men were the least effective. For example, Marshal Timoshenko was the more dependable because he had field experience since the beginning of the invasion, while Kozlov was an instance of the opposite state of affairs. . . ." Kozlov was a new general replacing one who had been purged, and he had to gain his experience at the expense of Soviet soldiers killed and wounded. But Marshal Tukhachevsky, and the eight top generals who died with him in the 1937 purge were all highly experienced army commanders of the 1918-1921 civil war, and at the 1942 stage of the war with Germany they would all have seen fighting against Hitler. Thousands of colonels, majors, captains, and lieutenants purged with them were likewise veterans of the civil war. Speaking frankly to Roosevelt and Churchill at Teheran in November, 1943, Stalin asserted that "in the winter war against Finland the Soviet Army had shown itself to be very poorly organized and had done very badly; that as a result of the Finnish war, the entire Soviet Army had been reorganized; but even so, when the Germans attacked in 1941, it could not be said that the Red Army was a first class fighting force."

Stalin had too much understanding of military affairs to risk committing a freshly purged army to a conflict with Germany in 1939.

Stalin might, however, have remained neutral, signing an agreement neither with the West nor with Hitler. Germany, as Litvinov stated in a Moscow broadcast on July 8, 1941, "intended first to deal with the Western states in order to be free afterward to fall upon the Soviet Union." Russia therefore would have been safe without a pact. It was not the pact that protected Soviet Russia from attack in 1939, but Hitler's decision to crush France and England first. In August, 1939, Hitler addressed his Commanders-in-Chief and said, "We must be determined from the beginning to fight the Western powers. . . . The conflict with Poland was bound to come sooner or later. I had already made this decision in the spring, but I thought I would first turn against the West and only afterward against the East." It was this orientation of Hitler's, not the pact, that saved Russia from attack in 1939. Stalin could have stayed out of the war and refrained from the understanding with Hitler. He would thereby have avoided the bloody war with Finland and the expensive occupation of the Baltic states and Eastern Poland. Within a week of his attack on Russia, Hitler had seized those territories together with hundreds of thousands of Soviet soldiers and vast military stores. Eastern Poland and the Baltics were no buffer. They were a drain. But Stalin wanted them because he had substituted Russian nationalism for revolutionary motivations.

It was thus the counterrevolutionary developments inside Russia, and especially Stalin's decision to liquidate the Bolshevik party as the ruling class (including the party leadership of the Army), that brought on his pact with the Fascist dictator.

For some unknown reason, moreover, perhaps because he thought Hitler a pure romantic, Stalin trusted him. In his long conversation with Harry L. Hopkins, President Roosevelt's special representative, on July 31, 1941, Stalin declared that "the Russian army had been confronted with a surprise attack." Stalin said he believed that "Hitler would not strike." So certain, indeed, was Stalin of Hitler's good intentions, that, as he told Mr. Hopkins, "Russia had one hundred and eighty divisions at the outbreak of the war, but many of these were well back of the line of combat, and could not be quickly mobilized, so that when the Germans struck it was impossible to offer adequate assistance." On the first day of the invasion, Russia lost one thousand planes, most of them on the ground.

Prime Minister Churchill, President Beneš of the Czechoslovak government-in-exile in London, and others had warned Stalin of an impending Nazi attack. Moreover, Assistant Soviet Foreign Commissar Solomon A. Lozovsky told foreign correspondents in Moscow on June 28, 1941, that between April 21 and June 21, the day before the invasion, Nazi airplanes had flown over Russian territory 180 times, and some penetrated as far as 400 miles, taking photographs. The Soviet government protested to the German government. Even that did not make Stalin believe what he did not wish to believe. The flight of Rudolf Hess, Number Two Nazi, to Scotland on May 10, 1941, made it clear to any politically literate person that Germany planned to attack Russia. Hess told official interrogators in Britain that Hitler sought peace with England and a free hand against the Soviet Union. Churchill telegraphed this information to Stalin. If Stalin nevertheless persisted in his view that Germany would continue the war on Britain till it ended with success, it can only be that his wish was father to the thought and, also, that he felt Hitler would keep his word not to assault Russia.

Stalin strongly resented Hitler's breach of faith. Stalin's first wartime radio broadcast to the Soviet people, on July 3, 1941, began, "It is I who am speaking to you, my friends. The treacherous armed attack of Hitler Germany on our fatherland, begun June 22, continues." The word "treacherous" occurs five more times in the text of the broadcast. Stalin frequently used the same term in subsequent public statements. It reveals his mind. He had been betrayed by Hitler. As a result, he hated Hitler with all his rich capacity for hate. "In Moscow, in the Kremlin," Harry L. Hopkins wrote in the *American Magazine* of December, 1941, after seeing Stalin, the Nazi attack "aroused a hatred of Hitler that nothing but the death of the German Chancellor could lessen. . . . The invasion was regarded in Moscow as the treachery of a partner who had suddenly revealed himself a rabid dog."

"Once we trusted this man," Stalin said to Hopkins of Hitler. When trust is rare its misplacement is resented the more.

Hitler had let Stalin down and, what was worse, proved him fallible and wrong.

The pact with Hitler gave Stalin the opportunity to throw his armed forces into Eastern Poland and the Baltics, where they were captured by Hitler; the opportunity to invade Finland, where his armies were seriously bled; and the opportunity to manufacture fewer arms than Russia had lost in Finland, Eastern Poland, and the Baltic states.

By contrast, the pact gave Hitler considerable Soviet imports in 1940 and 1941; the collaboration of the Communists, notably in France; popular support as a liberator from Bolshevism in Finland, the Baltic area, and Poland; and the advantage of surprise in his attack on Russia: all gains and, as far as historians have discovered, no losses.

Never had an infallible one failed so fully.

Stalin's relations with Hitler offer a unique insight into his personality. To rule the Soviet Union, Stalin avails himself of force. Force is not all; he also uses intelligence, guile, patience, and stubbornness. But force is a major element. In dealing with President Roosevelt and Prime Minister Churchill, Stalin likewise enjoyed the advantages inherent in strength; they needed his contribution to victory and he was shrewd enough to make them pay an exorbitant price for it. In relation to Hitler, however, Stalin's power was not dominant, he was the weaker partner. Here was scope for statesmanship, and it would have shone if he had displayed any. But in these exceptional circumstances, in which Stalin functioned without bludgeon, he was submissive and subservient. His arrogance and toughness disappeared. He curried favor with Hitler. He knew he was in the presence of a bigger bully and behaved accordingly. The summit of Stalin's wisdom was to take the worthless sop which Hitler threw him without anticipating the trouble bound to arise in the next, predictable phase when Hitler would either crush his Western enemies or turn in another direction for easier prey. Others saw this; Stalin did not. Superior strength deflates and confuses him. In the Nazi-Soviet pact period even Stalin's considerable reserves of intrigue were dormant. He did not dare use them. His foreign policy became a reflection of Hitler's and lost its independence. He promised Hitler to be good, and was good, and nothing probably could have surprised and irked him more than the reward: a hammer blow on the head. "This will teach me not to play around with dictators," Stalin may have reasoned mournfully.

CHAPTER XX

The Great Crisis

Hitler entered Russia with a mighty blitz which, in the first five months of the war, gave him an area inhabited by 40 per cent of the population of the entire Soviet Union. That lost territory, according to Politbureau member Voznesensky, produced 65 per cent of the Soviet Union's coal, 68 per cent of its pig iron, 58 per cent of its steel, 60 per cent of its aluminum, 38 per cent of its grain, 84 per cent of its sugar, 38 per cent of its cattle, and 60 per cent of its hogs, and contained 41 per cent of the country's railroad mileage. This was the ugly situation that faced Stalin in November, 1941. In the first week of December, German detachments entered Himki, a Moscow suburb twenty minutes by city bus from the Kremlin where Stalin sat and directed the war.

As soon as these speedy triumphs began, they sapped the morale of the Soviet people. Trained by Stalin to bow to power they bowed to Hitler's which seemed greater. If Hitler was destined to rule Russia it might be better not to oppose him. In the Western provinces, in the Ukraine, and in the North Caucasus, wherever Hitler's legions penetrated, they found numerous collaborators; the Tartar republic in the Crimea, the Kalmuck republic in the lower Volga region, and the Chechen-Ingushi republic in the North Caucasus were suppressed by Moscow and their inhabitants exiled to Siberia in hundreds of thousands for disloyalty. The non-Russian nationalities displayed the greatest reluctance to fight. They did not intend to die for the difference between oppression by Stalin and oppression by Hitler.

In the first five months of the war, the Red Army's spirit drooped. It was inadequately armed, miserably led, and disillusioned. Whole regiments were captured by Hitler and it is still moot whether they surrendered or were defeated.

From the moment Germany invaded Russia, Stalin knew his major problem: the Soviet people's lack of faith in victory. He told W. Averell Harriman that dictators "had always historically made mistakes because they could not keep the support of their people under the strain of the pressures of a hard-fought war." This was Stalin's worst worry.

After his first talk with Stalin on July 31, 1941, Harry L. Hopkins reported that the dictator was "anxious to have as many of his divisions as possible in contact with the enemy, because then the troops learn that Germans can be killed and are not supermen."

"History shows that there are no invincible armies and never have been," Stalin said in his first wartime radio broadcast on July 3, 1941. Napoleon, he recalled, was beaten by Russian, British, and German troops. "The German Army of Wilhelm in the period of the first imperialist war was also regarded as invincible," but it was finally crushed. "The same should be said of the present German Fascist Army of Hitler," Stalin urged. He then declared that "the best divisions of the German-Fascist Army have been smashed by our Red Army." In truth, the German advance was quick and relentless. But Stalin hoped his exaggerations would lift morale which was bad, for his broadcast warned against cowards, sowers of panic, and deserters "in our ranks." Stalin noted too that "the Great Lenin who founded our state" (the revolutionary Lenin thus became the nationalist Lenin) prized fearlessness in battle above all else. Russia's strength, Stalin insisted, was "incalculable"; moreover, "in this great war we have the peoples of Europe and America, as well as the German people who are enslaved by the Hitlerite despots, on our side."

Stalin struck the same high keynote in his next public address on November 6, 1941. In the first four months of war, he asserted, Russia's casualties had been 350,000 dead, 378,000 missing, and 1,020,000 wounded whereas Germany's losses were four and a half million. But since the Germans were advancing fast against negligible resistance it can be assumed that he arrived at the Russian figure by division and the German figure by multiplication. There was, however, method in Stalin's arithmetic. It was calculated to restore confidence. "The enemy is not as strong as some frightened intellectuals paint him," Stalin exclaimed. Yet he admitted that the "danger had considerably increased" since July. Leningrad was surrounded, Moscow threatened, and vast Soviet territories occupied. Nevertheless, England and America, he continued, had not wavered in their support of Russia (as Stalin had feared). The deeper the German Army moved into Russian territory, Stalin said, the more vulnerable it would be to Soviet blows. On the other hand, "there were many unfavorable factors as a result of which our army was suffering temporary defeats. . . . One of the reasons for failures of the Red Army is the absence of a second front in Europe, but," Stalin stated, "there can be no doubt" that a second front against Germany in Western Europe will be established "very soon."

Thus Stalin wove in and out between alibis for failures and hypodermics of confidence. Years later, on May 24, 1945, a fortnight after Germany's capitulation, Stalin disclosed that he himself had been not at all confident. "Our government," he admitted at a Kremlin banquet of Red Army officers, "made not a few blunders; there were moments of desperation in 1941 and 1942 when our army retreated, abandoned our native villages and cities in the Ukraine, White-Russia, Moldavia, Leningrad province, the Baltic area, the Karelian republic, abandoned them because it had no choice. Another nation might have said to the government: You have not justified our hopes, get out; we will set up a new government which will sign a peace with Germany and give us quiet. But the Russian people did not take that road because it had faith in the policy of its government. . . . Thank you, Russian people, for your trust." Unrolling the record of his memory, Stalin thus frankly revealed his dark fears that the government might be overthrown by a defeated, demoralized people. Stalin's private secretary, A. Poskrobeshov, wrote in the *Pravda* of December 21, 1949 that panic reigned in Moscow in the autumn of 1941. The Soviet press exhorted soldiers not to throw away their rifles. Desertions were numerous. The government had been moved deep inland to Kuibishev on the Volga River.

But Stalin remained in the imperiled Kremlin. This was a stroke of genius and, equally, a mark of his despair. Moscow's fall might have meant the collapse of the Soviet regime. Stalin probably had no wish to survive it. He would stake his life on success. This was the supreme test of his career and he met it well. Working assiduously, night and day, driving his underlings with animal fury, Stalin brought in unexhausted army reserves from Siberia and the Volga region. He planned a counteroffensive.

Hitler and nature collaborated. His head turned, his eyes blinded by the spectacular repetition in Russia of his earlier European blitzes, the Nazi chief—"cannibal," as Stalin called him—failed to concentrate on Moscow and, instead, sent the bulk of his forces into the North Caucasus. Hitler, Stalin said, was "hunting two hares: oil and the encirclement of Moscow." The oil was remote and meanwhile the environs of Moscow experienced their coldest winter in many years. Poorly clad, unaccustomed to sub-zero weather, the Germans crumpled. Their vehicles and artillery froze. Their morale and fighting ability dropped with the mercury in the thermometer. At that split second of history, Stalin launched his counteroffensive.

Moscow is a great Russian city and an important symbol. It excites a special urban patriotism. Its workers, equipped with pistols, shotguns, and shovels, marched out to the suburbs to check the invader. Everybody assumed that if Hitler took Moscow he would sow it with salt as proof that he had destroyed the Communist Mecca.

Winter, workers, and soldiers foiled the Nazis' design. The German Army withdrew from the ring around the city.

The Moscow victory pricked the legend of Hitler's invincibility. It signified that Stalin might win. The Soviet people's attitude immediately changed. They still had to reckon with Stalin.

Hitler contributed to the further rise of Soviet morale by keeping intact the hated farm collectives. The peasants had expected him to deliver them from this serfdom. But it was easier for the conqueror to confiscate grain from a collective than from innumerable small individual households. The Nazis, moreover, carrying their racist philosophy into the occupied Soviet territories, deliberately massacred old men, women, and children behind the front in order to clear out the "inferior" Slav and Jewish "under-men" and make room for German "Aryans" who would settle the land after the war. The reward was angry resistance to the invader by civilian partisans and a better combat spirit in the Red Army. They preferred their own tyrant who persecuted some of them to an outside conqueror who might exterminate all of them. Hitler's atrocities drove the Soviet people into the arms of Stalin.

While appreciating this Nazi-sent asset, Stalin was at first reluctant to encourage anti-German animosity among his troops; he feared it would bolster German morale just as anti-Russian acts by Germans had fortified Russian morale. Answering the charge that Soviet citizens "hate Germans as Germans and that the Red Army destroys German soldiers as Germans out of hatred of everything German and that therefore the Red Army was taking no German prisoners" but killing them instead, Stalin declared in an Order dated February 23, 1942, that this maligned the Red Army which "was free of all feeling of racial hate." But by November 6, 1943, Stalin had altered his tune. He compared the Germans with "medieval barbarians" and "the hordes of Attila." He called them "devils" and promised that "our nation will not forgive these criminal German perverts. We will force the German criminals to pay for all their evil doings." Soviet posters now called on the soldiers to "Hit the German," and Ilya Ehrenburg, a Red yellow journalist writing for the army newspaper, filled his articles with racist venom. The Kremlin was resolved to exploit fully any emotional factor which might convert failure into success, and it no doubt succeeded in arousing a patriotic feeling among the Russians who were seeing their country devastated. After the war Stalin paid a tribute to the Russian people, as distinct from other Soviet nationalities, for their "clear intelligence, stable character, and patience." They fought for Russia despite Stalin, or, perhaps, because they believed he had merged his "socialism" with their nationalism. In fact, several times during the war Stalin disputed the right of the Nazis to call themselves National-Socialists, and his London ambassador, Ivan Maisky, asked the B.B.C. to say "Hitlerite" instead of "Nazi."

The Moscow counteroffensive turned the tide and gave Russia confidence, but the crisis persisted. A Stalin Order dated May 1, 1942, summoned the troops to achieve, in 1942, the "final destruction of the German-Fascist Army and the liberation of all Soviet land from the Hitlerite scoundrels." This was propaganda; talk of victory might at least indicate that defeat no longer stared them in the face. Stalin himself was not yet free from the shock and consequent dejection which overtook him when Hitler invaded Russia. "In November, 1942, the danger to our fatherland," he said on November 6, 1943, was greater than when the enemy stood at the gates of Moscow in 1941.

This was the black truth.

The governments of the United States and Great Britain were even more pessimistic than Stalin and the Soviet people. Impressed by the Nazi blitz in Europe and depressed by Russia's poor military performance in Finland, United States Secretary of War Henry L. Stimson, Chief of Staff General George C. Marshall, and the War Plans Division of the General Staff were in "substantial unanimity," according to a document written by Stimson and reproduced in Robert E. Sherwood's *Roosevelt and Hopkins,* that "Germany will be thoroughly occupied in beating Russia for a minimum of one month and a possible maximum of three months." More specific yet equally gloomy, the British military thought "the first phase, involving the occupation of Ukraine and Moscow, might take as little as three, or as long as six weeks, or more." Prime Minister Churchill, broadcasting immediately after the invasion of Russia, let his rich imagination roam and saw Hitler using Russia as a "stepping-stone" to the possible seizure of China and India. "It is not too much to say here this summer evening," he declaimed, "that the lives and happiness of a thousand million additional people are now menaced with brutal Nazi violence."

These apprehensions ruled the counsels of Roosevelt and Churchill. Some, armed with postwar hindsight, now say that the West should have allowed the two dictators to slash and bleed one another to death. In 1941, everybody except a handful of amateur Machiavellis in the anti-Nazi world favored unstinting aid to Stalin. Any stiffening of Russia so that she held a month more, a fortnight more, would weaken Hitler and be that much gained.

Harry L. Hopkins of Iowa was the first airborne Anglo-American official to confer with Stalin after Hitler's attack. Sizing up his audience, Stalin stressed the moral aspect. There had to be a "minimum moral standard between all nations," he told Hopkins on July 30, 1941, but the Nazi leaders "knew no such minimum moral standard." He had only discovered it on June 22, 1941, when Hitler invaded Russia! Continuing, Stalin said, "The Germans were a people who would sign a treaty today, break it tomorrow and sign a second one the next day." After this ingratiating prelude, Stalin listed his needs in military supplies: 20,000 antiaircraft guns, a million or more rifles, large machine guns, tanks, aviation gasoline, steel, and nonferrous metals. "Give us antiaircraft guns and aluminum and we can fight for three or four years," Stalin promised. The aluminum was for making planes. "Fight for three or four years." No word of defeating Hitler. Indeed, Stalin said to Hopkins, "The power of Germany was so great that, even though Russia might defend herself, it would be very difficult for Russia and Britain combined to crush the German military machine." He said, Hopkins reported to President Roosevelt, "that the one thing that could defeat Hitler, and perhaps without ever firing a shot, would be the announcement that the United States was going to war with Germany." This may have been more compliment than sober appraisal, yet it reflected a hope. How eager Stalin was to win American aid, or at least good will, may be judged from his next statement. Stalin, Hopkins noted, "wanted me to tell the President that he would welcome the American troops on any part of the Russian front under the complete command of the American Army."

The United States was not yet at war, and had not even sent soldiers to help Britain. Stalin could hardly have expected Roosevelt to put American troops on a Russian battlefield. Yet perhaps he was ignorant enough, and a dictator enough, to think that the President might. If America could ship supplies to belligerents without being a belligerent herself, why not men? Throughout the war, and despite the mountains of Lend-Lease Stalin received from England

and the United States, he rarely permitted one of their military observers to see the front let alone allow foreign fighting units to operate on it as an independent command. Nevertheless, the Russian situation was desperate when Stalin spoke with Hopkins, and to inspire confidence in his own people and for the practical military support, he perhaps would have welcomed an American Army on Russian soil.

Stalin's offer sounds insincere because of what developed subsequently. Stalin is supple, which may be another way of saying that he is unscrupulous. During the Russo-German war, his mood, and his treatment of the Western Allies, sensitively reflected the course of battle. He was cordial or brutal or a mixture of both depending on the fortunes of war and on his estimate of what results a given tactic was yielding. He could, with equal facility, turn on the charm, thin as it was, or the rudeness, or alternate them, watching all the while for their effect on the statesmen who came from abroad to pay in homage and metal for the blood which the Soviet peoples shed so profusely to perpetuate and glorify his dictatorship.

In September, 1941, for instance, Lord Beaverbrook, British Minister of Production, and W. Averell Harriman, later United States Ambassador to Russia, went to Moscow, with supporting missions, to interview Stalin. "At the first meeting with Stalin, cordiality prevailed," Sherwood writes, basing his account on the Hopkins papers and official files. Stalin told Beaverbrook the British "might send forces to join the Russians in the Ukraine." Beaverbrook thought England could put some divisions into the Caucasus. "There is no war in the Caucasus but there is in the Ukraine," Stalin barked. Harriman mentioned President Roosevelt's concern with religious tolerance in Russia because this issue influenced the attitude of the American public toward Russian aid. "Stalin said that he did not know much about American public opinion toward Russia and did not seem to attach much importance to it." He always judged others by himself. Pleased with small favors, Harriman nevertheless wrote, "Beaverbrook and I considered the meeting had been extremely friendly. . . ."

The second session, the next evening, was even worse. According to Harriman, "The evening was very hard sledding. Stalin seemed discourteous and at times not interested, and rode us pretty hard. For example, he turned to me and said, 'Why is it that the United States can only give me one thousand tons of steel for tanks—a country with a production of over fifty million tons?.' "

"Over sixty million tons," Harriman corrected, but there was, nevertheless, no armor plate. Stalin glumly subsided.

Of the same two-hour meeting, Beaverbrook noted, "Stalin was very restless, walking about and smoking continuously, and appeared to both of us to be under an intense strain." Neither of the men, writes Sherwood, could account for Stalin's mood, "But their likeliest guess was that he had just received some alarming news about the imminent German drive on Moscow."

At the third conference with Stalin, Beaverbrook and Harriman handed Stalin a list of the supplies their countries could forward to Russia immediately. Stalin received the list "with enthusiasm." "It was sunshine after rain," Beaverbrook wrote.

To foreign notables, Stalin showed himself now wildly mercurial, now coldly calculating. The total impression was of an enigmatic, illusive, impulsive person capable of sudden, unexpected deeds—a separate peace with Hitler, for instance—in an emergency. It cannot have escaped Stalin that this impression made him the object of a persistent Anglo-American courtship instead of the reverse. Hard-pressed as he was by Hitler, Stalin should have begged the West for help. But they begged him to take it. Or he demanded it. They were ready to meet him 90 per cent, 100 per cent of the way so long as he continued to fight. Russia had the only land force capable of facing Hitler. Her military collapse or diplomatic defection might have multiplied America's and Britain's casualties tenfold and prolonged the war infinitely. To avoid this was the subtle task of Roosevelt and Churchill during the early critical years of Russia's involuntary involvement in the anti-Hitler struggle. "Of first importance," Harriman said in a speech in Los Angeles on April 30, 1951, "was to keep Russia as an effective fighting ally."

No sooner, therefore, had the Red Army won its first victory outside Moscow, and another in the temporary recapture of Rostov, than Stalin, sensing his advantage, made known to the British government his demands for territorial aggrandizement in many corners of the map: the Baltic countries, Finland, Rumania, Poland, Germany, and Turkey. Churchill decided to send his Foreign Minister, Anthony Eden, to Moscow.

At this juncture the Japanese attacked Pearl Harbor and then American, British, Dutch, and French possessions, warships, and airfields in the Far East. Germany and Italy forthwith declared war on the United States.

Faced now with a formidable enemy in the Pacific, England and America were more dependent on Russia's help in Europe. Nevertheless, and though Stalin, with customary toughness, claimed the Baltic countries and the same broad slice of Poland he received from Hitler in 1939, Eden did not accede. Neither did Stalin desist. Thus early in Russia's career as a still-shaky belligerent did her imperialist aims cast a black shadow on the future of the world.

In January, 1942, General Mason MacFarlane of the British Military Mission in Moscow reported that "the Red Army was in a bad way in the autumn but its tail is now up." However, an Anglo-American intelligence estimate, quoted by Sherwood, dwelt on the possibility of a "negotiated Russo-German settlement." Whenever fear of this development flagged, the Soviet press skillfully revived it. A second Stalin-Hitler pact signed behind the back of the Western powers was a constant bugbear to Washington and London and distorted their foreign policies. The mere thought of it softened any resolution to be firm with the Soviets or to restrict the flow of Lend-Lease supplies for Russia.

"The hopes of civilization rest on the worthy banners of the Russian Army," General Douglas MacArthur wired the Red Army on February 23, its birthday. Less grandiloquently, Churchill wrote Roosevelt on April 1, 1942, that "all now depends on the vast Russo-German struggle." The letter, quoted in Churchill's *The Hinge of Fate,* promised to keep "blasting Hitler from behind while he is grappling with the Bear." Stalin had informed Churchill that he expected the Germans to use gas on the Russian front. "I assured him," Churchill told Roosevelt, "that we shall treat any such outrage as if directed upon us, and will retaliate without limit. This we are in a good position to do."

Russia's military outlook remained bleak. Stalin's 1941 winter counteroffensive had relieved Moscow and recaptured much valuable ground. In the spring of 1942, however, Hitler released a powerful offensive. Stalin kept up a steady drumfire of telegrams to Roosevelt and Churchill insisting on a broad, uninterrupted stream of military materials. The main burden of delivering these goods lay on the British, and until February, 1942, their convoys had reached Soviet Arctic ports with only one ship sunk. But in March, Hitler dispatched the mighty battleship *Tirpitz* to prey on the convoys and assigned additional aircraft to molest them. The British suffered heavy losses and were reluctant to risk their precious ships. Supplies for Russia began to pile up in Icelandic, British, and American ports. Roosevelt pressed Churchill; on April 27, 1942, he wired, "About the shipments to Russia. I am greatly disturbed by your cable to Harry [Hopkins], because I fear not only the political repercussions in Russia, but even more the fact that our supplies will not reach them promptly."

In a dispatch to Churchill, dated May 6, 1942, Stalin said, "I have a request of you. Some ninety steamers loaded with various important war materials for the U.S.S.R. are bottled up at present in Iceland. . . . I am fully aware of the difficulties involved and of the sacrifices made by Great Britain in this matter. I feel however incumbent upon me to approach you with the request to take all possible measures to insure the arrival of the above-mentioned materials in the U.S.S.R. in the course of May, as it is extremely important for our front."

Unable to resist, and against his better judgment, the Prime Minister authorized a convoy for Russia. Thirty-four freighters, accompanied by a protective armada, sailed from Iceland for Archangel on June 27. The *Tirpitz* and other German warships came out to intercept. The British Admiralty ordered the convoy to scatter and proceed if possible to Soviet harbors. "Of the thirty-four ships which left Iceland," Churchill reports in *The Hinge of Fate*, "twenty-three were sunk, and their crews perished in the icy waters or suffered incredible hardships and mutilation by frostbite."

"In the months of April, May and June," Sherwood writes, "eighty-four ships carrying 522,000 tons left U.S. ports for Murmansk. Forty-four of these, carrying 300,000 tons, got through. Of the remainder, seventeen discharged their cargoes in Scotland and thirty-three were sunk by enemy or lost by shipwreck."

Churchill explained the difficult situation to Stalin in a lengthy cable. "I got a rough and surly answer," Churchill writes. The dictator felt that the British tale was "wholly unconvincing." "In wartime," Stalin said, "no important undertaking could be effected without risk or losses." The same message stressed the "serious situation" at the front, where the German spring attack was meeting with crushing successes, and demanded the immediate creation of a second front in Western Europe. "I must state in the most emphatic manner," Stalin declared, "that the Soviet government cannot acquiesce in the postponement of the second front in Europe until 1943." This hid a threat.

The convoys were resumed at heavy expense. Later, the Allies arranged to make deliveries to Russia via the Persian Gulf; and American planes were flown from Fairbanks, Alaska, to Siberia.

The question of an Anglo-American second front in Western Europe plagued relations with Russia. Stalin often and publicly stated Russia's case for a second front. "Assume," he said on November 6, 1942, "that there existed a second front in Europe just as in the First World War." The German position on the Russian front would be "sad." "In the First World War," he declared in the same speech, "there existed a second front in Europe which rendered the Germans' position very difficult, whereas in this war there is no second front in Europe." "In view of the absence of a second front in Europe," he repeated on February 23, 1943, "the Red Army is carrying the entire burden of the war." Exactly a year later he said, "The conditions under which Germany is conducting this war are more favorable to her than in the First World War when, from the very beginning to the end, she fought on two fronts. . . . History shows that Germany always won a war when she fought on one front, and lost when she had to fight on two fronts."

A simple statement answers these contentions: if Stalin had wished it, and if he had forbidden the French Communists to stab their country in 1939 and 1940, the Germans might have been engaged on two fronts from the very beginning of the Second World War. It was the Russian offensive in the summer of 1914 that saved France on the Marne. Stalin might have done the same in 1939. But at that time he did not foresee, as others did, the importance which two fronts would have for him a little later on.

Historic postmortems, however, bake no political cakes. Roosevelt and Churchill knew a second front was necessary to win the war and mollify Stalin. But when? On the second-front-in-1942 issue the Big Three were perilously divided. Stalin was adamant, Roosevelt willing, Churchill fiercely opposed.

Roosevelt favored a cross-Channel invasion of France either "in case of German internal collapse" or, as he wrote on July 16, 1942, "in the event Russian collapse becomes probable." Then it would be "imperative." But after much conferring and telegraphing, Churchill persuaded Roosevelt to agree, instead, to a landing in North Africa in 1942.

The Prime Minister had thus won part of his diplomatic battle. The more embarrassing task remained: to tell Stalin that there would be no second front in Europe in 1942. Churchill might have sent a telegram, or asked his Ambassador in Moscow to pass on the bad news. Characteristically, he decided to carry the information himself.

He had never met Stalin. He knew their first confrontation would be a stormy one. As reinforcements, he wanted an American representative to accompany him. Roosevelt delegated W. Averell Harriman.

Molotov met them at the airport and drove Churchill in his car to Government Villa Number Seven, eight miles out of Moscow, where "everything," Churchill remarked, "was prepared with totalitarian lavishness" in the midst of war and of a suffering population. Churchill also noticed that the windows of Molotov's limousine were two inches thick. "It is more prudent," Molotov explained. Stalin's glass would be at least as thick.

The first meeting between Churchill and Stalin took place on August 12, 1942, and lasted four hours. "The first two hours were bleak and somber," Churchill wrote. Churchill explained that an offensive operation across the Channel would, owing to weather conditions, have to begin in September, and the Anglo-Americans were not ready. They would prepare an expedition for 1943. But in 1943, the Germans might be stronger in the West than they are now. "At this point Stalin's face crumpled up into a frown but he did not interrupt." "The limiting factor," Churchill said, "was landing craft."

"Stalin, who had begun to look very glum, seemed unconvinced by my argument." He argued that there was not a single good German division in France. Churchill disputed this and presented refuting data. Stalin shook his head in disagreement. So they were unwilling to land even six divisions in France, Stalin grumbled mournfully. True, Churchill confirmed; no use wasting manpower when nobody but Hitler would gain thereby.

"Stalin, who had become restless, said that his view about war was different. A man who was not prepared to take risks could not win a war. Why were they so afraid of the Germans? He could not understand. His experience showed that troops must be blooded in battle. If you did not blood your troops you had no idea what their value was."

Their disagreement was total. Churchill changed the subject and discussed the Anglo-American bombing of Germany. Here, Churchill records, "Stalin emphasized the importance of striking at the morale of the German population. He said he attached the greatest importance to bombing, and that he knew our raids were having a tremendous effect in Germany."

At this point, Churchill unrolled a map and gave Stalin a detailed briefing on OPERATION TORCH, the planned landing in North Africa.

"May God prosper this undertaking," Stalin exclaimed. The Russian expression is more colloquial than pious.

After this unhappy encounter, Churchill felt, he said, "that at least the ice was broken and a human contact established." So he slept "soundly and long" in Soviet splendor. But the next morning he told Molotov that "Stalin will make a great mistake to treat us roughly when we have come so far." Molotov promised to transmit this plea to his Boss.

It did not help much. At eleven that evening Churchill saw Stalin again for "a most unpleasant discussion" lasting two hours. Stalin charged that the British Navy had abandoned the vessels it was convoying to Russian ports, whereupon Churchill defended British sea prowess in a dithyrambic retort so compelling oratorically that the British interpreter, entranced, had to be reminded to take notes. Stalin then reopened the argument about the second front and again accused the British of being afraid of Germans. "I repulsed his contentions squarely," Churchill writes, "but without taunts of any kind. I suppose he is not used to being contradicted repeatedly, but he did not become at all angry, or even animated. . . . I interposed that I pardoned the remarks which Stalin had made on account of the bravery of the Red Army. . . . Finally Stalin said we could carry it no further. He must accept our decision. He then abruptly invited us to dinner at eight o'clock the next night."

Churchill accepted but told Stalin bluntly that "there was no ring of comradeship in his attitude." Reminding Stalin that the British had stood alone for a year against the might of Germany, and of Italy, he stressed the need of unity now when victory appeared possible. After that the atmosphere grew "somewhat less tense."

"I make great allowance for the stresses through which they are passing," Churchill commented charitably. The stresses were there. But in addition Stalin had felt it his duty to try to shake or break Churchill's resolve. When he failed he was resigned but recorded the fact for future accounting.

Always the curious urchin and probing journalist despite his multitudinous war cares, Churchill was very much interested in the man Stalin. How did Stalin bear up under the strain of a heartbreaking ordeal for the preservation of the nation, Churchill wondered. "Tell me," he said to Stalin one evening past midnight, "have the stresses of this war been as bad to you personally as carrying through the policy of the Collective Farms?"

"Oh, no," Stalin replied without hesitation, "the Collective Farm policy was a terrible struggle."

"I thought you would have found it bad because you were dealing not with a few score thousands of aristocrats or big landowners, but with millions of small men," Churchill cross-examined without revealing whether his tongue was in his cheek.

"Ten millions," Stalin agreed, holding up his hands. "It was fearful. It lasted four years." The Communists argued with the peasant and tried to convince him, Stalin said, "but he always answers that he does not want the Collective Farm and would rather do without tractors."

"It was very bad and difficult," Stalin continued, "but necessary." Russia was intent on solving her food problem and expected that collectives would do it. "Millions of men and women being blotted out or displaced forever" rose in Churchill's mind, but he did not convey the vision to Stalin. Nor did he repeat Burke's dictum, "if I cannot have reform without injustice, I will not have reform."

"On the whole," Churchill summed up in a message to his War Cabinet and to Roosevelt, "I am definitely encouraged by my visit to Moscow. I am sure that the disappointing news I brought could not have been imparted except by me personally without leading to really serious drifting apart. It was my duty to go. Now they know the worst, and having made their protest are entirely friendly; this in spite of the fact that this is their most anxious and agonizing time."

The unbreakable decision conveyed to Stalin by Churchill was announced to the Soviet people in a widely diffused communiqué. For them it was a painful blow. The enemy was still only fifty miles from Moscow. The spring-summer offensive brought Hitler to Sevastopol in the Crimea, Voronezh in Central Russia, Stalingrad on the Volga, Novorossiisk on the Black Sea, Pyatigorsk in the North Caucasus, and Mozdok near the Caspian Sea. In some places, Stalin stated on November 6, 1942, the Germans advanced "as much as 500 kilometers," or more than 300 miles, all "on account of the absence of a second front in Europe." A major Anglo-American offensive in the West in 1942 would have cut Russia's casualties and saved many vital areas from Nazi devastation and rapine. Stalin's insistence on it was comprehensible, legitimate, and politically astute.

While mustering his armed forces to stem the German drive, Stalin performed another prodigious feat: thirteen hundred defense factories, with all their heavy machinery and workingmen, were lifted up and carried into the Urals and Siberia where they would be safer if Hitler took Moscow, reached the Volga, and occupied the Caucasus. The panic had ended; food was being distributed in cities, the police was dealing with idlers and weaklings. "The people in the rear have been transformed," Stalin observed on November 6, 1942. "They have become less slack, less slipshod, more disciplined . . . they have come to recognize their duty to the fatherland. . . . Bunglers and slackers, without a sense of civic obligation, grow fewer and fewer in the rear."

To prevent defeatism Stalin nevertheless withheld from families the news of the deaths of their sons in battle. Morale was better but not good; Stalin still felt he had to falsify Hitler's casualties in Russia. He put them at eight million without even mentioning his own. He admitted that the military threat was greater.

The crisis continued. Further withdrawals might prove necessary. Plans were ready for flight beyond the Volga. Relegated to the Ural Mountains, Stalin would have been a lesser world figure. His future and that of his regime still swayed in the balance. He knew it. He would not tempt fate, but he waited eagerly for a chance to alter it.

CHAPTER XXI

Stalingrad and Teheran

During the four years of war, Stalin never went to the front. No photograph has ever been seen of Stalin on a visit to the front; if he had gone, a photographer would certainly have recorded the event for publicity and posterity. War to Stalin was a scientific, mechanical operation. He excluded the personal from it. Besides, he was physically and politically safer in the Kremlin or in his deep, luxurious air-raid shelter where he could live and work. There do exist, however, numerous oil paintings of Stalin at the front, and cinema actors have played him viewing the front: "Socialist realism"—the presentation, in this case with Stalin's prior approval, of that which is not. One Soviet painting shows Stalin at the front in 1941, a veritable Hollywood general, broad-shouldered and tight-waisted, in resplendent uniform with decorations, standing alone on a hillock, with no staff, nobody near him; only far below in the snow, some soldiers lie in the trenches and gaze at him with mingled awe and love.

Stalin conducted a war, not people.

No important Soviet military decision in the Second World War was taken without Joseph Stalin. His ego and mistrust saw to that. Nor would any general or marshal, much less civilian leader, willingly accept the responsibility and attendant risk of determining major strategy without the approval of the all-highest in the Kremlin. Inevitably, the supreme direction of the war was the dictator's peril and privilege. He would have been blamed for defeat. His is the credit for victory.

Whether he actually drew the plans of campaigns and the blueprints of battles remains to be proved. The claim has been made; indeed, Soviet fictional films portray Stalin giving orders by long distance telephone from the Kremlin to front-line bunkers. But this merely grows from the Soviet principle that whatever is right in Russia originates with Stalin. He himself has tried to feed the impression of his military ability; in speaking, once, to an American general who, he knew, held Soviet Marshal Zhukov in high esteem as a military leader, Stalin sought, with scant success, to undermine Zhukov's reputation and enhance his own.

Nobody knows what happened in the inner circle where strategy was fixed. Stalin may have approved what seemed to him the best of several proposals submitted by professional soldiers. Or the amateur conception, based on astute political calculations, may have been Stalin's; the experts then gave it finished military form. Stalin might have planned campaigns; he did not have the technical knowledge to plan battles.

The greatest single Soviet military triumph in the Second World War, and probably its turning point, was Stalingrad. Stalin could not have wished it otherwise. Just as Moscow is a symbol of Russia, so Stalingrad, the City of Stalin, is a symbol of Stalin's personal dictatorship. Its four hundred thousand inhabitants, its few big factories, and its geographic position did not make it more important than a dozen other towns under German assault. But Stalin's association with its defense during the civil war, when it was still called Tsaritsyn, after the absolute monarch, had been transformed by history-falsifiers into a legend of his military genius. Now history would build up the Battle of Stalingrad into a true epic.

The Nazi attack on Stalingrad, which stretches for miles in a very thin line along the banks of the Volga, began in August, 1942. Stalin would not let it fall. Hitler hurled more troops and air power against it. Stalin reinforced the defending garrison. Hitler redoubled his effort to take the city. Its significance to Stalin gave it special meaning to Hitler. Soon giant armies were locked in the fight for the city. Germany used 330,000 men in the battle in and around Stalingrad.

The Nazis shelled the city from the land side and from boats on the river. Bombs rained on it from the air. Hardly a building, or factory, or home, remained intact. In time, the Germans entered Stalingrad and fought for the ruins. One part of an industrial plant was held by the Germans, another by the Russians. The Red Army occupied the cellar of an apartment house and the Nazis were in the upper floors. Night and day the battle raged.

Finally the Nazis had possession of most of the city. Now the besiegers became the besieged. The Russians besieged Stalingrad. Winter froze the river and the Germans and cut down their air support. Field-Marshal von Paulus, with a large army, was shut in the city. Hitler sent a big force under Field-Marshal Erich von Mannstein to relieve Paulus. Stalin, with magnificent strategy, cut it off. Paulus had no choice. On January 31, 1943, he came out and surrendered with over 80,000 troops and eighteen generals.

After the horror of battle, the Russians, Stalin said on November 6, 1943, buried 147,200 dead Germans and 46,700 of their own casualties found in the debris of Stalingrad. But many more thousands of human bodies had been mashed into unrecognizable pulp by falling ruins and falling explosives. They could not be counted.

"Stalingrad," Stalin declared, "was the sunset of the German-Fascist Army."

Russia and Germany continued in mortal combat for two years, three months, and one week after Stalingrad, but the outcome was no longer in doubt, and Stalin mellowed. In May, 1943, he gave a fair and friendly public analysis of the Anglo-American military effort in North Africa, took the title of Marshal, disbanded the Comintern following a suggestion by President Roosevelt, and congratulated Roosevelt and Churchill in separate telegrams on the victories of their armies in Tunis. Previously, in a message to Churchill, he had approved of the use which the Americans made of French Admiral Darlan, a Nazi collaborator abominated for that reason by Western liberals. "Military diplomacy," Stalin said, "must be able to use for military purposes not only Darlan but 'even the devil himself and the devil's grandmother' (a Russian proverb)." Later that year he paid a tribute to the success of the Allies in southern Italy and welcomed their air raids on Germany. "The aviation of our Allies," he stated on November 7, 1943, in an Order to the Red Army, "has subjected the industrial centers of Germany to serious bombardments. There is no doubt that the Red Army's blows against the Germans in the East, supported by the blows of the main force of our allies in the West will crush the military power of Hitler Germany and bring about the complete victory of the anti-Hitler coalition." Now he was really confident.

President Roosevelt had been eager to meet Stalin. It was curiosity, no doubt, but chiefly it was the need of tying Stalin more closely to the West. On April 11, 1942, Roosevelt suggested to Stalin with typical neighborly casualness that "perhaps next summer you and I could spend a few days together near our common border off Alaska." Stalin was unwilling. At the time of the Churchill-Roosevelt talks in Casablanca in January, 1943, the President again invited Stalin, but he refused. In May, 1943, Joseph E. Davies conveyed to Stalin the President's idea that if they could get together with Foreign Minister Molotov and Secretary of State Cordell Hull "all questions could be settled." "Stalin," in the words of Hull's published *Memoirs*, "replied that he wondered whether this really was true. He finally inclined toward a personal meeting with the President; but when Churchill suggested that he too should be present Stalin pulled back."

Still pursuing, Roosevelt cabled a proposal that the Three meet in Bagdad, capital of Iraq. Stalin suggested Teheran. The President wired back saying he had made a careful check of time and distances and discovered that Teheran "was impossible for him" because he had to be in a place where, within the ten days provided by the U. S. Constitution, he could receive and return bills passed by Congress for his signature. He offered, as alternatives, Asmara in East Africa and Ankara in Turkey. Stalin said, Nothing but Teheran.

"It was not a question of protection," Stalin cabled Roosevelt, according to Mr. Hull's *Memoirs*. That "did not worry him." But he had to maintain "personal contact with the High Command," and for this purpose there was a direct telegraph and telephone connection between Teheran and Moscow. The President offered to run a special wire from Moscow to Basra, in Iraq: that would save Franklin D. Roosevelt, who was a cripple, hundreds of miles. Stalin said, Only Teheran. Roosevelt was ready to travel some ten thousand miles to meet Stalin. Stalin would go no more than six hundred miles beyond the Soviet border to meet Roosevelt.

According to one source, Stalin gets dangerously ill when he flies, not airsick, but violently nervous. Or Stalin did indeed have to keep in close contact with the High Command; perhaps he feared an Army "palace revolution" to overthrow him. Alternatively, Stalin may have had an eye on political effects. The Big Two came to meet him at Teheran; they came to Soviet soil at Yalta in February, 1945; President Truman, Churchill, and Attlee were Stalin's guests, on Soviet-occupied territory, at the Potsdam Conference in June-July, 1945. For Stalin this was not without value: the world came to him. It raised his prestige with his own people and with foreign Communists; it fed his vanity too. Perhaps, in addition to all these considerations, Stalin simply found it selfishly convenient. "A man must conserve his strength," he said to Ambassador W. Bedell Smith in 1946; "President Roosevelt had a great sense of duty, but he did not save his strength. If he had, he would probably be alive today."

In the fall of 1942, Stalin agreed to a foreign ministers' conference, and at his suggestion it convened in Moscow. Past seventy years of age, Hull had never been in an airplane when he flew to Moscow in October, 1943, to sit with Molotov and Eden. Hull was a silver-haired, soft-spoken, long-distance-spitting, Southern-Colonel type of gentlemen. Yet of all the foreign statesmen who visited Stalin during the war, none understood him better than Hull. Both were sons of the mountains, and it appears that Tennessee is not far from Georgia. The first subject Hull and Stalin discussed was wheat planting. "I told Stalin," Hull writes, "about planting wheat six inches deep in Tennessee, which seemed something new to him." Then "we discussed rafting. I described how we bound logs into rafts in Tennessee, using hickory walings. Stalin described how his people had bound rafts together with vines."

The foreign ministers' conference dealt with the postwar problem of punishing enemy leaders. "If I had my way," Hull drawled mellifluously, "I would take Hitler and Mussolini and Tojo and their arch-accomplices and bring them before a drum court-martial. And at sunrise on the following day there would occur an historic incident." The Russians laughed with delight.

But when Hull, seconded by Harriman, took up with Stalin the matter of the place where the Big Three would gather, he got nowhere. Harriman said each head of state could have his own camp at Basra, guarded by his own soldiers. Stalin replied that he was "not at all worried on the subject of protection." Knowing full well how much Roosevelt desired the conference, Stalin hinted that perhaps it ought to be postponed till the spring when the two could meet in Alaska. That would have left out Churchill.

They accepted Teheran.

Three more contrasting men had rarely met. Churchill, the offspring of a noble, historic family. Roosevelt, the rich country squire. Stalin, the grandson, on his mother's side, of serfs, the son and grandson, on his father's side, of poor peasants who became poor cobblers. Churchill felt the romance of the past which bound him and the excitement of the present which fascinated him. To conserve the present was his dream for the future. Stalin coldly used the past as a ladder and pillar; the present perpetuated was his goal for the Russia of coming ages. Roosevelt gloried in change; to change institutions, traditions, and men's minds was his greatest pleasure. He loved plans.

Roosevelt had no dogma; Stalin had none either. Stalin was the least progressive. Churchill wanted to save an empire, Stalin to create one. That was the big clash at Teheran. Roosevelt saw himself as conciliator. He trusted his personality to smooth out differences. Stalin trusted only his power and remained immune to Roosevelt's charm and Churchill's rhetoric.

Roosevelt was there to win the war and reduce inter-Allied friction. Stalin thrived on friction. The more there was the more the others would pay him to eliminate it. Churchill understood Stalin better than Roosevelt did. Churchill and Stalin were both imperialists, whereas Roosevelt thought of the postwar in terms of internationalism which his partners scorned or ignored.

Stalin could unstintingly throw unlimited manpower into the mouth of Mars, as he had at Stalingrad. Churchill knew his country of forty-five million inhabitants, already badly bled in the First World War, could not afford to lose many more in this one. Roosevelt hoped to save American boys by giving freely of her steel and machines.

Roosevelt wanted nothing but peace in Teheran and good will in the Big Three. Stalin came for more practical prizes. Churchill could give Stalin little. Roosevelt was rich, pliable, accommodating, easygoing. Stalin let himself be wooed, but only on the promise that there would be no triangle. In conformity with his usual strategy, he aimed to drive a wedge between his two opponents; he never regarded them as anything else. He had no illusions. Only Roosevelt had illusions and Stalin therefore must have thought him quite naïve for a successful politician.

Roosevelt was spontaneous and joyous, Churchill zestful but sad, Stalin repressed and as emotional as an adding machine. Stalin was playing for added power, Roosevelt for a conference with a happy ending. Stalin played closed poker; Churchill played patience, alone; Roosevelt tried to do card tricks.

Roosevelt was optimistic by temperament and by the fact of victory over ailment; Churchill was pessimistic because his country's survival was being purchased at the price of its decline. Watching the two, Stalin was very optimistic.

Though Stalin came only a short distance, he arrived at Teheran after Mr. Roosevelt and Mr. Churchill. This may have been accidental. But the same thing happened at Yalta and again at Potsdam. At the two latter conferences he was host and, being Georgian, he knows the laws of hospitality extremely well. Perhaps there was purpose in his tardiness:

Stalin first met Lenin, his idol, at the party conference in Tammerfors, Finland, in December 1905. "I expected to see the mountain eagle of our party," he recounted in a speech on January 26, 1924, a few days after Lenin's death, "a big man, a big man not only politically but, if you please, physically, for Lenin appeared in my imagination as a Titan, stately and impressive. What was my disappointment when I saw a most ordinary person, of less than average height, differing from ordinary mortals in nothing, literally nothing.

"It is assumed," Stalin continued, "that a 'big man' should usually arrive late at a meeting so that the people at the meeting wait for him with bated breath, and then, just before the 'big man' arrives, members of the audience give notice: 'Tst, quiet, he's coming.' All this did not seem to me to be superfluous, because it makes an impression and inspires respect. But what was my disappointment when I learned that Lenin had arrived at the conference before the delegates and, stuck somewhere in a corner, was carrying on a conversation, a very ordinary conversation, quite simply, with the most ordinary delegates at the conference. I will not deny that at the time this appeared to me as somewhat of an infringement of some indispensable rules." Later, Stalin said, he understood that this modesty was one of Lenin's strongest characteristics.

But respect for humility was something superficially learned, whereas the disposition to stage-manage an entrance for the enhancement of prestige was deeply ingrained in the big man who had all the props of a big man but was not really one.

However, once Stalin had arrived at Teheran he conducted himself with civilized urbanity and Communist circumspection. He immediately invited Roosevelt to quit the remote American Embassy and come live with him in the spacious Soviet Embassy which was under strong Red Army guard. "Some kind of plot was afoot," Stalin intimated. The secret-police psychology, which envelops Stalin apparently traveled with him. Roosevelt subsequently told Mrs. Frances Perkins, for many years his Secretary of Labor, that he did not believe the story of the plot. He accepted nevertheless. It was a convenient arrangement; Churchill lived next door, in the British Legation, protected by an Anglo-Indian brigade, and the Big Three were accordingly neighbors. Yet the trio had been subtly divided into a two and a one.

Though Roosevelt and Stalin now shared the same quarters, the gulf between them remained. "For the first three days," Roosevelt explained to Mrs. Perkins, who reproduces his words in her book, *The Roosevelt I Knew*, "I made absolutely no progress. I couldn't get any personal connection with Stalin, although I had done everything he asked me to do. I had stayed at his Embassy, gone to his dinners, been introduced to his ministers and generals. He was correct, stiff, solemn, not smiling, nothing human to get hold of."

It is easy to imagine Roosevelt's frustration.

"I felt pretty discouraged," he admitted to Frances Perkins, "because I thought I was making no personal headway. What we were doing could have been done by the foreign ministers." The President had gone to Teheran to win Stalin's friendship.

"I thought it over all night," Roosevelt continued, "and made up my mind I had to do something desperate. I couldn't stay in Teheran forever. I had to cut through the icy surface so that later I could talk by telephone or letter in a personal way. I had scarcely seen Churchill alone during the conference. I had a feeling that the Russians did not feel right about seeing us conferring together in a language which we understood and they didn't.

"On my way to the conference room that morning we caught up with Winston and I had just a moment to say to him, 'Winston, I hope you won't be sore with me for what I am going to do.'

"Winston shifted his cigar and grunted. I must say he behaved very decently afterward.

"I began almost as soon as we got into the conference room. I talked privately with Stalin. I didn't say anything that I hadn't said before, but it appeared quite chummy and confidential, enough so that the other Russians joined us to listen. Still no smile.

"Then I said, lifting my hand to cover a whisper (which of course had to be interpreted), 'Winston is cranky this morning, he got up on the wrong side of the bed.'

"A vague smile passed over Stalin's eyes, and I decided I was on the right track. As soon as I sat down at the conference table, I began to tease Churchill about his Britishness, about John Bull, about his cigars, about his habits. It began to register with Stalin. Winston got red and scowled, and the more he did so, the more Stalin smiled. Finally Stalin broke out into a deep, hearty guffaw, and for the first time in three days I saw light. I kept it up until Stalin was laughing with me, and it was then that I called him

'Uncle Joe.' He would have thought me fresh the day before, but that day he laughed and came over and shook my hand."

Nobody probably ever paid a higher price for a laugh. For the scene had its serious counterpart. About a month earlier, from Washington, Roosevelt had telegraphed Churchill the text of a proposed message to Stalin offering to admit Russian military representatives to secret Anglo-American Joint Staff discussions. The proposal "filled me with alarm," Churchill writes in *Closing the Ring*, as well it might have. "Considering they tell us nothing of their own movements, I do not think we should open this door to them," Churchill replied. Properly concerned with building a solid wartime and postwar Big Three coalition, Roosevelt was making a valiant effort to uproot ineradicable Soviet suspicions. To dispel any notion in Russian heads that the Anglo-Americans were "ganging up" on them, Roosevelt advised Hull against traveling with Eden from Cairo to their Moscow conference in October, 1943, and in Moscow Hull wanted to give the Russians "every indication possible that both the American and the British delegations were ready separately to discuss any matters with them." At Teheran the President took the next step down and discussed separately only with the Russians. Churchill resented his isolation, and the result was unfortunate. "The fact," Churchill writes, "that the President was in private contact with Marshal Stalin and dwelling at the Soviet Embassy, and that he had avoided seeing me alone since we left Cairo, in spite of our hitherto intimate relations and the way in which our vital affairs were interwoven, led me to seek a direct personal interview with Stalin." Churchill "felt the Russian leader was not deriving a true impression of the British attitude" from Roosevelt. Before he undertook to dispel the misinformation he assured Stalin he was not disloyal to America.

Thus the "plot" and the laugh fall into a pattern. By taking Roosevelt into his palace, Stalin separated the two statesmen and stirred Churchill's fears. By holding Roosevelt at arm's length with no effort at all, Stalin challenged the President's talent to vanquish with charm. Intuitively Roosevelt knew, after thinking it over all night, that the way to make Stalin happy was to mock the Englishman. Stalin was cozy in the middle. Churchill came to set him straight about Roosevelt; Roosevelt strained to please him. Stalin did nothing. He had merely set the stage. No irreparable harm was done to Anglo-American or Churchill-Roosevelt relations. But Stalin received every indication that he could spoil them. He had muddied the waters and would now fish for discord. In the disunity of others lay his strength.

Differences had existed between the British and American points of views and Stalin heard their echo during the four-day Teheran conference.

Roosevelt was aided at Teheran by General George C. Marshall, General H. H. Arnold, Admiral Leahy, and Admiral King. Churchill came with the highest officers of the British armed services. But Stalin observed at the first session at 4 P.M. on November 28, 1943, according to Churchill, that "he had not expected that military questions would be discussed at the Conference, and he had not brought his military experts with him." The Russian generals Roosevelt met were Stalin's guards.

Of course Stalin knew in advance what Allied military chiefs would attend the sessions. But since his own were absent, he himself gave a brief summary of the position at the Soviet front (the Germans had resumed the offensive after Stalingrad and taken or retaken valuable ground); for the rest, most of the meetings were devoted to a consideration of Western war plans. Stalin's main concern at Teheran was the projected Anglo-American cross-Channel invasion of France, known by the code name of OVERLORD.

Roosevelt and Churchill felt somewhat guilty in this matter toward Stalin. OVERLORD had not occurred in 1943 as he had hoped. Now it was scheduled for May or June or July, 1944.

Churchill wanted to bring Turkey into the war and, with this in view, he urged the capture of the island of Rhodes. He had tried several times to persuade Turkey to fight on the anti-Nazi side. "I am all in favor of trying again," Stalin commented. "We ought to take them by the scruff of the neck if necessary." Yet he did not think the Turks would join. "All neutrals," he said, remembering his own role as one, "regard those who were waging war as fools to fight when they might be doing nothing."

Stalin opposed any military sideshows in the East Mediterranean, Balkans, or elsewhere. He even spoke against the Anglo-American advance to Rome, or if Rome had to be taken, then the Italian campaign should stop there. The important blow must be struck in France across the English Channel. He asked Churchill to commit himself to launching OVERLORD in May. Churchill did not promise. It might be later.

During the first Teheran session, Stalin looked at Churchill across the big table and said, "I wish to pose a very direct question to the Prime Minister about OVERLORD. Do the Prime Minister and the British Staff really believe in OVERLORD?"

"Provided," Churchill replied, "the conditions previously stated for OVERLORD are established when the time comes, it will be our stern duty to hurl across the Channel against the Germans every sinew of our strength." The conditions were that Britain would contribute sixteen divisions to the operation, the United States nineteen; big divisions. The British would keep their divisions up to strength, but if reinforcements were needed to broaden the front, they would have to come from America. England, Churchill said, was too poor in manpower and was tending other fronts.

"Who will command OVERLORD?" Stalin then asked. He put the same question many times at sessions, lunches, and dinners. He would not believe the West was serious about the offensive till a commander had been named. Stalin favored General Marshall, because he knew Marshall was an enthusiastic supporter of OVERLORD. Stalin said, "The Soviet government lays no claim to a voice in the appointment. We merely want to know who it will be." Roosevelt did not tell him.

At his man-to-man interview with Stalin, Churchill assured the dictator that he was "not in any way lukewarm about OVERLORD." But he was interested in the Eastern Mediterranean, in Turkey, and Greece, as well as in OVERLORD.

Stalin suspected the attack might be delayed. He warned Churchill that "if there were no operations in May, 1944, then the Red

Army would think that there would be no operations at all that year. . . . Disappointment could only create bad feeling. If there was no big change in the European war in 1944, it would be very difficult for the Russians to carry on. They were war-weary." Again the specter of a separate peace with Germany.

Churchill assured Stalin that if Hitler did not reinforce his army in France, OVERLORD would surely take place. This was Churchill's way of demanding that Russia continue to occupy Hitler and prevent him from shifting his troops to the Channel ports in Normandy. Stalin promised to mount an offensive timed with OVERLORD.

The Americans were eager for OVERLORD. Churchill acquiesced. To Stalin it was a matter of life and death.

After leaving Teheran, Roosevelt appointed Eisenhower to command OVERLORD. The Anglo-American armies poured over the beaches of Normandy on June 6, 1944. Seventeen days later, as pledged, Stalin opened a mighty attack on the Nazi forces in Russia. This was the sweetest fruit of Teheran. It destroyed the Nazi dominion of Europe.

Teheran also produced bitter fruit, bitter memories, and idle talk.

Roosevelt sketched the peacetime United Nations organization built on the foundation of "The Four Policemen": the United States, the United Kingdom, the Union of Socialist Soviet Republics, and China. Stalin frowned on China as policeman; too weak. What would happen, Stalin probed, if one of the policemen became a bandit, if a great power committed aggression? Apparently, the question did not receive serious attention at Teheran. At one dinner, when the problem of postwar bases was mentioned, Churchill announced that Britain intended to keep all she had. And what, he asked, might be Russia's territorial ambitions? "There is no need to speak at the present time about any Soviet desires," Stalin parried, "but when the time comes we will speak."

Churchill's sixty-ninth birthday was celebrated at a dinner in the British legation on November thirtieth. Before the dinner the Soviet NKVD arrived in force at the Legation, searched it from roof to cellar, looked behind every door, under every piece of furniture and cushion, and then about fifty of them, commanded by a general, remained to stand guard at windows and doors till the banquet ended. They were joined by a detail of American Secret Service men. No doubt, Scotland Yard was represented too.

After the meal, the British Prime Minister made a gracious speech in which he called the Russian dictator "Stalin the Great." Stalin graciously said that "without American production the war would have been lost." Roosevelt generously volunteered to give Russia the Manchurian port of Dairen after the war. Stalin "immediately expressed the opinion," writes Sherwood, "that the Chinese would object." The President thought they would agree. He had, in fact, discussed it with Chiang Kai-shek in Cairo about a week before. Having given this Chinese gift to Stalin at Churchill's birthday dinner, Roosevelt gave Churchill a Persian porcelain bowl about six or seven inches across the top and five inches high which he had bought in the American Army PX that day.

From the talks on Poland at various sessions, Stalin was warranted in concluding that he could, with impunity, take what he wanted: half the country. But Churchill reminded Stalin that the Bolsheviks came to power in 1917 proclaiming "no annexations and no indemnities" as their motto.

"I have told you," Stalin countered, "that I am becoming a conservative." Stalin is deeply conservative and orthodox, as though the theological seminary had molded him; a Russian orthodox monarch with the priestly mantle and bible of a Bolshevik.

Germany, too, was discussed at Teheran. Churchill reports in *Closing the Ring*: "Stalin said that he would like to see Germany split up. The President agreed, but Stalin suggested that I would object. I said I did not object."

Roosevelt presented a plan for the division of Germany into five parts. "Stalin, with a grin," Churchill writes, "suggested that I was not listening because I was not inclined to see Germany split up." Churchill explained his approach: Prussia should be treated sternly, and isolated. The South Germans were different and not as "ferocious"; they might join a Danubian federation; if Germany was partitioned and the parts not allowed to join some other big unit they would seek to reunite in a restored Germany. Stalin objected to federations. He preferred Roosevelt's scheme. All Germans, including workers, were Germans, Stalin asserted, and South Germans were no different from North Germans; they all fought like "devils" and "fierce beasts."

All agreed that this haphazard, desultory conversation was preliminary. The German problem received further flippant attention at a dinner given by Stalin where, according to Sherwood, Stalin engaged in "unremitting" teasing of Churchill. The British Prime Minister says he took no umbrage "until the Marshal entered in a genial manner upon a serious and even deadly aspect of the punishment to be inflicted upon the Germans." After the war, Stalin proposed, fifty thousand German officers and military technicians should be shot.

"The British Parliament and public," Churchill remarked, "will never tolerate mass executions. . . . The Soviets must be under no delusions on this point."

"Fifty thousand must be shot," Stalin reiterated.

Churchill grew angry. "I would rather," he exclaimed, "be taken out into the garden here and now and be shot myself than sully my own and my country's honor with such infamy."

Roosevelt poured a joke on the flame. Not fifty thousand, he said, only forty-nine thousand. "By this," Churchill suggests, "he hoped, no doubt, to reduce the whole matter to ridicule. Eden also made signs and gestures to me indicating that it was all a joke. But now Elliott Roosevelt rose in his place at the end of the table, saying how cordially he agreed with Marshal Stalin's plan and how sure he was that the United States Army would support it. At this intrusion I got up and left the table" and the room. Stalin immediately followed him, put his hand on his shoulder, and said it was all in fun. But Churchill declares that "I was not then, and am not now, fully convinced that all was chaff and there was no serious intent lurking behind the 'teasing.'"

Stalin's jokes can be grim.

During the Teheran Conference, Churchill presented Stalin with a sword which the King had had "specially designed and wrought" to commemorate the Russian victory at Stalingrad. Roosevelt described the ceremony to Mrs. Perkins: "As Stalin rose to accept the sword he flushed with a kind of emotional quality which I knew was very real. He put out his hands and took the sword from the crimson cushion. There were tears in his eyes. I saw them myself. He bowed from the hips swiftly and kissed the sword, a ceremonial gesture of great style which I know was unrehearsed. It was really very magnificent, moving, and sincere."

The same scene described by Churchill: "I handed the splendid weapon to Marshal Stalin, he raised it in a most impressive gesture to his lips and kissed the blade. He then handed it to Voroshilov, who dropped it."

When Roosevelt returned from Teheran to Washington he said to Mrs. Perkins, "I wish someone would tell me about the Russians. I don't know a good Russian from a bad Russian." That was the plain truth.

President Roosevelt's unusual perceptivity, which sometimes amounted almost to clairvoyance, told him, long before many others realized it, that the fate of humanity would depend on Soviet-American relations. Identifying Russia with Stalin, he decided, at whatever sacrifice of dignity, to win over the dictator. That was his duty. But the President's inordinate faith in himself, which had sustained him in a long personal ordeal and grown in the process, misled him into believing that he had succeeded. He left Teheran under the impression that Stalin was, as he put it, "get-at-able." He was not. Roosevelt had never met anybody like Stalin. Stalin is not "get-at-able" by anybody. That is the dictator's strength. To be omnipotent he must be inhumanly impervious to human personality. Stalin considers policies, not men. He had his policies. The world would soon discover them, and before his death Roosevelt too would discover that Stalin had not been "get-at-able" in Teheran.

CHAPTER XXII

Yalta and After Yalta

I had tea alone with Lord Halifax in the British Embassy in Washington on January 18, 1944, a scarce six weeks after the Teheran Conference. That morning the American press reproduced a queer story which had appeared in the Moscow *Pravda* the day before. *Pravda*'s "own correspondent" in Cairo, where, it subsequently developed, *Pravda* had no correspondent, reported, on information received from "Greek and Yugoslav" sources, that "two leading British personalities" had been negotiating with Nazi Foreign Minister Ribbentrop "in the Iberian peninsula" about a separate peace. If the story had nothing else it at least had a lot of geography in it.

"Tell me," was the first thing Halifax said to me, "what are the Russians up to? Why do they accuse the British government of wanting a separate peace with Germany?" The same question agitated Secretary of State Hull, Undersecretary of State Edward R. Stettinius, Jr., Assistant Secretary of State Adolf A. Berle, Jr., and other American diplomats with whom I talked in the following days.

The purpose of the *Pravda* tale was to produce just this state of perplexity. It made Washington and London fret. They wondered whether this was a warning that Stalin might sign a separate peace with Germany. Had he done so he would have saved Germany from defeat and cheated himself of the extensive territories he gained from the collapse of her power. But if Western statesmen understood this they were too sure about Stalin, and that was not to his advantage. Better to worry them. Hence the *Pravda* invention. It had no known basis in fact.

Already, the inescapable defeat of Hitler was casting its black shadow before. "The nearer we come to vanquishing our enemies, the more we inevitably become conscious of the differences among victors," President Roosevelt said in his annual message to Congress on January 6, 1945. A few weeks later, at Yalta, the President, viewing the destruction wrought by war and the retreating Nazis, told Stalin, according to Mr. Stettinius's memoirs, that he felt "more bloodthirsty toward the Germans than he did a year ago."

"Everybody is more bloodthirsty than he was a year ago," Stalin remarked. A better description of him would have been land-hungry. Stalin said on May 1, 1942, "It is not our purpose to invade foreign countries or subjugate foreign peoples. Our aim is clear and noble. We wish to liberate our Soviet soil from the German-Fascist scoundrels. . . . We have no other goals." Two years later, to the day, Stalin announced that three fourths of Soviet territory previously held by the foe had been rewon and soon, he hoped, all Russian lands would be liberated. "But our aims," he added, "cannot be limited to the expulsion of enemy troops from our fatherland." "The wounded animal" must be given no opportunity to "heal its wounds." They must pursue the enemy and release "our brother Poles and Czechs" and other peoples from Nazi slavery.

Military success had gone to Stalin's stomach and he was land-hungry. Churchill understood immediately that Russia was coming out into Europe; within a month of Stalin's statement Lord Halifax inquired of Secretary of State Hull how America would feel about an arrangement giving Russia the principal military responsibility for Rumania and Britain the same in Greece. Hull disliked the idea because he disliked spheres of influence; they subjugated peoples and bred conflicts. Halifax returned with a message from Churchill saying the projected plan was for military purposes only. President Roosevelt warned that military agreements quickly hardened into permanent political demarcations. Churchill proposed a three months' trial for the Rumania-Greece proposal. Roosevelt bowed.

In October, 1944, accordingly, Churchill visited Stalin in the Kremlin and together they designed a strange and useless crazy quilt of political patches. They agreed, says Stettinius, to fix in percentages "the degree of influence each would have in the Balkans." The Soviet Union would have "75-25 or 80-20 predominance in Bulgaria, Hungary, and Rumania; Britain and Russia would share influence in Yugoslavia 50-50; and the British would have full responsibility in Greece."

Behind this fantastic arrangement lay a two-fold purpose: England hoped to prevent Russia from taking all; Stalin wanted foreign sanction for his new expansionism.

Mussolini, meanwhile, had been deposed by his own Grand Fascist Council and arrested on the King's order. The United States favored Victor Emmanuel's abdication, but Churchill wished to keep the King on his throne and Marshal Badoglio, the conqueror of Ethiopia, as Prime Minister. Stalin too upheld Badoglio and so, therefore, did the Italian Communists.

This looked like an emerging coalition between Churchill, Stalin, and Communists in the interests of royalty, reaction, and empire. To spoil the picture, the Greek Communists, no doubt with Stalin's connivance, rebelled against Britain's "full responsibility in Greece" and inaugurated a bloody civil war. In October, 1944, Stalin, having received from Churchill all that Churchill was ready to give at the moment in the Balkans, including British help for Tito and British recognition of Soviet imperialism, "gave" Greece to England. In December, 1944, he tried to take Greece away from England. This is Stalin's one-step-at-a-time gradualness.

Stalin also stretched out a long arm to embrace Poland. As far back as 1941, a group of Polish Communists in Moscow formed what became known as the Lublin Committee. In 1944, Stalin urged the United States and Great Britain to recognize these Red puppets as the government of a new Poland. America and Britain refused.

It was against this background of conflicting aims that Roosevelt, Churchill, and Stalin met at Yalta in the Crimea from February 4 to February 11, 1945.

Three big military facts dominated the Big Three conference:

1. The Red Army had conquered most of Poland and Hungary, was deep in Germany, and deep in the Balkans.
2. The Anglo-American forces had not yet crossed the Rhine into Germany.
3. The high American military leaders at Yalta believed that the

war in the Pacific would continue until 1947. It was estimated that U.S. armed services would suffer an additional million casualties if Russia did not join in defeating Japan.

Stalin knew these facts and knew how to squeeze every advantage out of them. He was also extremely shrewd. During a plenary session on the second day of the conference Stalin asked the President to express an opinion on how long the United States would keep occupation forces in Germany. "I can get the people and Congress to co-operate fully for peace," Roosevelt replied, "but not to keep an army in Europe for a long time. Two years would be the limit."

"Europe is mine," Stalin might have said in his heart when he heard that fateful declaration of the President.

Roosevelt's assessment of the popular mood was correct at the time. Whether he need have stated it is another question. The mood changed; American troops remained in Europe far more than two years after war's end. Their presence there indicated America's determination to prevent Russian domination of the Continent. That is why Stalin asked the question. When Roosevelt said "two years," Stalin decided he would sooner or later have Europe; that helped shape his strategy at the Yalta Conference.

Considering his superior military position, Stalin was relatively conciliatory at Yalta. Considering they needed Russia to crush Germany and Japan, Roosevelt and Churchill were rather firm.

Roosevelt, and especially Churchill, insisted that France receive a zone of occupation in Germany. Stalin did not want to admit France into the Big Three "exclusive club." "I cannot forget," he said, "that in this war France opened the gates to the enemy." He forgot that he had encouraged the enemy to attack the gates and that the Communists helped turn the key. After he agreed to a French zone in Germany cut out of the American and British zones, he fought French membership in the four-power Control Commission. Finally he approved.

The Three also discussed the dismemberment of Germany and, formally, came to no conclusion. But the harm had been done long before Yalta when the British, American, and Soviet governments agreed that, in the words of Eisenhower, "the British and American occupation zones would be limited on the east by a line two hundred miles west of Berlin."

Reparations, writes James F. Byrnes in his book, *Speaking Frankly,* "were the chief interest of the Soviet delegation" at Yalta as far as Germany was concerned. Stalin asked that Germany's indemnity be fixed at twenty billion dollars of which Russia would receive 50 per cent. France, he said, had not exerted herself very much in the war and therefore did not have first claim on damages. Quoting scriptures at the devil again, Churchill reminded Stalin of the Communist slogan, "To each according to his needs." If only exertion counted, America would receive reparations, but she did not need any; France did. Stalin failed to reply.

In the end, the figure of twenty billion dollars in reparations was accepted "as a basis for discussion." An Anglo-American-Russian reparations commission would sit in Moscow to fix the total and apportion the shares.

Poland was the knottiest issue before the Big Three at Yalta. Secretary of State Stettinius felt that "as a result of the military situation, it was not a question of what Great Britain and the United States would permit Russia to do in Poland, but what the two countries could persuade the Soviet Union to accept." The battlefield dictated, the statesmen obeyed. Stalin asked for the eastern half of Poland up to the old Curzon Line. Roosevelt hoped Eastern Galicia and its capital city of Lvov could remain inside Poland, but Stalin demurred. East Galicia was Ruthenian, or Ukrainian, and he thought its annexation would win him support among the Soviet Ukrainian nationalists. For the territory Poland forfeited to Russia she would receive compensation in Germany. How much territory? Churchill said Poland should not acquire too large a slice of Germany: "It would be a pity to stuff the Polish goose so full of German food that he will die of indigestion." If, moreover, the Polish frontier were pushed westward to the Neisse River, as Stalin wished, nine million Germans would have to emigrate to the truncated postwar Germany and create serious inconveniences for the Allies who would be administering it. Stalin did not mind. He may have foreseen what subsequently happened: the inconveniences, both economic and political, arising from the presence in Western Germany of about ten million German refugees from the East, bothered America and England, not him. Final delimitation of Poland's frontier with Germany was left to the future peace conference.

But the real question was: what kind of Poland? Stalin had already set up his Lublin puppets as the Polish government in Warsaw. Roosevelt and Churchill told him they would never recognize it. They asked that non-Communist Poles from inside Poland and from the Polish government-in-exile in London be merged with the Warsaw unrecognizables. They named the names of these persons. Stalin replied that he would have to consult the Warsaw Poles; he would have to talk to himself, in other words. He tried to get the Warsaw Poles on the telephone but could get no connection, he reported. Nevertheless, he yielded to the recommendation of the President and Prime Minister: non-Communists would be introduced into the Communist regime at Warsaw, and the resulting twin-personality government would, "as soon as possible," conduct "free and unfettered elections" on the basis of "universal suffrage and secret ballot."

Other decisions at Yalta concerned the Balkans, the voting procedure and the membership of the United Nations, Iran, and so forth.

As the Three conferred in Yalta, the doom of Germany was already sealed; in three months Hitler would be dead. In six months Japan too would be vanquished. But Roosevelt and Churchill did not know this. Their top military staff chiefs did not know it. General Douglas MacArthur did not know it; he is quoted by Secretary of the Navy James Forrestal as saying to him, in Manila, on February 28, 1945, shortly after Yalta, that "we should secure the commitment of the Russians to active and vigorous prosecution of a campaign against the Japanese in Manchukuo [Manchuria] of such proportions as to pin down a very large part of the Japanese army."

The military trusted incorrect intelligence data. Perhaps their judgment was faulty. But the fact is that in their pessimism, which they thought was realism, they ceaselessly pressed Roosevelt and

Churchill to bring Russia into the Far Eastern conflict as soon as feasible.

The mistake was in imagining that this would be difficult. Cordell Hull writes in his memoirs that as he was sitting on Stalin's right at a dinner in the Kremlin on October 30, 1943, the dictator turned to him and said, "When the Allies succeeded in defeating Germany, the Soviet Union would then join in defeating Japan." Stalin, Hull states, "brought up this subject entirely on his own," and authorized Mr. Hull to give the information to the President "in the strictest confidence."

Likewise at the very first session at Teheran in November, 1943, Stalin asserted that after Germany's defeat the necessary Russian military reinforcements would be sent to the Far East and, "We shall be able by our common front to beat Japan." Why then was it necessary to pay Stalin at Yalta to enter the war against Japan? In view of Stalin's dynamically imperialistic mood, very much in evidence at the Crimea Conference, it should have been clear to the Western statesmen, and military, that they would have to pay Stalin to stay out of the Pacific war. Yet they agreed to reward him for joining the war three months after the defeat of Hitler. Russia would receive the southern, Japanese, half of the island of Sakhalin, the "internationalized" port of Dairen, a leased naval base at Port Arthur, and joint control with China of the two trunk railways of Manchuria. This assured Stalin of effective dominion over Manchuria and inevitably weighted the scales toward a Communist China despite his promise to support Nationalist China. In addition, the Kurile Islands, which Russia had never possessed, were assigned to her.

Since Stalin likes written commitments from others, he had these terms typed out on a paper which he, Roosevelt, and Churchill signed at Yalta. On Stalin's request, the document remained secret.

"The mood of the delegates, including Roosevelt and Hopkins," writes Sherwood, "could be described as one of extreme exultation as they left Yalta." James Byrnes, who attended the conference as adviser to the President and took shorthand notes at the sessions, called Yalta "the high tide of Big Three unity." This is remarkable.

The delegates may have been helpless, but there was little reason for their being hopeful, much less exultant. All the portents of an arrogantly expansive Russia faced them at the ruined Crimean resort. Stalin's stand on Poland, Germany, the Balkans, and China should have made it obvious at Yalta that trouble with Russia was in store for the West. General John R. Deane, the head of the U.S. mission in Moscow, had reported that the Soviet government was unco-operative and suspicious. Yet his chiefs remained innocent. Part of this was due to the simple fact that many top officials did not understand Stalin and still thought of him as nice "Uncle Joe." The focus on Hitler apparently obstructed a correct view of Stalin. Few persons are capable of double rejection. The politicians were unable to reject Hitler *and* Stalin. It is especially difficult to reject a dictator with whom one is collaborating. The tendency is to clothe him with enough virtue to make him presentable in polite democratic society. But foreign clothes did not make Stalin. He behaved like Stalin.

Within a month of Yalta, Soviet Assistant Foreign Minister Andrei Vishinsky went to Bukharest to see the King of Rumania whom Moscow had recently decorated with the Order of Victory for switching sides from Hitler to Stalin. Vishinsky, looking at his wrist watch, gave King Michael an ultimatum: dismiss the Radescu cabinet and appoint one entirely subservient to Russia or lose your throne. Michael, not knowing that he would soon lose it anyway, complied.

In the same month, Foreign Minister Molotov demonstrated that the Yalta agreement for a Polish government combining Communists and non-Communists would be treated by the Kremlin as a scrap of irrelevant paper.

Churchill expressed his apprehensions in a wire to Roosevelt who replied that he too had been "watching with anxiety and concern the development of the Soviet attitude" since Yalta. On April 1, the President dispatched a stern telegram to Stalin stressing his distress over Polish affairs and saying that "a thinly disguised continuation of the present government" in Poland, which is what

Moscow wanted, "would be entirely unacceptable, and would cause our people to regard the Yalta agreement as a failure."

During the first week of April, Ambassador W. Averell Harriman sent several cables from Moscow, quoted in *The Forrestal Diaries*, advocating a "tough" policy toward Russia and suggesting that friendship be "always on a *quid pro quo* basis." The Russians, he said, regarded America's "generous and considerate attitude" as a sign of weakness.

The Yalta honeymoon was ended. Roosevelt and Churchill were engaged in an acrimonious dispute with Stalin. Suddenly, on April 12, 1945, President Roosevelt died.

How explain the extremely rapid deterioration after Yalta? Secretary of State Stettinius offered the thesis that Stalin "had difficulties with the Politbureau" and that "certain members of the Politbureau may well have taken the line that the Soviet Union had been virtually sold out at Yalta." Stettinius believed that Anthony Eden inclined to the same view. It ignores the character and methods of Mr. Joseph Stalin. The record of his career emphasizes the importance he attaches to the installment-plan technique. He takes what he can get when he can get it and waits for more. He never butts a stone wall with a bare head. When he meets an obstruction he climbs over it or rides around it. At Yalta Roosevelt and Churchill withheld 100 per cent approval of Stalin's program on Poland. He took 75 per cent. Insistence on all might have caused a rupture which he did not want. A little while later the remaining 25 per cent could be wrapped in the confusion of technicalities, personalities, misinterpreted texts, the double meanings of words, etc. Maybe this would yield some additional ground. He might have to surrender part of it under pressure. It could be retrieved later. All these stratagems were employed by the Generalissimo in Poland and the end effect is a Russian colony without "free and unfettered elections" or a secret ballot.

Moreover, reports had reached Moscow of fierce anti-Communist opposition in Rumania and Poland. This made it imperative for Stalin to deny the West the limited influence which the Yalta decisions gave them in those countries. He felt he had to act with speed because shortly after Yalta the military situation became fluid. The Western armies were now advancing rapidly into Germany, and Stalin did not know where they would stop. The Germans might open the front to the Anglo-Americans and resist only the Russians. If the Western armies moved too close to Poland, Rumania, Czechoslovakia, and Hungary Stalin's plans to hold those nations might have been threatened. He therefore hastily consolidated his position in them even though this involved a breach of the Yalta agreements.

Nevertheless, Stalin tried not to alienate the West's friendship. In January, 1945, Molotov had handed Ambassador Harriman a memorandum proposing a six-billion-dollar, fifty-year American loan to Russia with a view, as Molotov put it, to reducing unemployment in the United States. The memorandum listed the machinery, notably heavy railway equipment, which the Soviet Union would, under the terms of the loan, be ready to accept in order to aid American capitalism during the expected postwar depression.

Stalin accordingly maneuvered deftly, taking what he wanted in contravention of his Yalta pledges yet trying to keep American good will. He wanted the loan. Above all, he was intent on fighting Japan, and American hostility might have interfered.

But Harriman was already completely convinced that relations with Russia would go from bad to worse. Visiting Washington in April to consult President Truman, Harriman warned that if Stalin entered China to fight Japan he would entrench himself there. "How urgent is the necessity for quick Russian participation in the war against Japan?" Harriman inquired.

Other skeptics appeared. In July, 1945, General Eisenhower went to Antwerp to meet the cruiser bringing President Truman and Secretary of State Byrnes to the Potsdam Big Three conference. "I told him [the President]," Eisenhower writes in *Crusade in Europe,* "that since reports indicated the imminence of Japan's collapse I deprecated the Red Army's engaging in that war. I foresaw certain difficulties arising out of such participation. . . ."

At Potsdam, Stalin was cruder than in Teheran and Yalta. He demanded Turkish territory and rights over the Dardanelles which would have made Turkey a Russian vassal. He asked for a colony in North Africa. He showed that he would do as he pleased in Poland and the Balkans, make trouble in Greece, and endeavor to spread his power over Germany. "We thought, however," Secretary Byrnes writes, "that we had established a basis for maintaining our war-born unity." The thought was deplorable. "We" should not have been blind and deaf. The idea of "unity" among national states is rather illusory at all times, and in relation to Stalin's Soviet Union it flew in the face of visible, audible circumstances.

Politicians, of course, do not work in a vacuum. They operate in the atmosphere of their countries. Two factors dominated the international democratic climate in 1945: (1) the desire, especially in America, to bring the soldiers back from Europe; (2) a widespread and profound admiration of Russia's performance in the war which protected Stalin from much adverse criticism in the United States and Great Britain. Some persons who foresaw the coming rift with Russia found themselves quite unpopular. This being the case it is noteworthy that the American and British leaders resisted Stalin at Potsdam as much as they did.

In Yalta Stalin had said he did not believe that England ever would have a Labour government. His dogma taught him that the capitalist class would not surrender power except under the compulsion of revolution; the bourgeoisie would yield to bullets, not ballots. Stalin must have been very surprised, therefore, when Churchill and Eden left Potsdam in mid-conference to vote in the British national elections and did not return. In their places, two days later, came Labour Prime Minister Clement R. Attlee and Labour Foreign Minister Ernest Bevin who proved to be no less anti-Communist than their Tory predecessors. Together with President Truman and Secretary Byrnes they stood firm against the Soviet attempt to achieve domination of Turkey, a foothold in the Mediterranean, and partial control of the Ruhr industrial area in Germany which normally would produce more steel than Russia. Nobody has next year's hindsight. If the Western statesmen at Potsdam can be accused of anything it is that they were not responsive to their own forebodings. They pitted their rosy hopes against black facts. Their hopes were father to the thought of unity. The record should have made them expect acrid rivalry.

The Potsdam illusions brought disaster to Asia. During the conference Stalin was pantingly, frantically eager to enter the war against Japan. He had concealed from America two Japanese offers to surrender. From Potsdam an Anglo-American-Chinese warning went out to Japan to capitulate before the homeland suffered "utter destruction." Stalin tried to delay it. The facts are stated in Byrnes's *Speaking Frankly*. Stalin feared that Japan might indeed surrender before Russia could make territorial gains in Asia.

Eisenhower, but not the Combined Chiefs of Staff, expected Japan's early collapse. Harriman suspected Stalin's motives in China. The atom bomb was about to be used on Hiroshima. Yet Mr. Byrnes did his best to facilitate and hasten Soviet participation in the Far Eastern conflict.

The first atomic bomb was dropped August 6; the second, on Nagasaki, August 8; Russia declared war August 9; Japan offered to surrender August 10; the war ended officially August 14.

Russia was in the Japanese war for five days, at most. This did not embarrass Stalin in showing Byrnes a film in Moscow in December, 1945, that depicted how Russia won the Eastern war and how Japan signed the terms of surrender on an unnamed battleship with none but Russian victors. Those five unnecessary days gave Stalin commanding strength in North Korea and Manchuria and altered the power relationships in the Pacific. A more skillful hand at Potsdam might easily have barred rather than smoothed Russia's entry into the war. Quick military action, by paratroopers if need be, could have forestalled an illegal Soviet invasion. The world would thus have been spared much pain and blood in Korea and elsewhere. Stalin had luck.

At long last, the costly Second World War was now finished. Russia had become a mighty power in Europe and Asia, far mightier than when the war began in 1939. What would Stalin choose to do?

CHAPTER XXIII

The Doodler

During the war Stalin's personality enjoyed fullest expression and soared to great heights. Wartime leadership gave free rein to his talents for organization, regimentation, hate, destruction, deception, and diplomatic maneuvering. It also put an enormous physical and nervous strain on him.

There is considerable restlessness in Stalin. He cannot sit still at meetings, and he likes to doodle. During the six-and-a-quarter hour interview which I attended in 1927 he did sit still, and did not draw. But with time the tendency to wander and sketch has grown, and especially in the war years and afterward his visitors noticed a propensity in him to doodle.

In September, 1941, Lord Beaverbrook saw Stalin make "numberless pictures of wolves" with black pencil and then fill in the background with red. Their significance is anybody's guess. Subconscious self-portrait perhaps.

When Eric Johnston visited Stalin in 1944, Stalin doodled on a large white sheet of paper. "During the interview," Johnston writes, "he drew wolves, girls, castles, geometric designs until the page was filled. He then folded the paper carefully from bottom to top, doodled again, repeated the process, until the paper was folded to a narrow strip. Then he threw it away and started all over again. I noticed that his hands were square, powerful, with well-manicured fingernails. He didn't look at me. He was absent-mindedly interested in the pencil marks on his paper."

Mr. Johnston may have been annoyed by Stalin's preoccupation with the paper and pencil, but at one point the drawings began to fascinate him too, and he thought he discerned the silhouette of a young woman in a tortured position. He asked Stalin whether this was a representation of "Miss America" during an economic depression.

"No," Stalin replied rather apologetically, "I am just playing. I am not trying to draw anything specific." After that, Stalin stopped doodling and paid more attention to the interview. Mr. Johnston's remarks may have inhibited the subconscious.

General Walter Bedell Smith, U.S. Ambassador in Moscow, also comments on Stalin's doodling in 1946. "His drawings," General Smith reports, "repeated many times, looked to me like lopsided hearts done in red, with a small question mark in the middle."

Wolves are a favorite and so is red. Repetitiveness is especially accentuated in Stalin's psychological art work.

Psychologists and psychoanalysts agree that doodling is an expression of the unconscious and subconscious. Stalin is a complicated person. To say that he is cruel is to simplify. Cruelty may result from fear. Stalin is full of fears, repression, and aggression.

CHAPTER XXIV

Self-portrait

One of the secrets of Stalin's personality seems to be a desire to substitute an unreal Stalin for the real one. It is as though he were unhappy about his true self and hoped, by his control of all Soviet media of communication, to be reborn with different attributes. Almighty ruler, he is not satisfied with having recreated Russia in his image; he would recreate himself in a more appealing image.

Stalin is free from criticism, control, and penalty, free from the checks imposed by law, theory, and morality. He is the only free man in Russia. Yet his natural habitat is behind a wall. Whether this is due to fear or policy, the effect is to make him a little-known person who therefore is uninhibited in the use of colors and contours for a self-portrait.

To the many, Stalin is a photograph, a hunk of clay, words on a piece of paper, an actor who plays him on the stage or in the films. They delineate the official legend. They present the person Stalin aspires to be.

Stalin is that rare man who can paint himself as he wishes. None will dare to contradict or correct.

It is not unusual for a man to be one thing to his employees and another to his children, or one thing to his public and another to his stenographer. Every politician has an official side which differs from his private self. But nobody can shield that image so successfully as Stalin does from the melting glare of the searchlight or the strictures of an opponent or the revelations of an intimate. Behind this immunity, the Soviet propaganda machine enjoys complete liberty to enlarge, embellish, and subtract, in a word to sculpt the heroic idol according to Stalin's meticulous specifications. It conforms to his idea of the perfect Stalin.

The outstanding feature of Stalin's self-portraiture is flight from reality. This starts with the radical retouching of his photographs and ends by attributing almost godlike qualities to him.

Soviet laboratories remove all pockmarks and most wrinkles from photographs of Stalin's face. Drawings erase the lines around his eyes, especially near his left eye, which spell cunning and guile; they elongate his head, straighten his receding forehead, square his shoulders, and fill out his chest. The look in the eye becomes direct and stern but loses its hardness. The artist's pencil or brush takes at least fifteen years off his present age. He seems tall, youthful, beautiful, attractive.

Stalin's disposition to be something he isn't, and to wear a disguise which might evoke an illusion, began to show long ago. Russian revolutionists often adopted party names to mislead the police but more generally to signalize a break with the past. Thus Ulyanov became Lenin, Bronstein Trotsky, Skryabin Molotov. Almost everybody used one pseudonym throughout his life. Stalin used more than ten. The nickname he preferred in his early career was "Koba." Koba, the hero of a novel called *The Patricides* by Alexander Kazbegi, a Georgian author, was a romantic mountaineer, an Alpine Robin Hood. That, at the moment, was Stalin's dream figure. When this pretension, redolent with sentiment, appeared too limiting to its unsentimental bearer, Djugashvili dropped "Koba" and rechristened himself "Stalin" which, being a Russian word, has a national rather than local, Georgian, connotation. It reflects a more sober yet equally ambitious self-evaluation, a realistic sense of what he was plus a dream, charged with hope, of the peaks to be scaled. As "Stalin" he met the 1917 revolution.

For several years after the revolution, while Lenin lived, Stalin seemed to revel in being secondary. He was all modesty, compliance, and submissiveness. But Lenin's eye pierced the mask of retiring self-effacement and detected the ominous signs of grandiose self-aggrandizement.

Stalin always plays two roles. He fills both imperfectly, yet neither is alien: the revolutionist is a theological student; the Georgian is a Russian nationalist; the Communist is an imperialist;

the humble servant of Lenin hides a hunger for orgiastic glorification. Subservience is a camouflage for the amassing of power.

When he had acquired the power to satisfy his appetite for glorification there began the systematic distortion which, in the last quarter of a century, has given Russia a retailored Stalin. What it most resembles is a juvenile's dreams of glory come true. He springs full-blown into the revolutionary movement. The official Soviet biography of Stalin, 243 pages long, devotes the first 16 lines to birth, childhood, and youth, and then suddenly he is a revolutionist. When he joins a study circle he immediately becomes the teacher. When there is a street demonstration he heads it, his chest bared to the bullets that are not discharged. In a strike, he leads. He was never a subordinate, according to the myth.

Stalin goes to the Bolshevik party conference in Finland in 1905. He was in fact an unimportant delegate. A painting, now widely reproduced, shows him talking to an informal group of leaders, of whom Lenin is one. They listen with rapt attention and Lenin looks as though nothing could be more important than to know what Stalin thinks. A similar canvas of the 1907 London congress depicts Lenin bending over to hear every precious word of Stalin's.

This was glory indeed, but it is nothing compared to what the riotous imagination does with Stalin's part in the revolution. October, 1917, Lenin returns from his hiding place to the capital. As he enters the Smolny Institute, headquarters of the Bolshevik party, he presses his hand on Stalin's shoulder. Stalin, handsome in semi-military uniform, is the only political lieutenant present. Other figures are soldiers and sailors. Obviously, to judge by this proletarian art, Lenin needed Stalin's support.

Further proof is found in a current film. Lenin sits in the Smolny baffled by a problem. Stalin, a popular actor, stands over him. "What would you do, Comrade Stalin?" Lenin says twisting his head around. Calmly, smilingly, Stalin removes the pipe from his mouth and speaks a few quiet words of wisdom. Yes, Lenin agrees, that is the solution.

The text of the official biography which, necessarily, is also a history of Soviet Russia, mentions only Lenin and Stalin, and the generals in the Second World War; all other names are those of enemies. Stalin worsted them in single combat, the lone knight aided by impersonal forces such as the party and the true doctrine. This is "Koba" in steel armor, Robin Hood with machine guns.

"Stalin is Lenin today" runs the theme song of Soviet propaganda. Stalin is Lenin. This has an element of tragedy. In 1917 Lenin was little known in Russia. He led the country through three and a half years of painful civil war, then three more years of hard times. During the succeeding decades Stalin has built up a tremendous chain of new industries and cities, revolutionized agriculture, enormously expanded educational facilities, and raised a new generation to whom Lenin is only a remote reputation. Yet Stalin is not Stalin, he is Lenin. This may seem like humility, and it could be. It suggests a consciousness of inadequacy, a feeling that as himself he would not reach the hearts and minds of the people. The real Stalin, with all the face-lifting, plastic surgery, literary falsification, and artistic inventiveness remains, in Stalin's view, unpresentable. A quarter century of glorification, which exaggerates every quality and achievement, still does not suffice to pile-drive Stalin into the affections of the country. The suitor fears that the courtship will fail unless the maid is made to think that he is not he but the lover who died.

Stalin likewise encourages comparisons with Ivan the Terrible and Peter the Great. They have been whitewashed and exalted by the literary and cinematographic hirelings of Stalinism into crowned rulers who regretfully performed unpleasant tasks and inflicted cruelty on the nation for its own good, obviously. The masses hated it while it lasted, but the reward of those Czars is in the heaven of history. That is where Stalin may expect his reward. He is raising Russia to greatness; why count the current victims? That is the implication of Stalin's identification, through fiction and films, with Peter and Ivan who, accordingly, is no longer called the Terrible but the Fourth.

Stalin is clear-eyed enough to recognize his need of a self-portrait which is actually a composite personality-photograph of Lenin, royalty, and historic field marshals. Yet the output of the myth-grinding Soviet propaganda machine shows that he has other thoughts too. Stalin combines a sense of inferiority with megalomania. The legend-makers suggest that nobody who ever lived in Russia was greater than Stalin. He himself has said, in sorrow of course, that he accomplished more than Lenin. Indeed, who in world history can compare with Stalin? Genghis Khan? His empire crumbled. Napoleon? A failure. Hitler? A suicide. The Roosevelts, the Churchills? They are run-of-the-mill, passing phenomena. Stalin the Great builds for eternity and differently. He created a new world. If full recognition is still withheld it is because humanity does not yet know that when Stalin jumped into the sea of history he started a wave which will engulf and drown those who deny him. His hatred is as high and icy as the summits of the Himalayas and is generously applied to all; for mankind without exception, even his closest co-workers, force him to work unceasingly on a self-portrait which is never Stalin. That is the ultimate in rejection; there could be no greater rejection.

Rejection may be the key to Stalin's life. His father rejected him. Lenin rejected him in his last testament; Trotsky was the mirror of that rejection. Stalin's wife rejected him by committing suicide. The Russian people reject him though he tries to identify himself with them. The world rejects him. Family brought him no love. Conquest brings him no friends. The most powerful man on earth cannot command a single heart.

Stalin arouses hate and anger. He is to be pitied. He is an outcast; outcast in a castle. He has isolated himself from humanity, and humanity has isolated him. He is powerful and insecure, omnipotent yet unloved, "infallible" yet afraid, afraid to be seen for what he is, so afraid of his true self that he envelops himself in a cloak designed to make him an invisible man. He can only resent this. It could explain his insatiable passion for power over others and his inexhaustible drive.

CHAPTER XXV

Stalin's Postwar Blueprint

Humanity was hungry for peace after the Second World War. The United States demobilized. Britain liberated India and turned inward to mend her broken economy. Stalin had the friendship of America, Europe, and Asia, and could have kept it. The governments would excuse his land grabs. In effect, at Teheran, Yalta, and Potsdam, they had.

Why should a new antagonism have flared so soon?

In Europe, the Soviet empire has not advanced beyond the line held by the Red Army when the Second World War ended. Within that perimeter, Stalin has, at varying times and speeds, merely consolidated the power which was inevitably his as a result of military victory. Nothing indicates that the United States or Britain would have gone to war, or taken less drastic action, to reduce the percentage of Soviet domination over Czechoslovakia, Hungary, Poland, or Bulgaria. The fact is they did not. They were powerless and they knew it and were reluctantly reconciled to living with the enlarged Soviet empire. No foreign nation was in a position or mood to dispute Russia's wartime expansions. Stalin could have had his present European satellites and Western friendship too.

Other possibilities were open to Stalin. He could forfeit Western friendship and expand.

The temptation to expand was great: American troops leaving Europe by the shipload every day; England in the depths of an economic crisis; Greece fighting a civil war; Germany in dissolution and rubble; Communists riding high in France and Italy; China divided between Nationalists and Communists; Hindu-Moslem dissension rampant in India; Arabs and Jews at loggerheads in Palestine. No place for the dove of peace to come to rest. The Red Army in Berlin and Vienna. In six days it could be anywhere in Europe.

That Stalin did not order his soldiers to march in 1946 and 1947 shows his restraint and reveals his concepts. He did not wish to invest Soviet military personnel in expansion. The American atomic bomb may also have served as a deterrent. But the chief factor was probably his belief that after an exhausting war, and before the world could regain hope and conservatism, some capitalist countries would go Communist and thereby give Russia an additional advantage in the long-term struggle between the soviet and non-soviet systems of society.

In postwar talks with Harold E. Stassen, Eric A. Johnston, and others Stalin made it clear that he expected a serious economic depression to develop in America in conformity with his doctrinaire principles. That would have accelerated capitalist decay in Europe and Asia.

But Russia was exhausted. Extensive areas had been churned up and laid waste as million-headed armies marched to and fro over the land. Soviet casualties, officially admitted to include seven million dead, no doubt numbered fifteen million military and civilian dead and perhaps thirty million wounded and incapacitated. It was not till November 7, 1944, that Stalin dared to honor the dead. "Eternal glory," he exclaimed, "to the heroes fallen in battle for the freedom and independence of the fatherland." Too many had fallen; aggressive military adventures were unthinkable.

Stalin put his trust in Communist penetration, capitalist economic collapse, civil wars, and Soviet "nonintervention." These could augment his power.

In the 1930's, Stalin was a pessimist about Russia's chances to prove her superiority in competition with the rest of the world. The war, with its heady victory, made him somewhat more optimistic. Russia would survive. Capitalism might even succumb.

The polarization of the world toward Russia and America, which Stalin had foretold in his interview with the American group in 1927, was now a fact. Until 1939, Russia's only preparation for the historic duel of the colossi was domestic construction. Since then Stalin had subtracted a large area from the capitalist world and added it to his own. But he needed further gains before the scales would be tipped against America.

It seems that a period of uncertainty intervened for Stalin immediately after the Second World War. He saw the opportunity and need to make new gains abroad, but he hesitated to apply force. Yet he began to turn his back on Russia's allies. Peace had hardly commenced when the Soviet press attacked Great Britain. For several months, however, America remained in favor. In September, 1945, the United States too became the object of vituperation. Yet the floodgates of antiforeign propaganda were not yet wide open. Indecision apparently dominated the upper Bolshevik counsels.

"In the many talks I had with Stalin I felt that he himself was of two minds," Ambassador Harriman revealed at Los Angeles on April 30, 1951; the alternatives, according to Mr. Harriman, were: (1) building for prosperity at home with foreign help, or (2) "external expansion" which would antagonize the West.

Harriman wished to know which of Stalin's "two minds" would prevail. "In October, 1945," he reports, "I went to see Stalin in his country place in Sochi in the Caucasus."

The Ambassador traveled south with his American interpreter and on arrival at Sochi was given a house several miles from Stalin's estate and a car for use during his stay. Stalin received Harriman twice in a large office; on each occasion they remained together, with their translators, for four hours, from 7 P.M. to 11 P.M. Stalin never hurries his foreign visitors; they may linger as long as he feels they have something to say.

Stalin served no food or drink to Harriman. They discussed numerous aspects of the world situation and particularly Russo-American relations. "After two long nights of arguments over the disagreements we were having, he as much as told me in a moment of anger," Harriman has stated publicly, "that he had decided to go his own way."

Years later Harriman commented especially on Stalin's word "decided." Two minds had become one. "America was isolationist after the First World War," Stalin said to Harriman. "We will be isolationist after the Second."

A slight duality nevertheless continued to manifest itself in Stalin's postwar political line. It showed in his speech of February 9, 1946. The speech was a milestone in history and a searchlight into Stalin's thoughts, particularly since he took the long view and defined Russia's plans for the next fifteen or twenty years. Only six months had passed since the defeat of Japan. Outwardly at least, Stalin's attitude toward the Western powers remained one of friendship. The democracies, he said—and this reversed his lies of 1939, 1940, and 1941 which were repeated at the time by foreign Communist parrots—had been attacked by the Fascist aggressors. "The Second World War against the Axis powers, unlike the First World War," Stalin declared, "assumed from the very outset the character of an anti-Fascist war, a war of liberation, one of the tasks of which was to restore democratic liberties. The entry of the Soviet Union into the war against the Axis powers could only augment—and really did augment—the anti-Fascist and liberating character of the Second World War." The speech contains no word of complaint or criticism which would diminish these friendly references to his wartime allies.

"This war," Stalin continued, "was the fiercest and most arduous ever fought in the history of the motherland. But the war was not only a curse." It tested the Soviet system, he explained, and the system passed the test. "More than that. . . ." Stalin asserted, "the Soviet social system has proved to be more viable and stable than the non-Soviet social system . . . the Soviet social system is a better form of organization of society than any non-Soviet social system." Why it was better than the British system or the American system which had also won the war and, in addition, helped Russia to win with billions of dollars' worth of their industrial products, he did not say.

The Communists had known long ago, which means he had known, Stalin affirmed, "that war was approaching, that it would be impossible to defend the country without heavy industry, that it was necessary to set to work to develop heavy industry as quickly as possible, and that to be belated in this matter meant courting defeat." From 1928 to 1941, therefore, Russia had concentrated on heavy industry. Hence victory.

What now were his plans for the future? "As regards long-term plans," he announced, "our party intends to organize another powerful upswing of our national economy that will enable us to raise our industry to a level, say, three times as high as that of prewar industry. We must see to it that our industry shall be able to produce annually up to fifty million tons of pig iron, up to sixty million tons of steel, up to five hundred million tons of coal, and up to sixty million tons of oil. Only when we succeed in doing that can we be sure that our motherland will be insured against all contingencies. This will need, perhaps, another three Five-Year Plans, if not more. But it can be done, and we must do it."

Stalin was calling on the Soviet people to work hard until 1960 or later to produce not things to wear, or to eat, or to live in, but iron, steel, coal, and oil "against all contingencies," in other words, for armaments. The country was tired, the people were spent, they had fought in the hope that life after victory would be better. Instead Stalin demanded more strain and striving.

Stalin has said many times that heavy industry—iron, coal, steel, oil—makes a nation strong, and a strong Russia is the monument he desires. Moreover, given his dogma of conflict, he may believe that in fifteen or more years the Soviet system will face another test, another war to decide the contest between the Soviet and non-Soviet systems. Meanwhile, added industrial and military power would cow the satellites, reinforce Moscow's diplomatic arm, encourage foreign Communists, and perhaps win a minor war instigated by Moscow but fought by a colony.

Heavy industrialization meant a further postponement, for more than a decade, of the relaxation and better living which the Soviet population craved after the horrors of war. "Soviet persons," Andrei Zhdanov, top member of the Politbureau, said on November 6, 1946, "are accustomed to put the interests of the national state above all else. They are accustomed to regard the common cause as their own private cause." Custom or compulsion, Zhdanov's words showed what the Kremlin expected: more sacrifices.

The Soviet people had no easy way of refusing the sacrifice, yet their incentive to work hard would depend, especially in view of the scarcity of consumer goods, on the degree of their conviction that the continued emphasis on war preparations was necessary. Soviet citizens had seen the food, arms, and other materials given free of charge to Russia by America and Britain. Millions of Red soldiers had seen foreign countries and brought back neither hostility nor revulsion. Quite the contrary; they found that Kremlin propaganda had lied to them about the extent of capitalist antagonism to Russia. Two million Soviet citizens taken out of Russia by Hitler as prisoners or slave laborers were so favorably impressed by the bourgeois world, despite its rubble, that they tried to desert, but the Allies, under a Yalta agreement, returned a million and a half of them. Five hundred thousand did become Soviet "displaced persons" abroad, permanent, voluntary exiles from Stalinism.

After the war, the Moscow press began publishing contemptuous articles about the rottenness of Rumania. The glitter is not gold, they warned the Soviet soldier on foreign duty. Even the tarnished tinsel of the Balkans seemed to attract men bred in drabness and fed on privations. Russians returning from Nazi prisoner-of-war camps were not allowed to go home but sent to "re-education centers."

Stalin wanted to cleanse his people of any kindly feeling for the givers of Lend-Lease and toward the outside world in general. He himself had been surprised by Lend-Lease and thought he had to pay for it. Friendship, when, according to dogma, the capitalist West might have united with Hitler to crush communism, puzzled Stalin. It delighted the country.

Now, in the postwar period, capitalist friendship for Soviet Russia had to be denied or explained away or forgotten. American businessmen made millions shipping sausage to Russia while Soviet soldiers gave their blood, Alexei Surkov sang in an ode "To a Chicago Manufacturer," written in 1942 but published in the July, 1947, issue of the Moscow *Novi Mir*. The Chicagoan was a "jackal," the Russian soldier a "lion." That exemplified the postwar Stalinist attitude to Lend-Lease. Hate instead of gratitude.

How, the Kremlin argued, could capitalists be true well-wishers of a Soviet state? The acceptance of capitalists as permanent collaborators of Communists would have left the Kremlin without a target for invective, without a source of hate, and without a spur to popular incentive.

Dictatorship is tension. A country under a dictatorship is like a powerhouse that continuously shivers and throbs. Stalin tries to give his people a sense of urgency, of emergency. "No time to relax," he is always saying. Relaxation would be fatal to a dictatorship.

Two days before Stalin's speech of February 9, 1946, Lazar Kaganovitch, a Politbureau member, said in Moscow, "Our country continues to be within a capitalist encirclement. Therefore there is no place for complacency. We must not relax." The Soviet leadership obviously feared a postwar letdown.

Stalin must have been at the peak of his form during the war—after he was sure he would not lose. War provides the perfect climate for a dictator. It requires maximum discipline and generates maximum tension. It justifies the hard hand of the ruler. He thrives in the atmosphere of violence. He takes all and need give nothing.

Peace, so eagerly sought, so dearly bought, threatened to become a political and emotional vacuum in which Stalin would suffocate. He had to fill it quickly with the air of war, cold war, rumors of war, preparations for war.

A dictatorship must have enemies. If they are at hand it inflates them. If they are absent it creates them to have an excuse for the terror, hardships, and tension. Stalin told Henri Barbusse, his French Communist biographer, that he would have abolished the death penalty but for the enmity of the capitalist world. In the 1950's, Stalin said several times that while of course the state should wither away under socialism, the Soviet Socialist state could not wither away, it had to grow, because Russia was "encircled" by enemies. Foreign foes are cited to explain the rigors of the all-powerful despotism.

In the fourteen years I lived in Soviet Russia I saw one enemy succeed the other as the official warrant for the dictatorship: first there were the Soviet-made petty capitalists or Nepmen of the cities and the relatively prosperous peasants or kulaks, then Trotsky, then the sabotaging engineers, then Zinoviev, Kamenev, Bukharin, Rykov, and Tomsky, then the other defendants in the Moscow "trials," then spies, diversionists, "wreckers," counterrevolutionaries, and so forth, and always Germany and Japan. During 1939 and 1940, when Germany and Japan were Russia's "friends," Stalin used England, France, and America as enemies.

In 1946, Stalin could no longer avow the existence of hostile elements at home. Germany and Japan had been crushed. Amicable relations with America, England, France, and the rest of the non-Soviet world would have left Russia with no enemies, with no excuse for the guns-instead-of-meat-and-houses program of heavy industrialization. Stalin soon found that he could not maintain tension within the country if he did not maintain tension with other countries. The needs of the Soviet dictatorship determine the nature of Soviet foreign policy. Postwar industrialization and the desire to eradicate the people's warm sentiments for the West dictated the isolationism which Stalin had announced to Harriman.

Gromyko's glum face and Vishinsky's rasping voice at United Nations meetings are the visual and auditory reflection of Stalin's wish to cut Russia off from friendship. They could smile and coo if he pressed a different-colored button. Even the peace propaganda of the Communists reeks with calculated hatred. "Peace or we will pillory and destroy you," is the bellicose spirit of the Communist peace campaign. Moscow had gone to the length of altering the size and shape of the dove of peace. The French, whose humor is so sharp you cannot feel the blade till it has passed through, have drawn a picture of this changed creature; it is huge and steel-plated and its beak is a cannon's mouth. They call it "The Dove That Goes BOOM."

Communist "peace" agitation converts the dove of peace into a parrot of Bolshevik hate-mongering. Pacifism and humanism are repugnant to the Communists. In their mouth, "peace" is a battle-cry, a military weapon. They say "peace" with a hiss and without human kindness.

Communist hate merges with Stalin's aversion to the West which is kin to the traditional contempt of the Slav "Easterners" for Europe. Together they erect a barrier between Russia and the West; they stimulate a desire to benefit from Western decadence. Messianic Slavism, married to Bolshevik antihumanism, has produced twins: Isolation and Expansion, who look very much like Czarist children.

General Walter Bedell Smith, United States Ambassador in Moscow, put a direct question to Stalin on April 4, 1946. "What does the Soviet Union want, and how far is Russia going to go?" General Smith asked.

Nine months after the close of the war, suspicion was already rife.

In reply, Stalin talked about Iran and the exposed position of the Baku oil fields. "Beria [the head of the Soviet secret police]," Stalin said, "and others tell me that saboteurs—even a man with a box of matches—might cause us serious damages. We are not going to risk our oil supply." This implied the need of annexing Iranian territory as a protection for Soviet territory, but how that would keep away the man with a box of matches Stalin did not explain. His agents had already set up a puppet Soviet government in the Iranian province of Azerbaijan.

Stalin also alluded to hostility in England and America toward Russia. "Is it possible that you really believe that the United States and Great Britain are united in an alliance to thwart Russia?" Smith demanded.

"Yes," Stalin replied curtly.

The Ambassador denied it.

At the end of the interview, General Smith still had no answer to his original question. "How far is Russia going to go?" he repeated.

"We are not going much further," Stalin stated.

"You say 'not much further,' but does that 'much' have reference to Turkey?"

On March 19, 1945, the Soviet government had unilaterally denounced the 1925 Russo-Turkish treaty of friendship and nonaggression. On June 7, 1945, Foreign Minister Molotov summoned Turkish Ambassador Selim Sarper and told him that the Soviet government laid claim to the Turkish provinces of Kars and Ardahan and to joint control over the Dardanelles. Stalin repeated the same demands to President Truman at Potsdam in July, 1945. It was these Russian measures which aroused the West's concern for Turkey and prompted General Smith's questions to the Generalissimo.

Stalin promised not to make war on Turkey, but he said, "The Turkish government is unfriendly to us. That is why the Soviet Union has demanded a base in the Dardanelles. It is a matter of our security." Stalin added that Russia was ready to accept a United Nations mandate over Turkey. This would have been a polite disguise for annexation.

Every conqueror justifies his brigandage against "unfriendly" nations on the grounds of "security." Hitler did so repeatedly. The imperialist takes one piece of territory to protect the territory he already has, then he requires the next piece of territory to protect the new territory, then he wants the adjoining area for further "security," and so on till somebody is frightened by endless land grabs, and then it is war. That is how the Second World War came.

In his conferences with Roosevelt, Churchill, and Truman, Stalin made no secret of his utter contempt for and impatience with weak countries; they belonged within the sphere of influence of one of the three great powers. The Soviet-Nazi pact of August, 1939, was a spheres-of-influence treaty and so was the 1944 Stalin-Churchill agreement on the Balkans. The power-man never understands why available power should not be used against the powerless.

General Smith indicated to Stalin that the United States would not permit Turkey to be subjugated. Turkey was too much "much"; if Turkey fell under Russian domination, Greece and the Middle East would follow. The Ambassador's statement is historic, for in the Czarist period it was England that had prevented Russia from seizing Turkey and coming out into the Mediterranean. After 1945, Great Britain lacked the strength to cope with Russian aggression. The role descended upon America. But for American power the Soviet government could submerge any nation in Europe or Asia.

That explains the special, unremitting virulence of Russia's anti-American propaganda.

The present Soviet empire results from the weakening of England and France and the disappearance of Germany, Italy, and Japan as great powers. Politics is as hostile to a vacuum as nature. Stalin moved into the power vacuums created by the war. He did that during the war. He thought he could go further after the war. There were signs of incipient vacuums in Turkey, Greece, China, and Germany, and social portents in Italy and France which could only have encouraged Stalin. The withdrawal of American troops from Europe two years after the war and an economic depression in the United States, both expected by Stalin, would have perfected Russia's opportunity for further expansion.

Stalin's postwar policy of trying to bite off bits of the outside world—Turkey in 1945; a piece of Iran in 1946; Berlin, by means of blockade, in 1948; South Korea in 1950—was sure to widen the gulf between Russia and the "enemy." This suited Stalin's purpose. He intended to isolate his empire. On July 4, 1947, the Czechoslovak Cabinet decided unanimously to accept the invitation to attend the preliminary Marshall Plan conference in Paris. Five days later, summoned to Moscow to see Stalin, the Czech Foreign Minister Jan Masaryk and other members of the Czech government obeyed the dictator's orders and rejected the invitation. Under the same iron pressure the Yugoslav and Polish governments reversed their decisions to join the Marshall Plan. Stalin knew that collaboration between America and the satellites would weaken his monopoly hold on them and offer them a choice of markets and loyalties.

When Georgi Dimitrov, the celebrated Communist hero of the Leipzig Reichstag Fire trial, and later Moscow-appointed Prime Minister of Bulgaria, suggested in 1946 and 1947 that Bulgaria unite in a South-Slav federation with Communist Yugoslavia he was reprimanded by the Moscow *Pravda* because Bulgaria had not yet been completely assimilated by Russia, and Yugoslavia was already restive under the Muscovite boot; Stalin therefore feared that in union the two would find the strength to break away from the Soviet "motherland." But shortly thereafter, when Bulgaria had been subjugated while Yugoslavia was getting ready to escape from his embrace, Stalin astutely reversed his position and favored the federation of docile Bulgaria with Yugoslavia as a means of holding the latter in the empire. At the same time he brought the independent Dimitrov to Russia to die. The policy varies, the purpose is always total identification of the colonies with Russia and their total isolation from the outside world.

He also isolates Russia. The campaign of hate for the West, and first for the United States, is accompanied by repeated misstatements that Russian art and culture down the ages took nothing from the West and that Russian science was equally autonomous, indeed superior. Not Marconi invented the wireless but Popoff, a Russian, is the Soviet claim; not Edison made the first electric bulb, but Yablochkov, a Russian; a Russian named Paul Schilling invented the telegraph, and Russians also invented the steam engine, the loom, the airplane, the helicopter, the lighter-than-air balloon, the submarine, and the internal combustion engine.

The purpose of this childish game is to feed Russian national vanity but more particularly to demonstrate that the Soviet Union has no need of foreign cultural or scientific contacts. Actually, Moscow watches the outside scientific world avidly, and borrows, buys, copies, steals, kidnaps whatever and whomever it can. This may be merely the first phase of isolation. Travel is already strictly limited and so are personal relationships by correspondence between Soviet intellectuals, artists, and professional persons with their opposite numbers abroad.

Stalin, it would appear, is closing out evidence of Western superiority while feverishly trying to hide Russia's inferiority in a smoke screen of boasts until the day of her own ascendancy arrives.

In the long run a higher living standard and higher culture in the democratic West would be conclusive argument not only against the Soviet regime but against its further expansion. Having affirmed that the Soviet system was best in war Stalin must demonstrate that it is best in peace.

This is now a basic Stalin motivation and the keynote of universal

Communist propaganda. It requires exaggeration of Soviet achievements and belittling of the West.

Everything points to West-Russia competition as the axis of Stalin's postwar thinking. The corresponding Communist strategy would include efforts to confuse bourgeois governments, shatter capitalist economy, and destroy non-Soviet morale. An atomic scientist lured into the Soviet Union is one more for it and one less for the enemy. A bourgeois diplomat enticed into fleeing to Moscow is an asset less for the secrets he carries than because his disappearance may create a Kafka-like atmosphere that makes men distrust their fellows and thereby disrupts Western society.

All forms of internationalism, in a world which is bursting at its national seams and crying for unification, must therefore suffer at Stalin's hands. In July, 1945, President Truman took to the Potsdam Conference a plan for the hydroelectric development of the Danube River and the full exploitation of its shipping and irrigation capacities (a TVA on the Danube) to which America would contribute six billion dollars. Stalin rejected the offer. He wanted a Red Danube, exclusive artery of the new Russian empire.

Stalin is the supreme isolationist. The Soviet government uses the United Nations as a podium for propaganda and a divisive tool, but it abstains from all the specialized agencies of the UN created to cope with the problems of food and agriculture, world health, international trade, and so forth; the Kremlin is not dedicated to the solution of world problems even though Russia would benefit. Moscow has repeatedly denounced efforts at world government and international federation.

Internationalism, scorned as "cosmopolitanism," is persecuted in Russia, for it implies ties with the rest of the world. Instead, Stalin's two-hostile-worlds policy requires: (1) a walled-off Russia holding her satellites by a short leash, and (2) Russian efforts to destroy or at least divide a maximum number of non-Soviet states. That would tip the scales against the democracies.

The record of Stalin's absolutism at home shows that he destroys what he cannot control. Having achieved great power abroad, he is prone to see the international situation too in terms of the patient, piecemeal destruction of the enemy. The enemy is any resisting object of desire, whether capitalist or defiant Communist like Tito.

An internationalist in Stalin's lexicon—he has said it repeatedly—is one who works for the good of Russia. Tito sinned by serving Yugoslavia and refusing to subserve Stalin. The published 1948 correspondence between Moscow and the Yugoslav Communists proves that Stalin insisted on control of the Yugoslav Army and secret police by Russia through Russian personnel. He wished to convert Yugoslavia into another colony. Insubordination made Tito a "Menshevik," "Fascist," "Bukharinite," and "Turkish assassin"; no epithet is too harsh. Stalin regards an independent Communist as worse than no Communist. Stalin now realizes that an independent Communist state can join the predominantly capitalistic West in order to escape the Russian threat. This has intensified his abhorrence of independents. Tito's defection inspired purges in all other satellite states of those who might wish to imitate his example, and since, in Stalin's mind, everyone is suspect and everyone retains a lingering longing for liberty, the purge has become a permanent feature in Russia's colonies too. The natural end of the process would be the imposition of Muscovite viceroys and Russian bureaucrats on all Soviet satellites.

Tito's "disloyalty" must also increase Stalin's hostility toward revolutionists. Inside Russia, Stalin never had any use for revolutionists. A revolutionist is a nonconformist, a rebel, a troublemaker for the power-man. All recognizable Russian revolutionists have been liquidated. Now the same operation shakes Russia's empire.

Stalin believes in revolution from above. Referring to the collectivization of Soviet agriculture, he boasted in the *Pravda* of June 20, 1950, that "we were able to do this because it was a revolution from above, because the revolution was accomplished on the initiative of the existing government with the support of the bulk of the peasantry." The support of the peasantry is open to question; Stalin himself has said that when, in response to violent protest, pressure on the peasants was briefly relaxed in 1930, a third of the collectivized peasants abandoned the collectives. But there can be no doubt that collectivization was a revolution from above.

Stalin has carried out the same kind of revolution in the Balkans. It is the only kind of revolution he understands. Stalin's political philosophy is based on the supremacy of organization and the suppression of people. The organization suppresses the people.

Tito had a people's army forged in the battle of the mountains and he had popular support. Unlike the other satellites, Yugoslavia was never completely occupied by the Red Army. That gave Tito the strength to break from Moscow's grip.

Stalin wants no more self-assertive Titos.

All foreign Communist parties would be stronger minus the link with Russia which compels them to zigzag with Soviet foreign policy (including the Soviet-Nazi pact), apologize for Stalin's deformations of communism, and weaken their own countries in order to make Russia stronger. Yet they remain linked. This is not merely a matter of financial subsidies. The foreign Communists promise a model Communist society and if they turned their backs on the biggest and oldest Communist society they would be telling their followers that the promise had soured in the Soviet Union and might sour at home as well.

Tito was in a different position. Having established a Communist government in Yugoslavia he was judged by his own performance, not by fantasies about the distant Red paradise.

Tito would resist an invading Russian army. A Communist Italy or a Communist France might resist an invading Russian army. "Why should Russia invade us?" they would wonder. "And why indeed except to dominate?"

Thus, Communist parties abroad are unmixed assets to Moscow whereas, in some circumstances, real revolutions from below could embarrass the Kremlin, and a truly Communist or Socialist world revolution, a most unlikely development, would spell the end of Stalinism in Russia.

"The export of revolution—that is nonsense," Stalin said to Roy Howard in 1936. Instead, Moscow has exported the Red Army and set up reactionary puppet governments in occupied Eastern and Central Europe. This was the most effective way of extending Russian power. Always distrustful, Stalin and his heirs will try to keep those states weak by forcing them to collectivize rapidly against the wishes of the peasantry, by making them trade with and through Moscow at a loss rather than with the rest of the world at a profit, and by reducing their standard of living lest Russia's suffer by comparison. If necessary, Moscow will involve other Communist states in antagonisms with non-Communist countries so as to make them dependent on Soviet arms.

Soviet imperialism has all the characteristics of classic capitalist imperialism. Theoretical differences are apparently less important than practical power similarities.

Where the Russian empire cannot grow by adding to its bulk what it subtracts from the enemy it will not spurn the alternative of undermining the non-Soviet world by Communist subversion; it will exploit every deficiency outside its domain while concealing its own.

Without military intervention, however, Moscow is unlikely to acquire any country covered by the steel umbrella of Western armaments. Inside this protected region, the advanced, industrialized, more or less welfare-state nations: Denmark, Norway, Sweden, Finland, Western Germany, Switzerland, Holland, Belgium, England, the United States, and Canada ("capitalistic" is an insufficient description of any of these) have adequate inner social and economic balance to reduce to a minimum the disturbances caused by Communists. This is not a danger area in the two-world rivalry.

France and Italy are also shielded by the military might of the united Western nations. But during the Second World War the Communists' talent for conspiracy, violence, and underground work enabled them to collect disproportionate political power which is fed now by the low productivity of industry and the low income of labor. The resulting economic depression of the middle classes as well as France's decline as a leading power, prepares new recruits for the irrational parties of despair, Rightist or Communist—where one is strong the other is strong, for they spring from the same source.

The "after me the deluge" attitude which the richer strata manifest in the evasion of taxes, the export of capital, the disinclination to invest, and the attachment to offensive luxury has its political counterpart in the irresponsibility of the parties in France and their social intransigence in Italy. The widespread feeling of helplessness in the face of an entrenched yet unprogressive industrial class and of hopelessly divided or stagnant political groups breeds frustration and bitterness, and a tendency toward radical solutions and violence; in France and Italy, therefore, the Socialists, the party of moderate reform, are weak. Conservative reluctance to change strengthens the Communist advocates of drastic change.

Unless national income in France and Italy is raised by more modern production techniques, by the fuller exploitation of used and untapped natural resources, by the scrapping of superfluous units of production and trade, and by the integration or federation of nations, and until that augmented income is more equitably distributed, both countries will remain disturbed, and their political democracy will be ground thin between the upper and nether millstones of extremism.

Where the lower end of the Italian boot dips deeper into the sea, Italy joins that vast belt of countries stretching from Gibraltar to Singapore in which modern industry and capitalism are a rickety superstructure on a social edifice essentially feudal. From the Iberian peninsula, around the Mediterranean littoral, through the entire Moslem world, except Turkey, which is uniquely firm, and Israel, on to Southeast Asia, the defenses against communism and other forms of totalitarianism are weak. It is in this mammoth region, inhabited by far more than a billion persons living in the nineteenth, eighteenth, seventeenth, and sixteenth centuries, that the rivalry between Russia and the West will rage with special fury for years. Stalin is too old to direct this struggle to its end. He will bequeath the task to his successor. The Kremlin begins with many advantages.

Already, communism has spread to China. The proximity of Russia and some of her acts, as well as the blunders of this or that Western agent were factors in the rise of Red China, but in perspective they are little more than foam on the ocean of Chinese discontent. Similar unhappiness fills the feudal regions from Spain to

Indo-China and, in addition, much of Africa and Latin America. Everywhere a thin wealthy upper caste shamelessly flaunts its luxury under the eyes of the hungry, diseased peasants and shepherds who are deprived of the education, organization, and political power to improve their lot. Techniques date back to Noah and the population increases faster than production. Industry is puny, the middle class weak, the working class small, and the farm population in feudal servitude. Army, bureaucracy, and police cruelly oppress and consciously delude the poor, and for these services to the rich they are allowed to consume the bulk of the national budget. Politics by assassination flourishes and palace revolutions multiply. Leadership goes to the unenlightened nobility or plutocracy who pay or to the trigger-quick military and unscrupulous demagogues who enflame the patriotic passions or religious fanaticism of the mass. Masters come and go, foreigners are ousted, national independence is achieved, but bread, rice, milk, medicines, water, shoes, shelter, schools remain in short supply. Loans from abroad reach the pockets of the haves; the have-nots have only their envy and hate.

Into this dark, humid atmosphere comes the voice of Russia or of domestic extremists of various colors who either think they have solutions or think they can gain power through wild promises. Communism, fascism, and kindred forms of totalitarianism must luxuriate in such a swamp of unhappiness and despair. Unrest will continue in that vast retarded region until the Stalinists seize power by forceful coups and modernize the ancient feudalism as Stalin has in Russia, or until the advanced nations of the world carry out a social transformation, or a social revolution, which, concretely, means the conscious fostering of new classes equipped with new economic and technical means to produce. Either the democracies revolutionize the feudal world from below and guide it speedily into the twentieth century, or the heirs of Stalin will revolutionize it from above with their Stalinist combination of eighteenth-century obscurantism and modern technique and tyranny. If parts or all of this colossal belt are absorbed or intimidated by Russia, the world balance will move in her favor. Asia's inclusion in the Soviet orbit would cripple Europe and damage America and thereby, in turn, ruin Asia. The democratic world must find a mutually beneficial substitute for the earlier, obsolete colonial exploitation of the East and Africa.

During the long period, decades perhaps, in which the Soviet and non-Soviet worlds will compete for superiority and supremacy, Moscow will probe for weak spots and take what she can take with impunity. But the record testifies that despite her overwhelming military power, Russia desisted where she met opposition: Iran in 1946-1947; Greece and Turkey; the Berlin blockade. Nor did Stalin attack rebellious Yugoslavia. The postwar strategy mapped by Stalin immediately after the Second World War would defeat itself if Russia were directly involved in a major armed conflict. For that might be a gamble with her national existence and imperial strength. Better, at least in the present stage, to equalize the balance between the two worlds by prolonged, wasteful guerrilla wars in non-Soviet countries or colonies or by social upheavals not always fomented by Moscow but never discouraged either. "I will not go too far," Stalin told Anthony Eden. This restraint is part of the scheme and of Stalin's character. But he is not the only judge of "too far."

The Stalin blueprint of postwar heavy industrialization, isolation, imperialist expansion when it is cheap and revolution or subversion when it is expensive to the enemy is less the product of his mind than of his temperament and of the political system he has created. Stalin is a prisoner in his own jail. If Muscovite efforts toward expansion stopped, collaboration with the West would again become possible, Russia would have no enemies, her people would be more relaxed and better fed and clothed, and the dictatorship would crumble.

This raises the question whether the fortress that Stalin built can never be opened to admit foreign friendship. Or would democracy enter with foreign friendship and end the dictatorship? The riddle is: Can a dictatorship which grew gradually to its present rigors gradually relax? The problem faces Stalin in his declining years and it will be the preoccupation of his heirs.

CHAPTER XXVI

The Death of Stalin

The question, "What will happen when Stalin dies?" is asked so frequently that it begins to sound more like a prayer than an inquiry. Millions in non-Soviet countries would like to hope that his passing will bring peace to the world and freedom inside the Soviet empire.

When a man has ruled a country for more than twenty-five years it is natural that some of his subjects should yearn for a change. But Soviet citizens know that only death can remove Stalin.

In the circumstances, Russians who remember their national history would inevitably think of assassination. Except for a member of Stalin's intimate entourage the chances of coming close enough to kill him are small, and inside that limited circle personal calculations and political considerations might stay the hand of a conspirator. Is it certain that the man who eliminated Stalin would succeed him? The murderer might be murdered by an ambitious rival. The attempt on Stalin, moreover, might fail, and then the would-be assassin and his family, friends, acquaintances, associates, and many thousands of innocents seized at random would die. The July 20, 1944, plot on Hitler's life failed although it was carried out by military staff men experienced in planning and killing. The bunglers paid a heavy toll.

Stalin's co-workers, who are partners in his tyranny, would condemn themselves by assassinating the tyrant. They would also condemn and weaken the system which is their only political future. Stalin has so completely identified the Soviet regime with himself that to reject him by killing him would be to reject the regime. An assassin, therefore, would have to proceed against the regime and kill not only Stalin but all his important colleagues. In self-defense, the colleagues oppose assassination as a political method. Moreover, the Soviet leaders are probably so impressed by Stalin's ability that they wish to postpone as long as possible the dread day when they must rule without him.

A foreign Stalinist could say, "This is wicked speculation. Why not assume that Stalin's comrades agree with him and adore him?" They may. But that too would be speculation. One cannot believe what they say because they would not dare say otherwise. A dictatorship expunges evidence in its disfavor and invalidates evidence in its favor. The observer is simply forced to the conclusion that where so much effort is expended on machinery to suppress opposition there must be much opposition and that it reaches into levels high enough to be best informed on the cruelty and cost of Stalin. But their share in perpetrating his horrors and the awe of pigmies facing a giant emasculates them, and their hands are still.

Stalin, however, is past seventy and some day death from natural causes will make the inconveniences of assassination superfluous. He will receive a mammoth funeral commensurate with his mania for bigness. How many will mourn him cannot be anticipated. Nor is it predictable whether he will be mummified and placed in a glass showcase beside Lenin. Stalin's last testament may provide for a separate mausoleum. There is room in the Red Square for two, and many Soviet citizens are no doubt eager to visit the second. For though they are too skeptical to expect drastic reforms from his heir or heirs they would naturally anticipate some relief.

It is not necessary to enter the miasma of prophecy to foresee that one thing will not happen: there will be no party controversy such as followed Lenin's death. Then the Communist party was a vital, vocal organism with power to decide and the right to speak. Now it is an automatic machine tool of unanimity.

The people had no voice in selecting Lenin's successor and will of course have none when Stalin dies. The only possible conflict for the succession could take place on the steppes or in the palace. The Red Army might try to seize the reins of government and elevate a popular military figure to national leadership. Bonapartes are not in the Russian tradition. The nation would be slow to respond to a man on horseback. It rarely reacts to glamour. Its historic revolts have been low-calory brush fires spreading spasmodically from village to village and town to town. Their extent, remarkably great in the case of some peasant insurrections, testified to the inefficiency of the repressive agencies of pre-Bolshevik central governments. But the Soviet secret police is ubiquitous, potent and ruthless, and the success of an army *coup d'état* or of a popular uprising with military support would depend on the NKVD. It is a spy system. It controls the railways, roads, telephones, and telegraph. It is an armed force with numerous well-equipped military regiments, usually the best in the land. It would know in advance, from its informers and microphones, about any conspiracy. It could deprive the plotters of the means of communication and movement. Its armed units would march against any Red Army detachments that somehow did move on Moscow from the plains. A loyal NKVD means safety for the dictatorship.

Stalin has said at various times that "technology decides everything," "cadres decide everything," and so forth. The truth is, he decides everything and after his death the secret police will decide everything. This is normal in a police state. Stalin is supreme lord thanks to his complete command of the NKVD. When he goes the secret police will have the biggest share in determining who shall be the new dictator.

The head of the NKVD, or MVD as it is also called, is Lavrenti P. Beria, like Stalin, a Georgian. I interviewed Beria in his office prison in Tiflis in 1924, when he was head of the Georgian Cheka. He looks like a scholarly intellectual rather than a shrewd politician and is intelligent and urbane. His whole adult life has been spent in the secret police. In 1924 Stalin gave him the assignment of wiping out a brief anti-Soviet Menshevik rebellion in Georgia the dying embers of which I had seen in the mountains. Beria told me that enemies would receive no quarter and in fact he proved totally merciless and hence worthy of promotion first to chief of the secret police of the Caucasus and later of the Soviet Union.

Beria became a deputy member of the Politbureau in 1939, a marshal in 1945, and a full member of the Politbureau in 1946. The country knows nothing about his personal life or personality, but that is no handicap when Stalin knows, trusts, and favors him.

At a solemn meeting of Soviet notables in the Moscow Big Theater each November 6, the eve of the anniversary of the Bolshevik revolution, a Soviet leader reports on the state of the nation. During the four years of the Second World War, this annual address was given by Stalin, thus emphasizing its importance. The November 6, 1945, speaker was Molotov. The 1946 address was delivered by Andrei Zhdanov, since deceased, then frequently mentioned as Stalin's heir apparent. Molotov again gave the report in 1947, and again in 1948. The spokesman in 1949 was Georgi M. Malenkov; in 1950, Marshal N. A. Bulganin, Minister of the Armed Forces.

The address on November 6, 1951, was by Beria. That raised his status. It indicated that Stalin wished to cloak Beria's police power with political prestige.

The ultimate development in the leadership of a police state would be the identity of the head of police and head of state. Beria's nationality, however, is an obstruction. If Beria succeeded Stalin as dictator the Russians might wonder how long Georgians were destined to rule over them. "Are there no Russians?" they could say to themselves.

This consideration, especially in view of the Kremlin's encouragement of Russian nationalism, suggests the likely emergence of a condominium after the death of Stalin consisting of Beria and one or more Russians.

As an organizer and manipulator, Stalin is a genius. It is clear that he has been allowing the battle for the succession to take place now, during his lifetime, while he can direct it into calm channels and prevent it from wrecking or disrupting the Soviet system. Stalin could arbitrarily choose his heir and appoint him second-in-command to manage affairs while he spends three to four months each year vacationing at his private winter villa on the beautiful Caucasus Riviera. But since this might cause bitterness, Stalin lets the Politbureau members compete for supremacy under his cautioning eye and with a little pressure here and there to make sure that his favorites do not lose. Stalin has always preferred to see his lieutenants expend their hostility on one another than to accumulate resentments against him.

So far, the battle for the succession has moved in Beria's favor. He is the foremost competitor for the still-occupied throne. But owing to his racial handicap he is no threat to Stalin and will not take the seat even after Stalin's death.

Beria's closest Russian ally appears to be Georgi M. Malenkov, long active in the party machine. He served as first assistant to Stalin's private secretary, Alexander Poskrobeshov; became a deputy member of the Politbureau in 1941; and a full member in 1946. His promotion thus parallels that of Beria.

Malenkov is known as an energetic, merciless organizer; Stalin used him during the war to repair critical breakdowns in the defense machine. Subsequently Malenkov performed several purge-and-intimidation missions in Russia's Balkan colonies. He and Beria are obviously a well-matched pair. This is the duumvirate that is likely to hold power when Stalin relinquishes it.

Beria was born in a Georgian village on March 29, 1899. Malenkov was born in Orenburg, now Sverdlovsk, a fast-growing industrial town in the Urals, on January 7, 1902. Both are children of the twentieth century. They are Stalin's political children. He has trained them as new-type Bolshevik headmen steeled in the Stalin furnace.

But it may be too early to hand Russia over entirely to this new generation of leaders. Malenkov could hardly succeed to Stalin's title; that would be somewhat derogatory to Stalin. Malenkov still lacks stature and reputation. He is too young to have a pre-Bolshevik past. He has no link to Lenin and the revolutionary myth.

For these reasons, Beria and Malenkov may be induced to join with Molotov to form a triumvirate.

After Lenin died, power passed to Zinoviev, Kamenev, and Stalin. But since the first two were Jews and the third a Georgian they appointed a Russian, Alexei Rykov, as chairman of the Council of People's Commissars or Prime Minister. Rykov thereby became the titular successor to Lenin but with far less influence than the man whose post he inherited. It is a fair assumption that Molotov will be the titular successor to Stalin. He would be Prime Minister. Stalin has given several signs of this probability. There are photographs showing Stalin smiling on Molotov. Molotov has been mentioned as the chief disciple of Stalin. He usually stands next to Stalin in group photographs. These are Soviet straws in the wind.

Molotov was born in Moscow in 1890; joined the Communist party in 1906; spent a year in a Czarist jail and two years and four months in Siberian exile. This record is an advantage. He is a bridge to the myth.

Molotov's advantages and long association with Stalin once gave him the illusion that he would not only sit on the throne but also inherit Stalin's power. Beria took another view. Considerable tension developed between Molotov and Beria. Molotov's surrender of the portfolio of Foreign Minister may have been one of the consequences. To be sure, Molotov's removal from that key post seems to have been part of a general reform which relieved several members of the Politbureau of departmental duties. But the secret police had always wanted to control the Foreign Office. Maxim Litvinov told me on a number of occasions about the troubles he had with the GPU which tried to read the Soviet diplomatic mail and place its own men in Soviet embassies and legations. It often did. Not infrequently the GPU subordinate was more influential than his ambassador.

Andrei Vishinsky, Molotov's successor as Foreign Minister, was considered an NKVD man. His Menshevik past, a discrediting circumstance, and his role as prosecutor in the Moscow "trials" would support this thesis which, if true, means that Beria is in effect the Soviet Foreign Minister acting through Vishinsky and Gromyko, his puppets. Neither has any domestic influence; they are Soviet career men, managers.

Beria's hold on the Foreign Office is a big victory over Molotov. Beria and Malenkov might prefer a man like Klementi E. Voroshilov or Nikolai Bulganin, the civilian head of the Army, as titular successor to Stalin. Voroshilov is too old to be ambitious and Bulganin would consent to play the role of an underling. But if the mighty Beria-Malenkov duumvirate must expand to admit Molotov they would first wish to shear him of his power and power lust. This process is continuing.

Beria can enjoy the support of other leaders who, for various reasons, do not aspire to supremacy: Anastasi Mikoyan, the Soviet trade lord, an Armenian; Lazar Kaganovitch, a Jew and distinguished organizer and "hatchet" man; Andrei A. Andreyev, the agricultural expert who acceded to the Politbureau in 1932 but has been reprimanded several times for blunders; and younger Communists trained in the fear of the secret police. In the 1920's, veteran Communists like Molotov and Voroshilov might have appealed to the party against the police. Now the party has no power and they could only appeal to the army and provoke a civil war which would damage the Soviet system. They would be reluctant to do that. The police is therefore paramount.

If Beria asserts his power, the Red Army will remain the technical, nonpolitical arm of the Soviet government standing furthest from the throne. The rivalry between the Red Army and the secret police is notorious. In theory at least, the Army is a threat to the police. Moreover, their functions are in conflict. It is the secret police, not the Army, which guards the frontiers. Both organizations maintain espionage systems abroad. With the party reduced to an appendage of the NKVD, the two power units in Russia are the secret police and the army, and they are rivals. Stalin rules both though he is in neither. But Beria is the secret police.

The choice in Russia is a military dictatorship or a police dictatorship, and at the moment the police is high in the ascendant.

Whoever succeeds Stalin, the quality of leadership will deteriorate when the reins drop from his strong hands. The men who possessed great ability, men like Valeri Mezhlauk, chairman of the federal Planning Commission, and Ukrainian boss Postishev, were purged for that reason, as was Ivan Maisky, Ambassador in London, just when he reached maximum usefulness. The surviving leaders are not without quality, but none has Stalin's talents as a juggler. He can keep several explosive balls in the air while balancing on a seesaw. If one of them crashed it might wreck the Kremlin.

The problems which Stalin has been juggling for some time will be passed on, unsolved, to his heirs. Three are major: (1) peasant opposition; (2) friction with national minorities; (3) the world situation.

About two thirds of the population of the Soviet Union till the soil. Almost all of them are in collective farms. Stalin is still not content.

Since 1917, the peasants have been the most irritating limitation on the dictatorship's power. Lenin and Stalin were forced to make concessions to them. Collectivization was designed to crush peasant resistance forever. But after studying them from 1928 to 1950 Stalin concluded that the collectives had failed to achieve this purpose.

A collective is the old Russian village managed by a few of its inhabitants who have become Communists. Its methods are different but the villagers are the same. The managers are often the relatives, sometimes the close friends, and always the neighbors of the peasants. The Soviet system requires the leaders to live in the tower and the masses in the cellar. But in a village collective this is impossible. Everybody lives on one level. For this reason, the managers cannot act with the severity which Moscow demands of its servants. They fear peasant reprisals; directors of collectives have been killed and mauled in the night. They also fear social boycott; their sons and daughters would not be accepted in marriage by embittered neighbors: their children would be bullied.

The collectives, consequently, are not as tightly regimented as Stalin had desired. The peasants retain some power—and that curtails the dictator's power.

The collective, moreover, retains a measure of capitalism. The members of a collective work on the common fields for a wage. But, in addition, each family has a plot of ground near the house to grow vegetables and fruit, and raise a cow, a goat, some pigs, poultry, and so forth. The produce of this personal acre is the peasant's property to be consumed or sold on the free market. He works better for himself than he does for the collective.

To eliminate the unsatisfactory economic and social features of the collectives, Stalin in 1950 inaugurated *agrogorods* or agricultural cities. The chief innovation consisted in merging two or more, sometimes five or six, collectives into one "town."

This sharp departure was officially justified on the grounds of economy and efficiency. But when a Soviet enterprise doubles its size it may triple its personnel and that saves neither red tape nor rubles. The excuse of technical efficiency is equally flimsy, for the single-village collective never had fences or ruts to separate it from an adjoining collective, and the farm machinery, operating from a government-owned, regional Machine Tractor Station, ploughed, harrowed, seeded, and harvested the land of several collectives, not one.

The aim of the *agrogorod* is political. It abolishes the private-capitalistic acre. It creates the gulf between people and managers which characterizes the entire Soviet system. Moscow plans to move all the peasants from their old villages and house them in the tenements of the new *agrogorod.* This would substitute urban diffusion for rural cohesion; universally, it seems, people are furthest apart when crowded together in towns.

A village, in which everybody knows everybody else—including the policeman—is apparently an anachronism in a police state. The Bolsheviks are intent on destroying the village by squeezing its inhabitants into citylike quarters where the secret police can observe and control them more easily.

With astounding courage and vitality, however, the Soviet peasants sabotaged the introduction of *agrogorods,* and within a year Stalin abandoned the idea. The peasants resisted their death as peasants. They refused to become completely regimented serfs. Stalin consequently retreated as he and Lenin had retreated in the past whenever resistance reached dangerous proportions. Stalin zigzags not according to any artificial, cerebral scheme but by the simple rules of political physics: he removes the lid when the pot boils; then, if it becomes too hot in his hands, he puts it back. The general Stalinist line is always in the direction of more pressure cooking.

The Soviet villages comprise approximately one hundred and thirty million persons. They are not, even at this late day, reconciled to Stalin. They will torment his heirs.

Many of these villagers are non-Russians whose grievances as peasants are compounded by the racial grievances which they share with urban non-Russians.

As a result of the post-1939 annexations of non-Russian peoples, Russians constitute only 50 per cent of the Soviet Union's population; the other half is divided among over a hundred national minorities. Stalin's policy of favoring and feeding Russian nationalism before and during the war paid dividends in the fight against Hitler. The Russians won the war; disaffection and the Nazis made their greatest inroads among the minorities.

Since 1945, the national minorities in the Soviet Union have lived amid the torments of a perpetual purge. The charge which Moscow levels against its victims is "bourgeois nationalism," but "bourgeois" simply signifies that Stalin disapproves. The accused are Communists and Soviet intellectuals. In fact, the Moscow *Pravda* of July 1, 1951, attacked the Central Committee of the Ukrainian Communist party for serious ideological defects in the matter of nationalism.

The basic difficulty is not the "bourgeois" nationalism of the minorities but Stalin's Russian nationalism. The Russians are taught to love Russia. Accordingly, a Soviet monthly prints a poem by V. Sosiura entitled "Love the Ukraine." Moscow protests and proscribes; to love the Ukraine means to love Russia less, perhaps to separate it from Russia. An Armenian novel, *Flames*, published in the 1880's, pays tribute to the Armenian struggle for independence from the Turks. Moscow ought to be pleased. But any struggle for independence could suggest another and is therefore suspect, especially since the novel fails to appreciate the help which Russians claim to have given the Armenians. The Armenian publishing house, is consequently reprimanded for reissuing the classic; it "foments bourgeois nationalism."

Since the Russians were glorifying their ancient martial, feudal heroes, a Kazan magazine began, in 1940, to republish a Tartar epic called *Idegay*. Idegay was a fifteenth-century Tartar khan, one of the leaders of the Golden Horde, who had fought and subdued the Russians. The Kremlin thought it wise not to remind them of their defeats and therefore banned the book.

Thus Stalin's Russian nationalism begets Tartar nationalism, and Ukrainian, Armenian, Uzbek, and other nationalisms, and Russian antagonism to those nationalisms.

Czarist Russia was never a melting pot. Lenin called it "a prison house of nationalities." The Czars elevated the Russians, subjugated all others, and simultaneously tried to Russify them. The attempt had to fail.

The Soviets, in their early international phase, abolished the inequalities between races and abandoned Russification. The result was peace among the nationalities, considerable cultural development, and considerable intermarriage and assimilation.

Stalin's cultivation of Russian nationalism reversed all these currents. Russification is back. The Latin alphabet, which Moscow gave to many retarded, chiefly Moslem, nationalities in place of the complicated, cursive Arabic script that had accounted for so much illiteracy, has been taken from them; the new script is Cyrillic or Russian. Over a vast area Russian has ousted the national language as the language of instruction in schools. All Yiddish-language Jewish dailies and several Jewish weeklies as well as the Jewish anti-Fascist Committee and the autonomous Jewish territory of Birobidjan have been suppressed by Moscow. Anti-Semitism and other interracial frictions have returned. Tension between the Kremlin and the regions inhabited by national minorities has returned; non-Russian minorities are being transported en masse to Siberia. The Czar muddled through; Stalin works thoroughly.

The discontent of the national minorities is matched by the unhappiness of the Soviet colonial satellites in Eastern Europe who, in effect, are Russia's new national minorities and subject to the same type of Russification, purges, and humiliations.

The mood of the satellites, of the races in Russia, and of the peasants reduces their economic productivity and complicates Moscow's task of governing. But the terror prevents them from organizing to overthrow the regime. Their only weapons are unnoticeable non-co-operation, slow, silent sabotage, and the subtle generation of an atmosphere which multiplies the Politbureau's fears of the people.

The people of a dictatorship are helpless. But a government whose deeds antagonize while its propaganda fails to convince is not entirely free either.

Material hardships further exacerbate the Kremlin's relations with the country. The fires of two-world rivalry burn at Russia's expense too; rearmament bends the backs of Soviet citizens no less than it burdens Englishmen, Frenchmen, and others. Stalin has no magic formula to dissolve the dilemma of guns-or-margarine. In a poor land like Russia, arms lower the living standard, just as in richer countries.

The disaffection in Russia and in the Soviet colonies are potent factors in the international situation. Stalin and his heirs will have to reckon with them. The Soviet government should have plenty of reason to doubt whether it could take its people into a war which did not begin with an obvious foreign invasion.

Ever since the postwar Russia-West antagonism became apparent, the line of Soviet propaganda has been: the capitalist enemy is bent on crushing us, therefore rally round Stalin and work hard; but the foreign Communists, the peace-loving "progressives" and proletarians abroad, and the millions of signers of the Stockholm "peace" pledge will frustrate the bellicose plans of Wall Street and the London City; therefore do not be panicky or hoard your crops, do not buy salt, continue to live normally. Moscow is afraid of its own alarms. It wants the benefits of antiforeign agitation without the embarrassment of war jitters.

Stalin's postwar juggling of the two balls, No Foreign Friendship and No War, has been impressively skillful. But no skill can erase the cost to Russia of world tension.

The dictatorship needs the tension yet Russia cannot afford it. It is Stalin's greatest failure that his policies serve the ruling clique and upper class, not the nation. Stalin tried to soften this clash of interests by blessing Russian nationalism, but the favorable wartime results of that measure have been canceled out by its subsequent effects on the national minorities and on a world alarmed by Soviet imperialism, the child of Russian nationalism.

These contradictions are Stalin's worst legacy to his heirs. They will face the difficult choice of hurting Russia by continuing Stalin's two-hostile-camps isolationism or negotiating a reconciliation with the West and thereby weakening the dictatorship.

Stalin has conducted the Soviet despotism into an impasse: cold war and a thriving dictatorship but a suffering Russia. The regime must seek a way out.

Consonant with its hatred of man, communism may be the new nihilism, born to negate and destroy. To wreak vengeance on mankind for resisting conversion, Stalinism might decide to perish with the Philistines by pulling out the supports of the temple of freedom. A war would achieve that result, for neither world can crush the other by force without succumbing in the debris.

But most signs indicate that rather than commit suicide in order to destroy the enemy, the Stalinists have a wager on the suicide of the democracies. To avoid the collapse of the dictatorship Russia invites the non-Soviet camp to go to its own death while she heats the fires of international tension and hopes they will not touch her.

The suicide of democracies consumed in the flames of their anger toward communism would obviously cause much pleasure in the Kremlin. The Stalin men watching from its towers no doubt rejoice whenever they discern the shrinkage of the democratic individual that results from fear of communism; they of course quickly recognize the familiar methods whereby Moscow reduced Soviet individuals to the convenient size of pigmies. Stalin knows that the real strength of democracy is an individual unhampered in self-assertion, free to grow, and free from crippling pressures toward conformity.

The more the democracies resemble dictatorships the less is their capacity to combat communism by nonviolent means. Two fear-dominated, tightly controlled systems, tense, spiteful, and hateful, repaying each ugly blow with one at least as ugly, and rejecting compromise, would soon catapult the planet into a war to end all civilization or would end civilization without war by the slower process of banishing moderation, political sanity, accommodation, tolerance, and justice, and reducing human rights and the standard of living.

Stalin's best possible victory is a foreign victory. Stalin's successes have been in the realm of power. He has established a powerful government and made Russia powerful. The Soviet Union has also achieved vast progress in industrial production; that is no capitalist monopoly. But within the steel cortex of power and regimented factory output, all the human problems fester. The relations between city and village, between classes, between races, between state and citizen, and between man and man have been aggravated and poisoned by Stalin. Ideals and Utopian ideas are dead; materialism is trumps. Soviet society is reactionary, cynical, and corrupt, a black monument to its creator. In the absence of war, its best chance of survival is in a world that has become like it though swearing undying enmity to it. That would be Stalin's big triumph. Judging by his postwar policies, that is his big hope. If Russia can draw attention to herself long enough, and thereby divert attention from the waiting problems of the non-Soviet world, the hope may be fulfilled.

On the other hand, decades of world peace during which the richer, advanced countries improve themselves and help half the human race lift itself out of its feudal poverty and unhappiness might sound the death knell of the Soviet system. It is doubtful whether communism in Russia or anywhere could survive twenty or thirty years of world tranquillity, prosperity, and progress. The maintenance of international peace and a mounting living standard for all would demonstrate the superiority of the free world, whereupon, in Stalin's opinion, the Soviet world would die. A regime predicated on tension within and without and on the disintegration of the democratic "enemy" could not in the long run coexist with a harmonious, democratic, non-Soviet world which looked critically at itself instead of fiercely at Russia and was solving its ethical, social, economic, and political problems. In such an era of peace the heirs of Mr. Stalin would be compelled to make gradual concessions to the Soviet people's yearning for more groceries and more liberties.

Stalin's fate is in the hands of the non-Stalinists. They can write history's verdict of him. They will determine whether his life was a success or failure.

Bibliography

Albom Dyeyatelyei V.K.P. (B.) (Album of the Leaders of the Communist Party of the USSR). Moscow: Izdatelstvo AXRR, 1927.

Alexandrov, G. F., and others. *Iosif Vissarionovich Stalin, Kratkaia Biografia* (Joseph V. Stalin, A Short Biography). Moscow: Gosudarstvennoe Izdatelstvo Politicheskoi Literatury, Second Revised Edition, 1950.

Alliluev, A. S. *Vospominaniia* (Memoirs). Moscow: Sovetskii Pisatel, 1948.

Alliluev, S. *Proidennyi Put* (The Road Behind). Moscow: OGIZ, 1946.

Barbusse, Henri. *Stalin, A New World Seen Through One Man.* New York: The Macmillan Company, 1935.

Beck, F., and Godin, W. *Russian Purge and the Extraction of Confession.* New York: Viking Press, Inc., 1951.

Byrnes, James F. *Speaking Frankly.* New York: Harper & Brothers, 1947.

Churchill, Winston. *The Second World War.* 5 vols. Boston: Houghton Mifflin Company, 1948-1951.

Davies, Joseph E. *Mission to Moscow.* New York: Simon & Schuster, Inc., 1941.

Deane, John R. *The Strange Alliance, The Story of Our Efforts at Wartime Co-operation with Russia.* New York: Viking Press, Inc., 1947.

Deutscher, I. *Stalin, a Political Biography.* New York: Oxford University Press, 1949.

Eisenhower, Dwight D. *Crusade in Europe.* New York: Doubleday & Company, Inc., 1948.

Falsifikatory Istorii, Istoricheskaia Spravka (Falsifiers of History, a Historical Reference). Moscow: Gosudarstvennoe Izdatelstvo Politicheskoi Literatury, 1951.

Fischer, Louis. *Men and Politics.* New York: Duell, Sloan and Pearce, Inc., 1941.

History of the Communist Party of the Soviet Union (Bolsheviks), Short Course. Edited by a Commission of the Central Committee of the C.P.S.U. (B.). Moscow: Foreign Languages Publishing House, 1939.

Knickerbocker, H. R. *The Red Trade Menace*. New York: Dodd, Mead & Company, Inc., 1931.

Konsultatsii, V Pomoshch Izuchaiushchim Marksizm-Leninizm, Sbornik Tretii (Reference Book, an Aid to Students of Marxism-Leninism, Volume III). Simferopol: Gosudarstvennoe Izdatelstvo Krymskoi ASSR, 1940.

Langer, William L., and Gleason, S. Everett. *The Challenge to Isolation, 1937-1940*. Published for the Council on Foreign Relations. New York: Harper & Brothers, 1952.

Levine, Isaac Don. *Stalin*. New York: Cosmopolitan Book Corp., 1931.

Lorimer, Frank. *The Population of the Soviet Union*. Geneva: League of Nations, 1946.

Marx-Engels-Lenin Institute. *Iosif Vissarionovich Stalin, Kratkaia Biografia* (Joseph Vissarionovich Stalin, A Brief Biography). Moscow: OGIZ, 1940.

Perkins, Frances. *The Roosevelt I Knew*. New York: Viking Press, Inc., 1946.

Pesni o Staline (Songs about Stalin). Moscow: Gosudarstvennoe Izdatelstvo Khudozhestvennoi Literatury, 1950.

Schueller, George K. *The Politburo*. With an Introduction by Harold H. Fisher. Stanford: Stanford University Press, 1951.

Sherwood, Robert E. *Roosevelt and Hopkins, An Intimate History*. New York: Harper & Brothers, Revised Edition, 1950.

Smith, Walter Bedell. *My Three Years in Moscow*. Philadelphia and New York: J. B. Lippincott Company, 1950.

Soiuz Sovetskikh Sotsialisticheskikh Respublik (Union of Soviet Socialist Republics). Special Volume of the Great Soviet Encyclopedia. Moscow: Gosudarstvennyi Nauchnyi Institut "Sovietskaia Entsikldpediia," 1948.

Sontag, Raymond James, and Beddie, James Stuart (eds.). *Nazi-Soviet Relations, 1939-1941*. Documents from the Archives of the German Foreign Office. Washington, D. C.: Department of State, 1948.

Souvarine, Boris. *Stalin, A Critical Survey of Bolshevism*. New York: Alliance Book Corporation, 1939.

Stalin-[H. G.] Wells Talk. The Verbatim Record and a Discussion by G. Bernard Shaw, H. G. Wells, and J. M. Keynes, Ernst Toller, and others. London: The New Statesman and Nation, 1934.

Stalin, Joseph. *Leninism*. Vol. I. New York: International Publishers (no date).

———. *Otchetnyi Doklad na XVIII Sezde Partii o Rabote TsK V.K.P.*

(B), 10 Marta 1939 g. (Report at the XVIII Congress of the Party on the Work of the Central Committee of the Communist Party of the Soviet Union [Bolsheviks], March 10, 1939). Moscow: Gosudarstvennoe Izdatelstvo Politicheskoi Literatury, 1950.

Stalin, Joseph. *O Velikoi Otechestvennoi Voine Sovetskogo Soiuza* (On the Great Patriotic War of the Soviet Union). Moscow: Gosudarstvennoe Izdatelstvo Politicheskoi Literatury, Fifth Edition, 1950.

———. *Sochineniia* (Collected Works). Vol. 1-13. Moscow: Gosudarstvennoe Izdatelstvo Politicheskoi Literatury, 1946-1949.

Stettinius, Edward R., Jr. *Roosevelt and the Russians, The Yalta Conference.* New York: Doubleday & Company, Inc., 1949.

Trotsky, Leon. *Stalin, An Appraisal of the Man and His Influence,* ed. Charles Malamuth. New York: Harper & Brothers, Second Edition, 1946.

Voznesensky, Nikolai A. *The Economy of the USSR During World War Two.* Washington, D. C.: Public Affairs Press, 1948.

Vstrechi s Tov. Stalinym (Meetings with Comrade Stalin), ed. A. Fadeyev. Moscow: OGIZ, 1939.

Wilmot, Chester. *The Struggle for Europe.* New York: Harper & Brothers, 1952.

Wolfe, Bertram D. *Three Who Made a Revolution, A Biographical History.* New York: Dial Press, Inc., 1948.

Index